T.R.

THE STORY OF THEODORE ROOSEVELT

T. R.

THE STORY OF
THEODORE ROOSEVELT
AND HIS INFLUENCE
ON OUR TIMES

BY

Noel F. Busch

REYNAL & COMPANY

NEW YORK

1963

For my daughters
Mary and Beatrix

I

"**R**oosevelt is not an American, you know. He is America."

This summation by the British writer, John Morley, after a visit to the White House in 1903, sheds considerable light not only on Theodore Roosevelt but also on the nation with which it identifies him. Likewise illuminating was Roosevelt's response to the compliment. Morley addressed it to a dinner companion in London who repeated it to Henry Cabot Lodge. Lodge brought it back to the President whose comment was:

"That was a very nice thing of Morley to say so long as it is confined to one or two of my friends who won't misunderstand it! Just at the moment people are speaking altogether too well of me, which is enough to make any man uncomfortable; for if he has any sense he knows that the reaction is perfectly certain to come under such circumstances, and that then people will revenge themselves for feeling humiliated for having said too much on one side by saying too much on the other."

Much indeed has been said about T.R.—he was, incidentally, the first President to be widely known by his initials—in the intervening years. The upshot of it all has been completely to confirm his prediction. For most of the twenty-five years preceding his death in 1919, T.R. commanded the attention of his contemporaries in a way that no American has done before or since. The reaction set in soon afterward—touched off, perhaps, by the astonishing discovery that the country could, if need be, get along without him. As T.R. had foreseen, people, having convinced themselves that he was indispensable, now blamed him for having tricked them into that illusion. Thus the stage was set for the further devaluation of T.R. that took place in the thirties.

By the thirties, three major historical developments had occurred. One was the Depression. Another was the capture of the Progressive movement in U.S. politics—which T.R. had led as a Republican in the tradition of Lincoln—by a Democratic party which attempted to conceal the kidnapping by giving its prize the new name of Liberalism. The third was that by now the occupant of the White House was a new and very different Roosevelt—(and one whose wife was T.R.'s by no means especially respectful niece).

The third factor was perhaps the most relevant to the consequences under discussion here. To what degree F.D.R. as a young man actually based his political credo on that of his then infinitely more renowned relative it is difficult to determine. Nonetheless, it was certainly no accident that his early career in New York and Washington followed an almost identical course—up to, and again after, his defeat for the Vice-Presidency in 1920. For many millions of American voters, to assume that the New Deal under Roosevelt II owed something of its character to the Square Deal under Roosevelt I was as natural as to assume three decades later that the New Frontier owed something of its character to the New Deal. In any case, Franklin Roosevelt stood for many if not most of the principles which T.R. had first proposed and fought for. Had F.D.R. been a Republican, he might well have been regarded, not without reason, as a staunch disciple of T.R. and the worthy inheritor of a proud family tradition. As things were, he came instead to be considered a rebel against all that T.R. represented and this view was confirmed rather than contradicted by the close connection through the distaff side of the family.

Once such a view gains acceptance, strong evidence that might contradict it is often dismissed in favor of weaker evidence which supports it. That T.R. had been the first advocate of a League of Nations, in his speech to the Nobel Prize committee in 1910, was, for example, largely ignored and emphasis placed instead upon the campaign against Wilson's version of the League led by T.R.'s close friend, Cabot Lodge. In 1932, the year of Franklin Roosevelt's first inauguration, there appeared an ably written and well documented biography of T.R.—the first since the no doubt overly devout official *Life* by Joseph Bucklin Bishop—by Henry Pringle, theretofore known chiefly as a contributor of profiles to *The New Yorker*. In his book, which won a Pulitzer Prize, Pringle treated T.R. in a manner that would have been unthinkable ten years earlier, before the cynicism of the twenties made it not merely permissible but praiseworthy to sneer at anything that could be regarded as "Victorian" or "unsophisticated." To Pringle, T.R. seemed an essentially ridiculous rather than heroic figure whose national leadership through two dramatic decades had consisted chiefly of posturing before the mirror of adulation held up by the naive public of his period.

During the thirties, this image of T.R. became the generally accepted one—especially among the writers and intellectuals who, in point of fact, were largely indebted to him for their recently increased prestige and influence in the community. Presently it became fashionable to regard T.R. not merely as absurd but even as a vaguely vicious "fascist" prototype. T.R.'s realistic recognition that war and the threat of war were, and would continue to be for the foreseeable future, important influences in international affairs was on occasion compared if not equated with the belligerence of Benito Mussolini—who, to be sure, like F.D.R. and many others, may well have found T.R. a master of political techniques well worthy of close study and occasional emulation.

The truth was perhaps merely that T.R. in common with other major historical influences, was susceptible to various interpretations and to appreciation by rogues as well as to derogation by sincere and talented writers. That this should be so was a measure of the stature which, almost as aptly as in Morley's apothegm, were summed up by Elihu Root —whom T.R. considered the ablest man of his era and one whom he would have chosen instead of Taft as his successor in the White House if he had supposed it possible for Root, as a Wall Street lawyer, to be elected. Root called T.R. "the greatest teacher of the essentials of popular government the world has ever known" and it is not difficult to find evidence in support of this dictum.

It was indeed precisely when, on the more superficial and therefore more apparent level, T.R. was being downgraded and dismissed as a serious force in American life that his influence was perhaps at its strongest and most pervasive. T.R.'s example, which was at the heart of his teaching, had by the 1930s become part of the blood stream of American life more completely, perhaps, though there is no way to prove it, than that of any other president before or since. To be sure, Americans had boxed and played tennis before his appearance on the scene but T.R.'s participation in such pursuits gave them a new prestige and popularity. The mania for sport in general which swept the country in the twenties and presently became world-wide can be traced at least in part to his wholehearted addiction to a wide spectrum of outdoor exertions. On writing, the most influential of the arts, his impact was equally striking—if only through its effect upon Ernest Hemingway, the most influential author of the period, whose strenuous philosophy derived from T.R.'s as obviously as his enthusiasm for shooting big game in Africa. For better or for worse, through his influence on the founders of *Time*, T.R. can be considered largely responsible for the invention of the U.S. news-magazine and all its world-wide off-shoots.

To cite specific instances however merely underlines the futility of attempting to define T.R.'s significance in such terms. His real importance lies deeper—and the very fact that his influence is nowadays so far taken for granted as to be in effect unrecognized is merely one more proof that T.R.'s character is still the inherent character of his country. He wrote that character across the sky for the world to read; and the real virtue of John Morley's comment is that it is, if anything, more true today than when he made it.

One interesting consequence of the diminution of respect openly accorded to T.R. during the thirties as distinct from that revealed unconsciously, is the corollary that he has been largely ignored by the psychoanalytic school of biography whose members would otherwise no doubt have given him the benefit of extensive attention. T.R. had, of course, begun to be the target of psychiatric diagnosis almost as soon as such a thing existed, starting at least as far back as the cam-

paign of 1912. An early disciple of Sigmund Freud at that
time hastened to render an opinion which, perhaps because it
was couched in jargon of a sort which did not achieve general
currency until a full generation later, made only a passing
sensation. According to this expert, the learned Dr. Morton
Prince, T.R. was sure "to go down in history as one of the
most illustrious psychological examples of the distortion of
conscious mental processes through the force of subconscious
wishes." Another psychiatrist of the period, Dr. Allen Mc-
Lane Hamilton, gravely considered the question of T.R.'s
sanity in an article for the New York *Times*.

One trouble with these early applications of analytic procedures to the career of T.R. was that they were perhaps
more politically than scientifically motivated. Partly on this
account, they may have discouraged further excursions into
what might well have been a highly rewarding field of enquiry. Actually, however, while T.R. would doubtless have
been the first to admit that his character and career offered
first-rate material for research along these lines, he had already done the job quite satisfactorily himself in the first
pages of his autobiography, without recourse to the cumber-
some terminology subsequently imposed upon such forms of
self-scrutiny. T.R.'s own account of the way in which during
frequent attacks of severe asthma, he was cradled in the arms
of his father, who often walked the floor with him for long
periods during the small hours of the morning, clearly suggests the mechanism of a precocious transfer of infantile affection. His subsequent strong sense of identification with his
father—in whose character, he notes, the masculine and
feminine virtues were effectively combined—is further confirmed by the eagerness with which he presently accepts this
parent's suggestion that he embark on a stern regimen of body
building. It helps to account for the process of over-compen-

sation whereby this regimen was eventually projected into T.R.'s lifelong philosophy of the strenuous life.

There is, of course, nothing whatsoever unusual, let alone unsatisfactory, about such an identification. Only maladjusted sons fail to make one sooner or later and it is perhaps merely another name for the way in which well-adjusted ones come to welcome the responsibilities and the prerogatives which accompany adult life. What was unusual in T.R.'s case was merely that the identification took place so soon and had such lasting intensity. Thus the portrait of his father hung—and indeed still hangs—on the wall above the desk in his sanctum at Sagamore Hill in Oyster Bay, where he could never raise his eyes without seeing it. According to his own account, his own capacities began first to make themselves apparent during the years of his early adolescence—at an age when most of his contemporaries were doubtless, like their present-day peers, just embarking upon the period of teen-age disaffection. In T.R.'s case, the only instance of even momentary hostility between himself and his male parent which he could recall occurred when he was four years old and this be-whiskered authority was obliged to pursue him under the kitchen table to punish him for a trifling misdemeanor. To this episode too, contemporary psychiatrists might trace some of his later activities, including, no doubt, encounters with grizzly bears and white rhinoceri.

One or two of T.R.'s critics have dwelt on what seemed to them to be T.R.'s occasional air of self-righteousness. Close reading of his autobiography suggests that what he really felt was not so much that *he* was always right as that his *father* was, and that he himself was merely, in a special sense, *in loco parentis*. Likewise, the conviction that those who opposed him were allied with the forces of evil, of which he was sometimes accused, may have been merely a projection of the feel-

ings he himself had expressed about those who opposed the
senior Roosevelt's confirmation as Collector of the Port of
New York—a post which he himself was later able to confer
upon an especially devoted disciple.

T.R.'s effort, explicit in his own writings, to be as much
like his father as possible may have helped not only to super-
charge his whole approach to life, but also to make him not so
much a dual, as actually a double, or twin-motored, personality. It may thus help to account for comments of various
admirers including, among others, that renowned White
House chief usher, Ike Hoover. A skillful and experienced
observer of the eminent, Hoover was so devoted to T.R. that,
when the latter called at the White House in 1910, he remarked that it was the only happy day the attendants there
had had for two years and that "not one of us would exchange
it for a hundred dollar bill." It was however, Hoover who,
in his knowledge and affection said of T.R. that he "seemed
to be forcing himself all the time; acting, as it were, and successfully."

T.R.'s own analysis of his youthful development goes far to
explain why his adult attitude toward authority was, in psychiatric terms, ambivalent—or, to use less technical language,
appropriately impartial. Far from feeling permanently committed to membership in, and sympathy exclusively for, the
tribe of "underdogs" and "underprivileged" persons, as do
those who have never fully come to terms with adult authority, he was nonetheless quite ready to endorse the viewpoint of society's victims whenever the facts justified it. On
the one hand, he was never in the least awed by authority,
and fully capable of defying and usually defeating it in any
guise whatsoever. On the other, he was also immune to the
ailment, endemic then as now in what he was the first to call

the "lunatic fringe," of supposing that the *status quo* exists only to be altered and rules only to be broken.

While in fact it may well be demonstrably harmless and even to some degree informative for outsiders to embark upon interpretative diagnoses of eminent personages long deceased, it cannot be denied that the practice has certain risks, if only for the practitioner. Research along such lines is likely to be mistaken for an attempt to belittle or disparage its object even though exactly the reverse may be the case. This is perhaps unfortunate; for if the proper study of mankind is man, it can also be urged that the proper function of psychiatry is not so much to cure the mentally infirm as to assist in the scrutiny of their betters.

In the case of T.R., for example, such scrutiny could be carried further along various lines. One might be to note that, having overcome hostility toward his parents before most children begin to indulge it, and certainly before he himself was aware of having any, he never suffered from the "repressed guilt feelings" which provide the sand in the gears of most less happily adjusted humans. T.R.'s total clarity of conscience can be deduced not only from his own by no means infrequent affirmations but also from circumstantial evidence in the form of other character traits and tendencies. One of the latter might be the capacity for intense and uninterrupted enjoyment, which he possessed to a degree unthinkable for anyone with a psyche clouded by any trace of self-doubt or accusation. Corollary evidence might be supplied by the excellence of his memory. Like a sundial which records only the shining hours, memory, most psychologists agree, tends to erase unpleasant experiences while taking full note of pleasant ones. Roosevelt's astounding ability to recall events, ideas and people may well have been derived at least in part from the obvious fact that for him all experiences tended to be happy ones.

Roosevelt's phenomenal clarity of conscience may likewise corroborate both his lifelong immunity to indecision and his own modest but undeniably shrewd appraisal of his character and capacities. The latter differs from that of most other qualified observers, most notably perhaps the outstanding U.S. assessor of creative talent, Van Wyck Brooks, who wrote: "If ever there was obviously a man of genius, it was Theodore Roosevelt." T.R. himself believed on the contrary that his achievements were due not to the possession of extraordinary capacities but to his unfailing readiness to use ordinary ones "up to the handle." Among many phrasings of this belief, the most revealing is perhaps his statement to the newspaperman, Oscar K. Davis:

"I am just an ordinary man, without any special ability in any direction. In most things I am just above the average; in some of them a little under rather than over. I am only an ordinary walker. I can't run. I am not a good swimmer, although I am a strong one. I probably ride better than I do anything else, but I am certainly not a remarkably good rider. I am not a good shot. My eyesight is not strong, and I have to get close to my game in order to make any shot at all. I never could be a good boxer, although I like to box and do keep at it whenever I can. My eyesight prevents me from being a good boxer, even if otherwise I could qualify. So you see that from the physical point of view I am just an ordinary or perhaps a little less than ordinary man. . . . I am not a brilliant writer. I have written a great deal, but I always have to work and slave over everything I write. The things that I have done in one office or another are all, with the possible exception of the Panama Canal, just such things as any ordinary man could have done. There is nothing brilliant or outstanding in my record, except perhaps this one thing. I do the things that I believe ought to be done. And when I make up my mind to do a thing, I act."

The question of whether or not T.R. was a genius must obviously depend mainly upon the definition put to a noun which is perhaps as little understood as it is vastly overworked. One way to reconcile his opinion with that of Brooks might be to suggest that what genius consists of is, precisely, the ability, which so few mortals ever attain, to use each talent to the utmost. How thoroughly T.R. contrived to do this was wryly summed up by another well-seasoned judge of character, Oliver Wendell Holmes, whom Roosevelt picked for the Supreme Court bench, with whom he later differed sharply. Of T.R., Holmes wrote to his friend, Sir Arthur Pollock, in February, 1921: "He was very likeable, a big figure, a rather ordinary intellect, with extraordinary gifts, a shrewd and I think pretty unscrupulous politician. He played all his cards —if not more. R.i.p."

For a generation to whom T.R. must necessarily appear as a figure in history, it may be pertinent to suggest that his period is by no means as remote as the chaotic nature of the Twentieth Century may make it seem. T.R. was only a few years older than Sir Winston Churchill and he might well have outlived World War II, as did his widow. Edith Kermit Carow was twenty-six when she married T.R. and not yet sixty when he died. A third of her life still remained to be lived out at Sagamore Hill, a period which must have been in sharp contrast to the eventful commotion of her earlier years there. In accord with an old-fashioned custom now rarely followed, the simple headstone over her husband's grave was inscribed with her name as well as his, the latter being complete except for the date of her death. This was

finally filled in after the death of Kermit and Theodore Jr.
in the second World War which T.R. had so clearly foreseen.
The brief inscription now reads:

> Theodore Roosevelt
> Born October 28, 1858
> Died January 6, 1919
> and his wife,
> Edith Kermit
> Born August 8, 1861
> Died September 30, 1948

Like Sagamore Hill, which was recently declared a national
monument, two other houses that formed an important part
of T.R.'s background are still on view to the public. One is
the cabin at Medora, North Dakota, where he lived during
his first days as a rancher on the open range country of the
Little Missouri. The other is the old house at 28 East 20th
Street, New York City, in which he was born and where he
spent his first and most formative years. The district is now
one of low-cost loft structures: a block East are Gramercy
Park and above it the region of Armenian restaurants, while
the lower reaches of respectably residential Park Avenue start
some fourteen blocks to the North. Nonetheless, at least for a
New Yorker, it is not hard to reconstruct the scene as it must
have looked a hundred years ago and to imagine the old
brownstone, set well back from the present building line, as
it appeared when Theodore Roosevelt, the future President's
father, brought his pretty bride back from Roswell, Georgia,
to live there.

II

N̲ew York in the late 1850's
was a city of less than a million souls in which the tallest edifice was the spire of Trinity Church. Elevated railroads, now
well in the past, were then still well in the future; carts, carriages, and horsecars clattered along streets cobbled with
stones brought from Europe as ballast in ships that then returned with cargoes of raw materials for the factories of the
old world. The well-dressed man was likely to wear a stove-
pipe hat, trousers without cuffs or creases and a black frock
coat; ladies wore hoop skirts and floppy bonnets; their stockings, rarely, if ever, exposed to public view, were made of lisle
rather than silk. The sound of the city nowadays is a deep
mechanized buzz punctuated by the wheeze of air brakes, the
clatter of power drills or riveting hammers and the intermittent humming and thumping of jet aircraft. Then it was a
different and less pervasive but, in a way, more vital one;
wheels rattling on the pavement, the slap of hooves, human
voices and, above Forty-second Street, the noises made by

steam locomotives that puffed and wheezed and whistled on the surface tracks along Park Avenue.

Nonetheless, all such signs of progress notwithstanding, the changes that have occurred in the past century may still be outnumbered by ways in which the city has remained the same. New York had a sense of urgency and purpose that had already enabled it to surpass Boston and Philadelphia as the major metropolis of the Eastern seaboard, and made it indeed the nation's capital in all respects except what New Yorkers considered the rather unrewarding specialty of politics. New York's air had, then as now, a special sooty, salty, stimulating tang. The space limitations of Manhattan Island, soon to push its architecture upwards into the marvelous creation of the skyscraper, had already produced what is still the characteristic New York house—a four-story brownstone box jammed against identical neighbors on both sides with windows only at front and rear, and a flight of steps in front running up to a small and rather grimy stoop, or porch. Nowadays, when fewer than five thousand New Yorkers live in private houses at all, most of the remaining brownstones have been converted into small apartments or rooming houses. In the fifties, the vast majority were still private residences. The town's aristocracy lived in them, mostly along lower Fifth Avenue or the cross streets on either side of it, North of Washington Square. It was in just such a house that Theodore Roosevelt was born on October 27th, 1858.

Theodore Roosevelt Sr., his father, was a prosperous importer of glassware and a member in good standing of the city's mercantile upper crust. The Roosevelts were nothing like as rich as the Vanderbilts or the Astors but they had been well-to-do a good deal longer. Their roots in the city went back to 1644 when the first of the clan had come over from Holland; in the six generations since then, its members had proliferated not only on Manhattan Island, where Theodore, Sr.'s direct forebears on the male side had all been born but in the nearby counties and up the Hudson River toward Albany. His wife, the former Martha Bulloch—somewhat surprisingly because the widespread social life of the Roosevelts rarely took them quite so far afield for their brides—was the daughter of an affluent plantation family which had been established at Roswell, Georgia, for several generations.

Known to the immediate members of his family as "Teedie," small Theodore proved to be a delicate baby who, as he outgrew infancy, was subject to increasingly severe attacks of asthma. When these kept him awake at night, as he became too big for his mother to carry comfortably in her arms, the chore of walking him to sleep fell regularly to his father. The especially close relationship thus established became, if anything, even closer as the years went by. The painful and untimely death of Theodore Roosevelt, Sr. from cancer when his son was a sophomore at Harvard was such a severe blow to the latter that his diaries for a year thereafter were devoted almost entirely to expressions of grief like the following:

"I remember so well how when I was a very weak asthmatic child, he used to walk up and down with me in his arms for hours together, night after night. . . . I owe everything I am or have to Father . . . Oh, how little worthy I am of such a father. . . . How I wish I could ever do something to keep up his name. . . ."

Many years later, when the younger Theodore Roosevelt had done much to keep up the name, his feelings, as described in a letter to one of his friends, remained unchanged.

"I was fortunate enough in having a father whom I have always been able to regard as an ideal man. It sounds a little like cant to say what I am going to say but he really did combine the strength and courage and will and energy of the strongest man with the tenderness, cleanness and purity of a woman. I was a sickly and timid boy. He not only took great and untiring care of me—some of my earliest remembrances are of nights when he would walk up and down with me for an hour at a time in his arms when I was a wretched little mite suffering acutely from asthma—but he also most wisely refused to coddle me, and made me feel that I must force myself to hold my own with other boys and prepare to do the rough work of the world. I cannot say that he ever put it into words but he certainly gave me the feeling that I was always to be both decent and manly, and that if I were manly nobody would laugh at my being decent."

Other contemporary estimates of Theodore Roosevelt, Sr. tend to confirm the high opinion of his namesake. The older Roosevelt owed his considerable eminence in the community as much to high spirits and friendliness as to his reputation for acumen, probity, and diligence in good works. His sidelines, along with worthy organizations like the Orthopedic (now the Roosevelt) Hospital, the Newsboys' Lodging House and the Y.M.C.A., included dining out frequently and driving a four-in-hand at such speed that "the grooms fell out at the corners." An old friend recalled seeing him "in full evening dress, serving a most generous dinner to his newsboys . . . and then dashing off to an evening party in Fifth Avenue." At parties, according to his daughter, he liked to stay until swept out with the favors.

Along with many other noted figures—among them J. P. Morgan, Elihu Root and Robert Lincoln—Theodore, Sr., although subject to draft during the Civil War, had chosen the then entirely conventional course of hiring a substitute to serve in his stead. In so doing, he was no doubt motivated by family considerations—since two of his wife's brothers were serving in the Confederate Navy, one as an admiral and the other as a midshipman. Nonetheless, Roosevelt still felt obligated to make some direct contribution to the Union cause and found a characteristic way of doing so. This was a plan whereby soldiers could allot a portion of their pay to their families, which he first helped to persuade Congress to enact into law and then, as one of the three allotment commissioners, helped to persuade the troops to utilize. In the course of getting political support for his allotment plan, Roosevelt frequented Washington where he became well acquainted with both President Lincoln and his young secretary, John Hay. Mrs. Lincoln took a liking to him; she invited him to accompany the family to church and to give her advice about buying hats. Hay called on the Roosevelts in New York and met young T.R. in his nursery. "This is a young man who will make his mark," the host said to his family in introducing his Washington visitor.

When, in the spring of 1869, Theodore Roosevelt, Sr. decided to go abroad, he arranged the trip in characteristic style, taking the whole family with him. In addition to ten-year-old Teedie and himself, the group included his wife, a pretty, fluttery person whom Teedie by his early teens had begun to address as "Motherling"; Teedie's fourteen-year-old sister, Anna, nicknamed "Bye" or "Bamie"; his nine-year-old brother, Elliott, later the father of Eleanor Roosevelt; and seven-year-old Corinne, nicknamed "Pussie" or "Connie." The itinerary planned for this formidable entourage would have presented serious logistic problems in the era of air and auto travel, let alone that of hansom cabs, slow trains, and paddle-wheel steamers. It called for a year's tour of England, Holland, Germany, Switzerland, Italy, Austria and France, with extensive travel in the interior of each and two visits to most.

Such a schedule would all by itself be enough to suggest that the younger Theodore Roosevelt's concept of the strenuous life owed much to his father's example. So would some of the activities undertaken en route, like walks of from thirteen to twenty-three miles along Swiss mountain paths which both Theodores mention casually in their numerous letters. The actual communication of the concept in specific terms took place during the summer of 1870. One of the objectives of the European trip had been to provide a beneficial change for Teedie. When his asthma persisted after their return, his father summoned him for a heart-to-heart talk and said:

"You have the mind but not the body and without the help of the body the mind cannot go as far as it should. . . . You must make your body. It is hard drudgery . . . but I know that you will do it."

In view of Teedie's feelings toward his father, it is not surprising that he took a vow to do exactly that and thereafter spent a large portion of his waking hours living up to it. During the winter, this involved an arduous regimen of pulling chest weights and swinging on parallel bars, first in a gymnasium and then in a room at home in which the necessary apparatus was installed. During the summer, like most well-to-do New Yorkers, the Roosevelts went "to the country" —the Jersey coast, Ardsley or Tarrytown on the Hudson, or the Adirondacks. At such resorts, Teedie took lengthy hikes or rides on his pony, Grant, named for the General.

Had little Roosevelt been packed off to a private school like most other urchins of his age and station, he might have been enrolled, willingly or otherwise, in the immemorial war between schoolboys and their teachers. Instead, he had lessons at home where, far from being laughed at, blunted or diverted, the enthusiasm for acquiring knowledge which, like many frail children, he rapidly developed, was directed into congenial channels. One such channel was a magazine called *Our Young Folks* which, according to the *Autobiography* which T.R. wrote in his fifties, "taught me more than any of my text books." In *Our Young Folks,* one of his favorite features was a serial correspondence between a schoolboy and his family, the influence of which can readily be traced in T.R.'s own later efforts in this field. Another was its complete coverage of Natural History.

Just as most contemporary small boys are much excited about outer space due to recent developments in astrophysics, those of the 1880's were much concerned about zoology, due to the discoveries of Darwin. Teedie's interest in this subject started at the age of seven when he saw a seal which had been killed in New York harbor displayed as an oddity on a wooden slab in a Broadway market. Presently he was entering descriptions of wood spiders, crickets, and other insects in a zoological notebook. At the same time he was collecting animal oddities, including the seal's skull, for a "Roosevelt Museum of Natural History" established on an upstairs porch at the rear of the Roosevelt town house.

Small Teedie's interests in zoology and in the concept of the strenuous life were not merely compatible but mutually complimentary and they became more so as he grew older. In addition to spying on small birds, beasts and reptiles in their native habitats, he began trying to shoot and preserve them. This led to the discovery of a further physical infirmity when, at the age of thirteen, he acquired his first rifle. Trying to use this weapon, he found that his companions often took aim at targets which he could not even see. The spectacles which were presently prescribed for him not only vastly improved his marksmanship but also enabled him to extend his exploration of zoology into the allied field of taxidermy. In this his mentor was a renowned Adirondack expert, John

G. Bell, who had worked with Audubon. The results of his efforts in this field provided additional specimens for display in the Roosevelt Museum.

The Roosevelt Museum of Natural History—and for that matter, Teedie's concern with zoology in general—reflected his father's interest in the American Museum of Natural History, which he had helped to found. Soon after leaving college, young Roosevelt formed a lasting friendship with Henry Fairfield Osborn, who, as head of the Museum many years later, helped support his strenuous trips to Africa and South America. Osborn was only one of many of his close associates among the famous outdoor naturalists of the period, who also included John Burroughs, John Muir, and Chancellor David Starr Jordan of Leland Stanford University. The latter in due course arranged to have Roosevelt's boyhood collections preserved at the University of Indiana and also to have a special variety of the Hawaiian Kali Kali fish—golden yellow with cross bands of crimson—officially named the *Rooseveltia*. When he called on Roosevelt at the White House in 1905 to enlist the President's aid in his proposed exploration of the deep seas off Japan in the Fish Commission steamer *Albatross*, T.R. pounded the desk and replied: "It was to help along things like this, Dr. Jordan, that I took *this* job!"

Even more significant in his development than small Teedie's visit to the oculist was another childhood experience which he describes in his *Autobiography:*

> Having an attack of asthma, I was sent off by myself to Moosehead Lake. On the stagecoach ride thither I encountered a couple of other boys who were about my own age, but very much more competent and also much more mischievous. I have no doubt they were good-hearted boys, but they were boys! They found that I was a foreordained and predestined victim, and industriously proceeded to make life miserable for

me. The worst feature was that when I finally tried to fight them I discovered that either one singly could not only handle me with easy contempt, but handle me so as not to hurt me much and yet to prevent my doing any damage whatever in return.

Had Roosevelt's encounter with the "mischievous" boys occurred at the beginning of his program of body-building it might not have made much of an impression on him. That it occurred instead after he had spent two full years, or a sixth of his life up to that time, in the effort to become physically self-sufficient was what made it especially painful. Under similar circumstances, many small boys might well have concluded that the whole theory of body-building was a delusion. Young Roosevelt, on the contrary, merely decided to intensify his regimen:

The experience taught me what probably no amount of good advice could have taught me. I made up my mind that I must try to learn so that I would not again be put in such a helpless position; and having become quickly and bitterly conscious that I did not have the natural prowess to hold my own, I decided that I would try to supply its place by training. Accordingly, with my father's hearty approval, I started to learn to box. I was a painfully slow and awkward pupil, and certainly worked two or three years before I made any perceptible improvement whatever. My first boxing master was John Long, an ex-prize-fighter. I can see his rooms now, with colored pictures of the fights between Tom Hyer and Yankee Sullivan, and Heenan and Sayers, and other great events in the annals of the squared circle. On one occasion, to excite interest among his patrons, he held a series of "championship" matches for the different weights, the prizes being, at least in my own class, pewter mugs of a value, I should suppose, approximating fifty cents. Neither he nor I had any idea that I could do anything, but I was entered in the lightweight contest, in which it happened that I was pitted in succession against a couple of reedy striplings who were even worse than I was. Equally to their surprise and to my own, and to John Long's, I won, and the pewter mug became one of my most prized possessions. I kept it, and alluded to it, and I fear bragged about it, for a number of years, and I only wish I knew where it was now. Years later I read an account of a little man who once in a fifth-rate handicap race won a worthless pewter medal and joyed in it ever after. Well, as soon as I read that story I felt that that little man and I were brothers.

During the winter of 1872, the Roosevelts took another trip to Europe which resembled the first except that this one included a boat trip up the Nile to Khartoum and a prolonged stay in the Holy Land. Teedie, who had been bored by the first trip, now had the strenuous zoological life—in the form of bird-shooting, horseback riding and taxidermy practice, on shipboard or in hotel rooms—to sustain him. When his father left Teedie, Elliott, and Corinne in Dresden, to live with a German family and pick up the language, the two boys devoted themselves even more diligently to boxing.

The Roosevelts' return to New York in the spring of 1872 coincided with several innovations. One was a new town house at 6 West 57th Street where, in addition to his gymnastic equipment, Theodore had access to Central Park with its rock-climbs, bridle paths and skating-ponds. Another was a country house at Oyster Bay—named, of all things, "Tranquillity"—where they spent the next several summers. Here rowing and swimming were added to Teedie's routine, as well as track and field competition with numerous Roosevelt cousins who lived nearby. The third was a tutor named Arthur Cutler, later the founder of New York's Cutler School, whose job was to prepare his charge for college. Under Cutler, in the years that followed he studied eight hours a day in winter and three in summer, devoting his spare time to systematic weight lifting, parallel-bar swinging, walking, climbing, skating, shooting, running, jumping, rowing, and swimming as the season and surroundings indicated. In September of 1876, he entered Harvard.

By the time Theodore Roosevelt got to Harvard, his intense campaign of strenuous exercise had done far more than rid him—except for increasingly infrequent relapses—of his chronic asthma. It had turned him into a sort of juvenile, all-around iron-man whose phenomenal endurance was presently to enable him to accomplish summer vacation feats like a twenty-five mile round trip across Long Island Sound in less than six hours rowing time or a sixty-mile ride from Oyster Bay to Lake Ronkonkoma on his horse, Lightfoot. To the casual observer, however, his athletic abilities were concealed by his appearance, which remained that of a spindly weakling.

That Roosevelt's stature gave no hint of his capacities was fortunate in view of the circumstances. Harvard, in the first years of Charles Eliot's presidency, was not a place where premiums were placed upon physical prowess or, indeed, effort of any sort. The emphasis, on the contrary, was upon languor and indolence. Undergraduates made a point of speaking slowly, in a "Harvard drawl"; they walked in a premeditated slouch, or "Harvard swing." This attitude was poetically expressed by Roosevelt's friend, George Pellew, official poet of the class of 1880, in verses composed to grace a gathering at the Hasty Pudding Club:

". . . We ask but time to drift.
To drift—and note the devious ways of man,
To drift,—and probing life's recesses scan

The truths that overarch and underlie
The surface faiths whereby men live and die . . .

We deem it narrow-minded to excel.
We call the man fanatic who applies
His life to one grand purpose till he dies.
Enthusiasm sees one side, one fact;
We try to see all sides, but do not act . . .
We long to sit with newspapers unfurled,
Indifferent spectators of the world."

In view of the contrast between the attitude of young
Theodore Roosevelt and that of his contemporaries, confusion of various sorts was bound to develop. A good example
of it occurred one afternoon in the Harvard gymnasium,
where he spent much of his spare time, as did one of his
classmates named Richard Welling. Watching Roosevelt
struggling first with the chest weights and then with some
other items of equipment that were new to him, Welling
judged him to be a weakling, and, out of pity, arranged to go
skating with him. He described what followed to a friend
long afterward:

". . . A long ride in a freezing horse-car and then Fresh
Pond, too big and too unprotected from the furious winds to
be good skating ground, rough ice, dull skates, wretched
skaters, scuffling about, mostly arms waving like windmills in
a gale—and when any sane man would have voted to go home,
as the afternoon's sport was clearly a flop, Roosevelt was
exclaiming, "Isn't this bully!"—and the harder it blew and the
worse we skated, the more often I had to hear "Isn't this
bully!" There was no trace of shelter where we could rub our
ears, restore our fingers to some semblance of feeling, or

prevent our toes from becoming perhaps seriously frost-bitten. Never in college was my grit so put to the test. . . . Nearly three hours passed before Roosevelt finally said, "It's too dark to skate any more" (as though, if there had been a moon, we could have gone on until midnight). . . ."

What made this incident especially noteworthy was that Welling, according to the official figures, was the strongest man in the class. Upon less resilient contemporaries, the impact of Roosevelt's strenuosity was often even less ingratiating. Some decided that he must be mentally unbalanced and William Roscoe Thayer, later his admiring biographer, who was a class behind him, recalled saying to himself, "I wonder whether he is the real thing or only the bundle of eccentricities he appears." He decided that Roosevelt was "a good deal of a joke . . . active and enthusiastic and that was all." Another classmate recalled the most serious offense of all when "it was not considered good form to move at more than a walk, Roosevelt was always running."

Upon his professors also, Roosevelt made a somewhat ambiguous impression owing to "his tendency to interrupt the lecturer and ask questions." His favorite course was, understandably, Natural History. Here his classroom contributions were so continuous that the lecturer, Professor Nathaniel Shaler, one day found himself moved to exclaim: "Now look here, Roosevelt, let me talk. I'm running this course."

In overcoming the equivocal reactions aroused in his teachers and contemporaries, Roosevelt had at least one substantial advantage. This was a naturally gregarious disposition which, now for the first time, he had an adequate opportunity to display along lines encouraged by his father and, perhaps, best defined by him in a letter to Corinne:

"Remember that almost everyone will be kind to you and love you if you are only willing to receive their love and are unselfish. This, you know, is the virtue which I put above all others and while it increases so much the pleasure of those about you, it adds infinitely to your own. . . ."

His father's specific advice in a letter to Theodore had been: "Take care of your morals first, your health next, and finally your studies." In adhering to this counsel, Theodore left little to chance, as indicated by his daily schedule during freshman year: 7:15, get up; 7:45, chapel; 8, breakfast; 8:30, study; 9, classes; 12, study; 1, lunch; 1:30, study; 2:30, class; 3:30, exercise; 6, dinner; 7, study; 8:30, see friends; 10:30, read; 11, bed. In addition to all this, he took part in a variety of extracurricular activities and taught an hour each week at Sunday School.

The combination of Roosevelt's diligence and his buoyant affability eventually proved enough to overcome the effects of his apparent eccentricity. His classmates forgave his unwillingness to drawl or slouch and he eventually became a definite social success. Along with Robert Bacon, considered the handsomest man in the class and its acknowledged leader, who later served briefly as T.R.'s Secretary of State and as Ambassador to France under Taft, he joined the elite Institute of 1770 and wrote articles for the Finance Club. By the end of his junior year, he was a member of Porcellian, Harvard's choosiest club, as well as secretary of the Hasty Pudding, president of Alpha Delta Phi, an editor of the *Advocate* and vice-president of the Natural History Society.

Although he gained twelve pounds while in college, Roosevelt remained too light to hope to make the varsity crew, for which his prowess as an oarsman might well have qualified him otherwise. His eye-sight as well as his stature ruled out football or baseball. The highpoint of his athletic career came in the winter of his junior year, when he reached the finals of the lightweight boxing championship, against the defend-

At eight, here wearing a velvet suit, Roosevelt was a delicate, precocious child, still subject to frequent attacks of acute asthma but intellectually advanced beyond his years.

From Stephan Lorant's *The Life and Times of Theodore Roosevelt* (Doubleday)

Alice Lee, (left) with her cousin (center) whom Roosevelt married in 1880, was a light-hearted pretty girl who died tragically after giving birth to a daughter on February 14, 1884.

T.R.'s oldest son was Theodore, Jr., who grew up to fight in both world wars, run for Governor of New York and die of a heart attack soon after D-Day in 1944.

As Colonel of Rough Riders, T.R.'s equipment included a Brooks Brothers uniform, a soft hat that later became famous and a dozen pairs of steel-rimmed glasses.

At Sagamore Hill, in the summer of 1903, the family included six children—from left to right, Quentin, Theodore, Jr., Archibald, Alice, Kermit and Ethel.

"He's good enough for me" was the quote from Uncle Sam under this famous Davenport cartoon that helped T.R. to be elected President in his own right in 1904.

The American Eagle gets a thorough scrubbing from T.R. in this Bernard Partridge drawing. T.R.'s strenuous demeanor made him a godsend to cartoonists.

"It was great!" said T.R. after his first plane ride—at Springfield, Illinois, in 1910. Aviator Arch Hoxsey was killed when his flimsy machine crashed a year later.

ing titleholder, C. S. Hanks. Hanks won the decision but not before Roosevelt had had an opportunity to impress the substantial crowd, which included a sportswriter for the New York *Times*, by a characteristic gesture. When he dropped his guard at the end of a round, Hanks gave him an illegal punch on the nose which drew blood and caused onlookers to hiss. Roosevelt held up his hand for silence and shouted: "It's all right—he didn't hear him," indicating that Hanks had inadvertently missed the timekeeper's signal. He then walked across the ring to shake his opponent's hand.

During the summer of 1876, Roosevelt's tutor, Arthur Cutler, a confirmed camping enthusiast, had made a trip to the Maine woods with Emlen and James West Roosevelt and their Oyster Bay friend, Arthur Weekes. In Maine, their host and guide had been a crack lumberman and guide named William Sewall who ran an informal hunting lodge near Island Falls in Aroostook County, the northernmost corner of the state. When Cutler reported to his former pupil that the trip had been highly satisfactory, Roosevelt resolved to take one like it. In the late summer of 1878, some six months after his father's death, he and his cousins Emlen and James West Roosevelt with their friend Will Thomson, spent the last three weeks of their vacation at Sewall camp. Roosevelt and Sewall soon found that, as Sewall later phrased it, they "hitched well together." The Maine woods proved so much to Roosevelt's liking that he made two more trips there, in March, 1879, and the following September.

Before Roosevelt's first visit to Island Falls, Cutler had written to Sewall that Roosevelt was in somewhat delicate health and should not be allowed to overexert himself. The lumberman, observing his guest closely, noted that, while Roosevelt made occasional asthmatic noises which Sewall described as "guffleing," he was always in good humor and thought nothing of walking twenty-five miles a day. Sewall considered this "a good fair walk for any common man." On Roosevelt, Sewall made an even more favorable impression which he recorded forty years later in his autobiography: "The kind of Americanism—self-respecting, duty-performing, life-enjoying—which is the most valuable possession that one generation can hand on to the next."

On Roosevelt's second trip to Island Falls, the snow was three feet deep and the temperature ten below zero. This made it ideal for a caribou hunt lasting a day and a half in the course of which the hunters spent one night on the trail with little food and no blankets. In a letter to his mother, Roosevelt commented on the scenery: "When it freezes after a rain, all the trees look as though they were made out of crystal." Years later he recalled "delicious nights under a lean-to . . . on balsam bows in front of a blazing stump."

The March trip made a good run-through or warm-up for the third one, on which his companions were Emlen Roosevelt and Cutler. The main objective this time was to climb Mount Katahdin, next to Mount Washington the highest peak in New England. Somewhat embarrassingly for Cutler, in view of his earlier comments, he and Emlen collapsed before gaining the summit, but Roosevelt reached it easily and noted in his diary that he could "endure fatigue and hardship pretty nearly as well as these lumbermen." That night it rained and they were "all soaked through" with no apparent ill effects. When Emlen and Cutler returned to civilization, Roosevelt stayed on for a nine-day pirogue trip with Sewall. It rained most of the time and a typical day involved ten hours in the water dragging the dugout around rocks, rapids, beaver-dams and log-jams. Roosevelt stated in his diary that he was "enjoying the trip greatly . . . am in superb health and as tough as a pine knot." After another ten days of hunting, hiking and canoe-paddling on a comparable scale, he reluctantly packed up to go back to college and summed up his impressions:

"What glorious fun I am having. . . . No fellow ever had a better time than I have. And my life has such absurd contrasts. At one time I live in the height of luxury; and then for a month will undergo really severe toil and hardship—and I enjoy both extremes almost equally. . . . By Jove, it sometimes seems as if I were having too happy a time to have it last. I enjoy every minute I live, almost."

In recovering from the deep emotional shock of his father's death, one thing that had greatly helped Roosevelt was his encounter with the Maine wilderness and with Bill Sewall, who became his friend for life and, eventually, like a quorum of T.R.'s other friends, wrote a book about him. Another was the example of the elder Roosevelt himself: he had believed in accepting God's will not merely bravely but happily, and, in his son's words, had "enjoyed life more than any other man I ever knew." Beginning in the autumn of his junior year, there was also a third influence which doubtless helped to explain, in his phrase about enjoying every minute of his own life, the use of the alien adverb "almost." That autumn he had fallen in love; and this experience, while vastly exhilarating, was by no means without its alarming aspects.

The object of Roosevelt's affections was Miss Alice Hathaway Lee, the cousin and nextdoor neighbor of his close friend and classmate, Richard Saltonstall. She was a pretty, willowy blonde with a retroussé nose and a disposition indicated by her nickname, "Sunshine." However, as the daughter of the eminently proper Bostonian, George Cabot Lee, of Chestnut Hill and Boston's top banking firm, Lee Higginson and Company, she was not without numerous other admirers and, at seventeen, in no hurry to make a final choice among them.

Before encountering Alice Lee, young Roosevelt's experience in romance had been, to put it mildly, limited. In New York and Oyster Bay, along with the other young Roosevelts and their friends, he had shared in rounds of youthful dinner parties, picnics and dancing classes. The only girls he had seen more of than the rest were his sister's friends, Frances Theodora Smith, Annie Murray and Edith Kermit Carow. Fanny Smith considered him then "the most original boy I ever knew" and more than sixty years later recalled "dreading to sit next to him at any formal dinner lest I become so convulsed with laughter at his whispered sallies as to disgrace myself and be forced to leave the room." Roosevelt regarded Annie Murray as "a very nice girl besides being very pretty" but the only one of the three in whom he had ever showed more than casual interest was Edith Carow. Even in her case, the evidence, so far as can be gathered from his usually explicit diaries, consisted of no more than an occasional row across Oyster Bay, one conversation in the summer house at Tranquility and a letter addressed to "Dear Eidie" from Sorrento, when he was homesick and eleven.

Outside the family-approved circle, Roosevelt's acquaintance with the opposite sex had been even less extensive. The studied indifference displayed by Harvard undergraduates on the campus sometimes deserted then under the stimulus of less rarified environments, especially that provided by the burlesque shows at Boston's Globe Theatre. There, indeed, their behavior was often so unruly as to shock even the performers and when the celebrated Emily Soldene took her troupe from Boston to Cincinnati, her anxious inquiry on arrival was, "Is there a University here?" Roosevelt and his set appeared to be more or less immune to the attractions of downtown Boston. Of his friends, he remarked in his diary that while "not brilliant" they were "plucky, honorable and rigidly virtuous." As for himself, mindful of the priority assigned to morals by his father, he was able to write that "Thank Heaven, I am at least perfectly pure."

The impression made by Roosevelt upon mixed society in suburban Boston's elite younger set was, on the whole, not greatly dissimilar from that made on his classmates. The future Mrs. Robert Bacon, a Boston debutante of 1879, recalled Roosevelt as being "studious, ambitious, eccentric—not the sort to appeal at first." Alice Lee's sister, Rose, many years later recalled that "He danced just as you'd expect him to dance if you knew him—he hopped." Roosevelt's tendency to turn the conversation to such topics as insects, snakes, or lizards was not calculated to captivate young ladies of Victorian sensibility nor was his propensity on occasion to produce dead specimens of such creatures from his coat pockets.

That, under the circumstances, his courtship encountered difficulties may be less startling than that it finally succeeded. According to entries in his diary, Roosevelt met Alice Lee on October 18th, 1878, and by Thanksgiving Day he had made up his mind to marry her. Her views on the subject did not coincide with his until considerably later. According to Rose Lee, her sister "had no intention of marrying him—but she did." Mrs. Robert Bacon later recalled a party at the Hasty Pudding Club at which Roosevelt pointed to Alice and said: "See that girl? I am going to marry her. She won't have me but I am going to have her."

Roosevelt's first proposal to Alice Lee apparently took place toward the end of his junior year and brought an indecisive reply. By the fall of his senior year—during which he had arranged a light schedule of courses so as to allow him ample time for other pursuits—Alice Lee's reluctance to reach a favorable decision was causing Roosevelt such perturbation that, according to his diary, "night after night I have not even gone to bed." His classmates finally thought it necessary to send for his cousin, James West Roosevelt, to come to Boston and talk him out of his habit of nocturnal wandering in the woods near Cambridge. Finally, on Sunday, January 25 of 1880, the day before the start of midyear exams, Roosevelt's diary contains a climactic entry:

"At last everything is settled; but it seems impossible to realize it. I am so happy that I dare not trust in my own happiness. I drove over to the Lees' determined to make an end of things at last; it was nearly eight months since I had first proposed to her, and I had been nearly crazy during the past year; and after much pleading, my sweet, pretty darling consented to be my wife. Oh, how bewitchingly pretty she looked! If loving her with my whole heart and soul can make her happy, she shall be happy. . . . How she, so pure and sweet and beautiful can think of marrying me I cannot understand but I praise and thank God it is so. . . ."

In view of the emotional turmoil he was experiencing during the last half of his junior year and the first half of his senior year, Roosevelt preserved an appearance of noteworthy equanimity. By this time he was enough of a campus social figure to be singled out for mention in a Hasty Pudding show which referred to him as "awful smart, with waxed mustache and hair in curls"—although photographs of the period show him wearing side whiskers but without the mustache. For his almost daily excursions to Chestnut Hill—six miles each way over rolling open country—Roosevelt either rode Lightfoot, usually at a gallop, or drove him, harnessed to the smart dog-cart that was the period's equivalent of an imported sports car.

Even more astonishing than Roosevelt's apparent equanimity was the genuine resilience and self-control that enabled him, despite sleepless nights and agitated days, not only to keep up a busy campus and social life but also to maintain respectable scholastic standing. Roosevelt's position in his class slipped slightly from that of his junior year, when he had been thirteenth out of one hundred and sixty-six, but his four-year record was good enough to qualify him for Phi Beta Kappa in his senior year, during which he also undertook a project that would have been astonishingly ambitious even for a college graduate with no other urgent problems on his mind. As a sophomore, Roosevelt had been thoroughly bored by two of his history courses; on further investigation he came to the conclusion that one reason lay in the textbooks. There was not, for example, anywhere that he could find an adequate treatment of the War of 1812. Roosevelt decided to rectify this omission at least by writing one himself. During his senior year he began to gather material and composed the first chapter.

Plans for his future upon leaving college presented something of a problem. Having inherited some $125,000 from his father, his position, as he later expressed it, was that "I had enough to get bread. What I had to do, if I wanted butter and jam, was to provide the butter and jam." A career as a naturalist promised little in this direction and by this time Roosevelt's interests, as indicated by his literary project, had begun to expand. A year of law at Columbia would give him time to work on his book and improve his equipment for whatever career he undertook afterward. Meanwhile his wedding, scheduled for October, gave him plenty to look forward to in his last spring at Cambridge. The diary became more exuberant than ever: ". . . Only four months before we get married. My cup of happiness is almost too full."

On March 26th, 1880, Roosevelt dropped in at the office of Dr. Dudley A. Sargent, the University physician, for a routine check-up. The doctor wrote down his measurements —five feet eight inches, a hundred and thirty-six pounds—put a stethoscope to his chest and finally imparted some confidential advice. His heart, said the doctor, had an irregular beat. It would be wise for him to choose a sedentary career, avoid undue excitement and never run upstairs.

The warning note supplied by his call on Dr. Sargent, like the experience with the mischievous boys en route to Moose-head Lake a decade before, posed a potential dilemma. What it might well have suggested was that the entire course of violent exertion upon which he had embarked on his father's recommendation at the age of ten had been totally mistaken. While increasing his endurance and helping his asthma, the exertion had perhaps at the same time been the cause of impairing his heart and thus gravely curtailing either the length of his life or his choice of a career. If Roosevelt ever allowed himself to consider such a possibility, there is no record of it.

The first six weeks after his graduation—*cum laude,* and twenty-first in a class of one hundred and seventy-seven— Roosevelt spent on an exchange of visits with his fiancée during which time he took her for long rowboat excursions around Oyster Bay and then climbed mountains in Maine. These pastimes were the prelude to a six-week hunting trip with his brother, Elliott, on which they spent long days tramping after game in Illinois, Iowa, and what was then the Dakota Territory. After a gala wedding in October, Roosevelt and his bride settled down for a winter in New York during which, while leading a busy social life, he studied law at Columbia University to which he walked back and forth some six miles a day from the family house on West Fifty-seventh Street. During spare moments, Roosevelt wrote what proved to be a definitive history of *The Naval War of 1812;* and in May, the young couple set off for a four-month tour of Europe which included visits to Ireland, England, France, Germany, Italy, Austria and Switzerland.

For Roosevelt, the climax of the European tour was, natu- rally, Switzerland. There, after warming up on a few minor Alps, he proceeded to climb Mount Pilatus and the Jungfrau, excursions which, he confessed to his diary, left him "rather tired." He was not, however, too tired for a third and more vigorous ascent involving what was then the world's classic test of mountaineering, the fifteen-thousand-foot Matterhorn.

The Matterhorn had, to be sure, been conquered for the first time some sixteen years before when—after fourteen un- successful efforts by previous expeditions—that of Edward Whymper managed to reach the peak, at the cost of four of its members in a fall down a four-thousand-foot precipice. Since then, others had made the climb but it remained almost as risky as it was arduous, even for trained mountaineers in tip- top condition. Roosevelt hired a guide at Zermatt, spent the night in an icy cave on a cliff face near the top, and arose at 3:45 the next morning, so as to see the sunrise from the summit. He and his guide were back at Zermatt early in the afternoon. This time Roosevelt was "not very tired."

For a young man who had been warned against running upstairs, an overnight ascent of the highest peak in Europe was certainly a feat worthy of comment, favorable or other- wise. In Roosevelt's case, even after he became one of the world figures of his era, it attracted little notice, for two reasons. One was that Roosevelt had kept Dr. Sargent's diagnosis to himself and only revealed it several decades later to his biographer, Hermann Hagedorn. The other was that, far from being a mere bit of foolish bravado, in defiance of the most rudimentary common sense, the climb was an entirely deliberate demonstration of the philosophy which Roosevelt later summed up in his famous phrase, "the stren- uous life," and of which practically everything else he did was an expression also.

III

WHILE never himself directly engaged in politics, the elder Theodore Roosevelt kept in touch with political developments and eventually got involved in a political fight of substantial proportions. This fight, which took place in the last year of his life and may have hastened the course of his final illness, concerned the post of Collector of Customs for the Port of New York, to which President Rutherford B. Hayes, elected on a reform ticket in 1876, appointed him the following year. In order to occupy the post, long regarded as a choice political plum, Roosevelt needed confirmation by the Senate where he was strongly opposed by New York's Republican boss, Senator Roscoe Conklin. When, led by Conklin, the Senate voted 31 to 25 in favor of the incumbent, Chester A. Arthur, it was both a sharp disappointment to Theodore Roosevelt, Sr., and a resounding victory for the machine.

To the younger Theodore, who followed the fight closely, his father's defeat for the collectorship was especially distressing and he recorded his feelings in a letter to Bamie: "I am glad on his account but sorry for New York." The influence of the incident upon his own choice of a career became apparent in his senior year at college when he remarked to his friend, William Roscoe Thayer, that after graduation he might try to do something to help the cause of better government in New York.

T.R.'s first direct contact with New York politics took place more or less inadvertently during his first busy winter in New York when, in spare moments not occupied by his marriage, his study of law, his marathon walks and his naval history, he made it his business to learn the whereabouts of his local Republican headquarters and then to join it. As noted in his autobiography, this project seemed to his friends a questionable one, to put it mildly. They explained to him that the headquarters was a disreputable sort of place.

> run by saloon-keepers, horse-car conductors and the like, and not by men with any of whom I would have come in contact outside. . . . I answered that if this were so it merely meant that the people I knew did not belong to the governing class and that the other people did—and that I intended to be one of the governing class; and that if they proved too hard bit for me I supposed I would have to quit but that I certainly would not quit until I . . . found out that I really was too weak to hold my own in the rough and tumble.

The Twenty-first District Republican Organization, which Roosevelt eventually found in a room over a saloon at the corner of Fifth Avenue and Fifty-ninth Street, was run by a local leader named Jake Hess, who tolerated Roosevelt's presence at meetings during the winter and spring of 1881. At these gatherings, Roosevelt became well acquainted with an Irish ward-captain named Joe Murray, a defector from Tammany Hall and a seasoned veteran of the rowdy free-for-all of New York municipal politics. In the fall of 1881, when Roosevelt returned from Europe, Murray was concocting a plan to unseat the Twenty-first District's representative in the Assembly at Albany. Roosevelt fell in with the plan and, when it became clear that Murray had rounded up enough votes to put it into effect, conferred with him as to whom they should nominate as a successor. Murray proposed that Roosevelt himself run for the seat and the latter, with some apparent reluctance, eventually agreed to do so.

Roosevelt's first political campaign got off on the wrong foot when, with Murray and Hess, he set out on a round of calls on influential local saloonkeepers. The calls started at an establishment run by a jovial German named Fischer who said that license fees were too high and that he hoped Roosevelt would treat the liquor interests fairly. Roosevelt replied that he intended to treat all interests fairly and asked Fischer what his fee was. When the barkeeper stated that it was two hundred dollars, Roosevelt replied: "I don't think you pay enough. I thought it would be at least twice as much." Appalled by this breach of political decorum, Murray intimated that thereafter Roosevelt's calls could be confined to his late father's influential friends while he and Hess took care of the riffraff. With this scheme in effect, the canvassing proceeded more smoothly. On Election Day, Roosevelt carried the district by fifteen hundred votes, or twice the normal Republican margin.

When Roosevelt turned up in Albany on January 2, 1882, reporters at the Delavan House found him an even more surprising figure than had his peers at Harvard some six years before. One noted that, although the temperature was only seventeen above zero, he walked back from a caucus at the Capital Building "wearing a broad smile instead of an overcoat." Others commented on his teeth, which "seemed to be all over his face," his eyeglasses carried foppishly on a cord, and a shrill voice which sometimes broke into a falsetto, along with an affected-sounding Harvard accent. His colleagues in the Assembly also found him a puzzling phenomenon. Isaac Hunt of Watertown, later a close friend, recalled that "We almost shouted with laughter to think that the most veritable representative of the New York dude had come to the Chamber." John McManus, a New York liquor dealer and Tammany stalwart, of whom it was said that he could "carry a ton on his back," thought that some gentle hazing might be in order and conspired with some of his friends to toss the dude in a blanket. Roosevelt, when he got wind of this scheme, went straight to the ringleader. "If you try anything like that," he said, "I'll kick you, I'll bite you, I'll do anything to you . . . you'd better let me alone." Whether impressed by Roosevelt's manner or merely disheartened over losing the element of surprise, McManus followed this advice.

Roosevelt's friendship with Hunt developed when, after a party caucus, Roosevelt crossed the committee room to introduce himself by saying: "You are from the country, I want to ask you how you manage caucuses like this in the country." Since Hunt was wearing a new Prince Albert coat which he had just had tailored to order in the hope of concealing his rural origins, the effect of this salutation was less than ingratiating. Nonetheless, he soon came to like Roosevelt and presently gave him the information that enabled him to win his political spurs. While investigating the receiverships of certain insolvent insurance companies, Hunt had found irregularities that caused him to suspect that Judge Theodore Westbrook of the State Supreme Court was in collusion with the receivers. On looking into the matter further at Hunt's suggestion, Roosevelt found grounds for an even more serious charge. This was that Westbrook had conspired with a group of financiers lead by the notorious Jay Gould to enable the latter to acquire control of the Manhattan Elevated Railway Company at a substantial cost to the state's taxpayers. On the basis of this, Roosevelt introduced a resolution calling for Westbrook's impeachment.

What gave Roosevelt's resolution for the impeachment of Judge Westbrook major significance was that it amounted to a deliberate attack upon the then widely accepted alliance between Big Business and the Law whereby one major function of the latter was to enable the former to do as it pleased. Normally a young man entering politics secured advancement by seeking the endorsement of both these allies, not by attacking them. By doing the opposite, Roosevelt was fighting the first pitched battle of what became his lifelong campaign against what he later termed "malefactors of great wealth."

The skill and energy with which he conducted his fight, against the opposition of an influential combination of members from both parties, attracted further attention. Ably coached by Hunt in tricks of parliamentary procedure and marshalling newspaper support through the State House reporters, he made his case from the floor with skill which, in sharp contrast to his youthful appearance, brought the issue to statewide and even nationwide attention. In the end, the chamber failed to impeach Westbrook and the affair ended with the Judge's sudden death, apparently from a heart attack partially induced by mental stress. Nonetheless, Roosevelt's handling of the issue caused him, as he said years later in a letter to his oldest son, to rise "like a rocket." In New York that spring, men like Cornelius Vanderbilt and his father's old friend, Chauncey Depew, attended testimonial dinners for him. Many years later, Charles Evans Hughes, then a young law student, described what Roosevelt's debut in politics had meant to the young men of his own generation: "It was a splendid breeze blowing through the legislative halls making everyone feel brighter and better."

During Roosevelt's second term in the Assembly—after a one-sided victory in the autumn of 1882, while his party was being roundly defeated—he made the acquaintance of a young man who introduced him to a side of life that was entirely new to him. The young man was Samuel Gompers, then head of the strongest local in New York's Cigar Workers' Union, and the alien environment was slum life on New York's East Side. At that time, immigration to the United States was running at the rate of some 800,000 a year. Many of the immigrants, not only unable to speak English but illiterate in their native tongues as well, became the prey of unscrupulous employers—often themselves earlier immigrants of the same nationality. Among such employers, cigar manufacturers were often the worst offenders. Cigar-rolling was customarily done in the homes of the employees—to save the manufacturers the cost of renting a loft—where the loose tobacco might be used as bedding for the children of the household and become mixed up with the household garbage.

Like most young men of his station in life, Roosevelt had little concept of living conditions among the poor. Lobbying for a bill to make it illegal for tobacco workers to work in their homes, Gompers persuaded Roosevelt to join him on a house-to-house tour of the cigar-manufacturing district. Roosevelt was appalled by what he saw and visited the district twice more, once alone and once with a committee of fellow Assemblymen. The bill got his wholehearted support and, though it failed to pass, opened Roosevelt's eyes to the defects of a judicial system which excused such inequities on the ground that to forbid the rolling of cigars at home would be to deprive the cigar workers of their freedom of choice. Even more importantly, he began to be seriously concerned about the injustices that then existed in the United States social order generally.

Between Election Day of 1881 and his first arrival in Albany, Roosevelt's *The Naval War of 1812* had made its appearance and been favorably reviewed on both sides of the Atlantic. Its success indeed was such that eventually it went into eight editions and was later reprinted almost verbatim as part of the official British history of the Royal Navy. Quite in keeping with the rise in Roosevelt's literary and political fortunes were the circumstances of his private life. During his first winter in Albany, he and Alice had rooms in Albany but spent their weekends either in New York with his family or in Boston with hers. During his second, they rented a New York house at 55 West 48th Street to which the young Assemblyman repaired from Albany every weekend. Meanwhile, far from diminishing his physical activities, Roosevelt's political obligations served to enlarge them. In New York, the length of his daily walks had been limited to the route between his house and law school. Now, the hilly countryside around the capital made it possible for him to increase both pace and mileage. Hunt, who accompanied him on one of his customary twelve-mile constitutionals, came back so exhausted he could hardly speak.

Roosevelt's less knowledgeable colleagues were often misled by his clothes, accent, and deportment into mistaking him for an effete dilettante. Mistakes of this sort often had lively consequences like those which developed one winter day when, in the course of an afternoon stroll, he stopped at a road house and encountered a tough Assemblyman named John Costello, with two cronies. "Won't Momma's boy catch cold?" asked Costello, calling attention to Roosevelt's overcoat, a short pea-jacket. When Roosevelt appeared to take no umbrage, Costello called him "a damned little dude."

Feeling that matters had now gone far enough, Roosevelt took off his glasses, put them in his pocket, and, utilizing the pugilistic dexterity developed during his career at Harvard, floored first Costello and then the closest of his cronies with one punch each. When the third member of the group withdrew from the action, Roosevelt instructed Costello first to "go and wash yourself" and then to "have a glass of beer. . . . When you are in the presence of gentlemen, behave like a gentleman," he said, before taking his departure.

Despite the exertions of his public and private life, Roosevelt, in the summer after his second term, suffered a recurrence of his childhood asthma accompanied now by a digestive ailment described in his diaries as "cholera morbus" of which the principal symptoms were vomiting and diarrhea. In the effort to effect a cure, he took the advice of a new doctor who sent him to a resort hotel in the Catskills. For a time, Roosevelt was able to endure this environment, with the aid of several sets of tennis followed by a long ride every afternoon, but before long the quietude began to pall. He expressed his feelings in a letter to Corinne:

". . . At first, the boiling baths were rather pleasant; but for the first time in my life, I came within an ace of fainting when I got out of the bath this morning. I have a bad headache, a general feeling of lassitude, and am bored out of my life by having nothing whatever to do, and being placed in that quintessence of abomination, a large summer hotel at a watering place for underbred and overdressed old girls, fat old female scandal-mongers and a select collection of assorted cripples and consumptives."

During the summer before his marriage, Roosevelt had

derived pleasure and therapeutic benefit from his shooting trip to the West. A chance to apply the same remedy again but in an even more arduous form had presented itself through an encounter—at a June meeting of the Free Trade Club in New York where he had made a speech—with a colorful personage named H. H. Gorringe. Gorringe had recently resigned his commission as a U.S. naval Commander after a public controversy with the Secretary of the Navy in which he had urged the necessity for a bigger fleet. Before that, he had distinguished himself by the unique and adventurous feat of bringing the famous obelisk known as Cleopatra's Needle from Alexandria to New York. If these accomplishments had not in themselves been enough to guarantee immediate congeniality with T.R., additional common bonds would have been provided by the wide range of Gorringe's other interests, among which was big-game hunting on the Western plains. When Gorringe proposed that Roosevelt join him on a September excursion to the settlement of Little Missouri, beyond Fargo on the Dakota Territory, Roosevelt naturally accepted with alacrity. Later on when the pressure of his numerous other concerns obliged Gorringe to give up the trip, Roosevelt resolved to escape the enforced lethargy of life in a Catskills resort hotel by going alone.

His second western trip—during which he made a practice of sleeping outdoors in the rain, pursued buffalo until he shot one and arranged to invest nearly half his patrimony in a cattle ranch—had a predictably beneficial effect upon Roosevelt's health and spirits. When he got back to New York in October, he was in fine trim for his third election campaign which, in a Republican landslide, he won by a majority so large as to make him a strong candidate for the Assembly speakership. He failed to win it, but the circumstances of his defeat were such as to strengthen his position in the party.

Since New York was sure to be a key state in what was equally sure to be a hard fight for the Presidential nomination the next spring, this meant that, at twenty-five, he was already a political figure of consequence not only on the Albany but also on the national scene.

To top Roosevelt's already brimming cup of good fortune, he was now about to become a father. In the last months of her first pregnancy, Alice was re-established in the Roosevelt house on Fifty-Seventh Street, where she could have the best of care and company during his weekly absences up-state. Here the Christmas holidays passed happily with the usual pleasant round of family festivities; and it was here that a few weeks later, with no warning whatsoever, there fell a blow which might have smashed most men for good and all and which was to test even Roosevelt's almost supernatural powers of endurance to the utmost.

During late January and the first weeks of February, Roosevelt had been in New York from Friday through Monday of each week to attend hearings of a special committee—for whose creation he was largely responsible, and of which he was chairman—that was inquiring into irregularities in the management of various departments of the municipal government. On Wednesday, the thirteenth of February, he was back in Albany to sit with the Cities Committee, of which he was also chairman and which had been considering his Aldermanic Bill, to deprive the Board of Aldermen of the right to confirm the mayor's appointments. On the thirteenth, the day the Aldermanic Bill was scheduled for a third and final reading, Roosevelt got a telegram in the morning announcing the birth of a daughter. He received the congratulations of his colleagues and, having requested a leave of absence, prepared to leave for New York. Before he caught his train a second telegram arrived indicating that his wife's condition was giving her doctor cause for alarm. This was disturbing to be sure, but as the late afternoon train crawled down the Hudson through a thick fog and rumbled slowly along the surface tracks on what is now Park Avenue, Roosevelt could not have had the slightest inkling of what was in store for him when his hansom cab drew up at 6 West 57th Street. It was nearly midnight when his brother Elliott met him at the door with the words: "There is a curse on this House! Mother is dying and Alice is dying too."

Roosevelt rushed upstairs to the third floor which Alice shared with his sister Corinne, whose baby boy had been born the previous April. There he found his wife desperately ill and scarcely conscious enough to recognize him. Two hours later, he was told that if he wished to see his mother while she was still alive—her winter cold had turned out to be acute typhoid—he must hurry to her downstairs room. Standing with his sister beside her bedside, in the room where his father had died six years before, Roosevelt repeated Elliott's words: "There *is* a curse on this house." After his mother's death at 3:00 A.M. he went upstairs again to the room in which Alice died of Bright's disease at two o'clock the next afternoon. It was St. Valentine's Day—and the anniversary of the one on which they had announced their engagement four years before.

Two days later, the Presbyterian Church at Fifth Avenue and Fifty-fifth Street was the scene of a double funeral service. In the front pews sat the Roosevelt family with Alice's father, George C. Lee. Behind them were assembled representatives of New York's social and political upper strata—Astors and Harrimans, ex-Mayor Grace and Mayor Seth Low of Brooklyn, and colleagues from the Assembly, which had adjourned for three days in an unprecedented gesture of respect and sympathy. After the services, the family went on to Greenwood

Cemetery where on a bitter cold afternoon both bodies were interred.

Roosevelt's diary is blank for the two days after the fourteenth. A year later, he gathered the newspaper tributes, letters of condolence and the seven speeches of sympathy made by his fellow Assemblymen into a book which he had printed privately by Putnam's. On the first page, he wrote his last words of love for Alice Lee:

> She was beautiful in face and form and lovelier still in spirit; as a flower she grew, and as a fair young flower she died. Her life had been always in the sunshine; there had never come to her a single great sorrow; and none ever knew her who did not love and revere her for her bright, sunny temper and her saintly unselfishness. Fair, pure and joyous as a maiden; loving, tender, and happy as a young wife; when she had just become a mother, when her life seemed to be but just begun, and when the years seemed so bright before her —then, by a strange and terrible fate, death came to her.
>
> And when my heart's dearest died, the light went from my life forever.

The record shows that Roosevelt never again spoke of his first wife to any other living soul. In his autobiography, she is not mentioned. Even to his daughter, christened Alice for Alice Lee, Roosevelt never once brought himself to mention her mother.

In a letter to Bill Sewall at Island Falls, Arthur Cutler wrote on the afternoon of the funeral: ". . . The family are utterly demoralized and Theodore is in a dazed stunned state. He does not know what he does or says." Sewall responded with a letter of condolence to Roosevelt which the latter acknowledged three weeks later: "It was a grim and evil fate but I have never believed it did any good to flinch or yield for any blow, nor does it lighten the blow to cease from working." In a note replying to the condolences of Carl Schurz a week after his wife's death, Roosevelt had put his feelings even more strongly: "Your words of kind sympathy were very welcome to me; and you can see I have taken up my work again; indeed I think I should go mad if I were not employed. . . ."

In fact, Roosevelt was back in Albany on February 20 with enough self-possession to speak the next day on behalf of his Aldermanic Bill, which the Assembly passed, by a vote of 70 to 51. That weekend he was in New York again, to chair the hearings of his Investigating Committee. Thereafter, with his daughter Alice entrusted to the able care of his elder sister, he went on to even more energetic activities. One was the completion of the work of the Investigating Committee which continued its work until the middle of March, concentrating attention on the activities of the police department of which Roosevelt was to become a Commissioner a few years later. Another was the passage of nine bills based on the Committee's findings of which, thanks to Roosevelt's indefatigable efforts in Committee and on the Assembly floor, no fewer than seven were enacted into law by the time the session ended on May 15th. However, even this record, which would have done credit to a seasoned legislator with no personal sorrows to distract him, was only a warm-up for Roosevelt's major effort in the spring of 1884. This was his fight to prevent the nomination of James G. Blaine for President of the United States at the Republican Convention in Chicago.

In order to understand the issues involved in the 1884 Republican Convention and the exciting election that followed —the closest in United States history until that of 1960— one essential point is some understanding of its central figure, James G. Blaine. Maine's longtime congressman and senator before becoming Secretary of State under President James Garfield, Blaine was an able, eloquent and urbane politician who was, however, suspected of having used his office as Speaker of the House in 1869 for purposes of personal gain. This suspicion had been enough to prevent Blaine's nomination for the Presidency in 1876 and 1880; now at last it appeared that his offense—an unethical rather than illegal one, of which he had never been either acquitted or convicted—might well have been more than counterbalanced by subsequent distinguished services. Nonetheless, while strongly supported by the Republican national machine, Blaine was strongly opposed by the increasingly powerful reform elements in the party. These elements felt, and not without substantial grounds, that in order to win the election, the party, lately under heavy fire for corruption in office, would now more than ever before need a candidate of conspicuous and demonstrable probity.

Blaine's most formidable opponent for the nomination was the former Port Collector, Chester A. Arthur, who had succeeded Garfield in the White House after the latter's assassination but who, while in office, had incurred the enmity of important factions of the party. In the event that the Blaine and Arthur forces were deadlocked, various dark horses were being put forward of whom at least two were preferred by reform elements to either of the principal contenders. One of these was General William Tecumseh Sherman, the sixty-five-year-old Civil War hero who, however, effectively took himself out of the race with a statement that he would consider himself "a fool and a mad man" to enter it. Another was George F. Edmunds of Vermont, a senator for twenty years and a man of unimpeachable honesty, who had neither formidable enemies nor outstanding qualifications.

To Roosevelt, President Arthur, as the beneficiary of his father's disheartening defeat a decade before, might well have been unacceptable on that account alone, and his status as a machine politician served to make him even more so. As for Blaine, he stood for all that Roosevelt despised in his own party and derived his strongest support from those of its members whom he most disdained. This left him only a choice among dark horses of whom Edmunds seemed clearly the soundest. Along with a substantial segment of his party including most of the reform element, he proposed to back the Vermont Senator with all the means at his command.

Roosevelt's campaign on behalf of Edmunds was by no means a forlorn effort in a lost cause; so astute an observer as Grover Cleveland had stated it as his considered opinion that, "The Republican situation demands the nomination of Edmunds and Edmunds will be nominated." Nor was Roosevelt without important allies, including Massachusetts' young Congressman Henry Cabot Lodge whom he had already met briefly while serving in the Assembly and with whom the closest friendship of his life was to develop from their association in the preconvention campaign. Roosevelt moreover conducted his fight for Edmunds with even more than his usual resolution and dexterity.

The scene of the first battle was the State Republican Convention at Utica which opened on April 23. Here, the business in hand was the nomination of four delegates-at-large whose votes at Chicago were likely to have a disproportionate significance as indices of the strength of Edmunds backing through the nation. With seventy of the 496 delegates for Edmunds and the rest about evenly divided between Blaine and Arthur, the numerical weakness of the former was partially offset by their possession of the balance of power. They held a further advantage in that for Arthur, a New Yorker, the choice of even one Blaine man among New York's four delegates-at-large might well mean disaster at Chicago. Roosevelt made the most of this advantage through the preliminary period of bargaining and jockeying for position. By the time the convention met for the first time, he had persuaded the Arthur forces to support any slate he picked—providing only that none of its members were for Blaine. The proceedings opened with the election, by a 251-to-243 vote, of Roosevelt's nominee for temporary chairman. When the ballots for delegates-at-large were counted, Roosevelt himself led the list with 472 votes and three other Edmunds's men were nominated with him, all four far ahead of the leader of the Blaine forces, who ranked a poor fifth with 243. What made this first step toward a defeat of Blaine at Chicago especially satisfactory to Roosevelt was that it represented also a victory over the forces who had done most to defeat him for the Speakership of the Assembly the winter before.

The National Convention that met in Chicago in June lacked the nationwide audience currently provided by radio and television but the scene itself was not vastly dissimilar from similar occasions three quarters of a century later. Now again, as chairman of New York's delegates-at-large, Roosevelt repeated the strategy that had helped him succeed at Utica by putting in nomination as temporary chairman a rival to the candidate proposed by the chairman of the National Committee. After a lively contest on the floor, the roll call began and when it ended, Roosevelt's candidate, a Mississippi Negro named John R. Lynch, had been elected by 424 to 384.

What followed then was the final struggle for the nomination. Easily the most eloquent of the nominating speeches was that of Ohio's blind orator, Judge William H. West, a tall, cadaverous old man who made full use of the inapposite pseudonym that nearly won Blaine the election: "Wherever blows fell thickest and fastest, there, in the forefront of the battle, was seen to wave the white plume of James G. Blaine, our Henry of Navarre. . . ." Martin Townsend of New York made a strong plea for Arthur. Governor John Davis Long of Massachusetts employed bitter sarcasm on behalf of Edmunds: "Gentlemen, I nominate as the Republican candidate . . . the Honorable—aye! the *Honorable*—George F. Edmunds of Vermont." Nonetheless, by the time the convention adjourned at 1:45 in the morning, it had become clear that the balloting the next day would be a contest of Blaine against the field.

On the first roll call the next morning, with 411 votes necessary to nominate, Blaine had 334½ to 278 for Arthur, 93 for Edmunds and 112½ scattered among five others. On two succeeding ballots when Blaine picked up some forty votes mainly from Edmunds while Arthur was losing four, Blaine's victory seemed assured unless the convention could be adjourned overnight and a new alignment of opposition organized to meet the threat. The move to adjourn—led by Senator Foraker of Ohio, a Sherman backer, and strongly supported by Roosevelt, threw the already tumultuous convention into complete turmoil but when the motion was finally put to a vote, it went down to defeat. The outcome then became inevitable. On the fourth ballot, Blaine had 511 votes and Roosevelt's long hard battle had ended in a smashing defeat.

So far as Roosevelt's political career was concerned, Blaine's nomination at Chicago left two alternatives, both thoroughly unrewarding. One was to bolt the party—the course taken by most of the influential members of the reform element from whom he had derived his chief support—which would have effectively ruled out further advancement through normal party channels. The other was to give Blaine his outspoken support in the forthcoming campaign, which—even if Blaine won in November and even if Roosevelt's principles had permitted him to follow it, which they did not—could hardly have been expected to produce very substantial benefits. In effect, then, the channel of vigorous, competitive political activity, in Albany and in the national arena, in which he had been able to find precious distraction in the first months after tragedy, had been abruptly closed to him. He found himself, suddenly, for the first time in his life, and as inopportunely as possible, with nothing particular to do.

At a deeper level than that of mere practicalities, the outcome of the Chicago convention seemed significant, as indication of a rhythm of failure and calamity. Just when all had looked brightest in his family affairs, unimaginable disaster had in a single day destroyed all his hopes and plans. Now, even the opportunity offered by his career "to so live as not to dishonor the memory of those I loved who have gone before me" appeared to have been snatched away from him. Certainly as he took the train West from Chicago the day after the convention, Roosevelt had every reason to reflect that —far from reaching the heights that had looked so accessible six months before—he had attained only the improbable distinction of a precociously complete failure at the age of twenty-five.

In fact, of course, as things turned out, the reverse was the case. The precocity in Roosevelt's case had been his overnight success at Albany. Had it continued unimpeded, he might have encountered even more serious reverses later on. The sudden pause in his progress that occurred after the Chicago convention was to prove more than an important breathing space in his career. Up to that time, despite his phenomenal endurance, he had been physically so frail that reporters at the convention had noted that his whole frame shook in the effort to make his voice heard above the uproar. The next two years, spent mostly outdoors in the Badlands of Dakota, would finally give him strength to match his energy but it would do even more than that. As Roosevelt said many years later, these were the years that gave him the understanding of men and of life without which he might never have been President. Naturally Roosevelt knew nothing of this as his train rumbled through darkness and daylight into the wooded country around St. Paul and then over the rolling, windswept prairies of the Dakota Territory.

At St. Paul, a reporter found him and got an interview—which Roosevelt later disavowed—indicating that he would support Blaine. As the campaign developed, however, he did so and in two trips East—one in July and another in October—made statements and speeches that accented the platform far more than the candidate. On the eve of the election, Blaine's apparent endorsement of a clerical supporter's ill-timed reference to the opposition as the party of "Rum, Romanism, and Rebellion" cost him New York's Catholic vote and, with it, the state and the White House. For Roosevelt, the result was that he spent most of the next two years out of politics and far from the public eye, on the plains of Dakota.

IV

ROOSEVELT's abrupt decision in 1883 to invest some forty thousand of the $125,000 dollars he had inherited from his father in a Dakota cattle ranch was by no means an altogether rash one. The Civil War had touched off a sudden increase in Eastern demand for beef which the newly opened West, especially Texas, had hastened to supply. Profits available in ranching and the means of making them were the subject of an 1881 best-seller named *Beef Bonanza or How to Get Rich on the Plains* by General James S. Brisbin, which suggested that Montana and the Dakota Territory were especially promising areas for such operations.

The reasons why the Northwestern plains seemed suitable for cattle ranching were eminently logical. Prior to 1873, this area had provided grazing land for the "Northern herd" of some three million buffalo upon which the Sioux and other Indians had lived comfortably for centuries. The arrival of the Northern Pacific Railroad at Bismarck in 1873 brought

complete and sudden change. Buffalo hunters, heretofore dependent on oxcarts as a means of shipping out hides which
were in great demand as rugs or coats in the East and in
Europe, suddenly had a fast and dependable means of export.
Thus encouraged, it took the hunters only about ten years to
wipe out the buffalo completely. By this time, most of the
Indians for whom the buffalo had provided both shelter and
sustenance had been penned up in reservations. Thereafter,
the Dakota prairies, where the grass was as plentiful as ever—
and far more so than further south—became simultaneously
safe for settlers and available as pasture for domestic cattle.
Dakota was closer to Eastern markets than Texas, and since
the land was still public domain, all that a rancher had to pay
for was his livestock.

In all of the Dakota Territory, the most promising region
appeared to be the so-called "Badlands," an extraordinary area
some two hundred miles long and twenty-five miles wide along
the northward course of the Little Missouri River, which
owed its peculiar character to a geological accident several
million years earlier. This was the arrival of a great glacier
causing the river, which had previously drained into Hudson
Bay, first to be dammed up into an enormous lake and then
to find a new outlet via the Mississippi, into the Gulf of
Mexico. As the lake drained, the land which it had covered
was eroded into an amazing labyrinth of buttes, bluffs, pyra-
mids, gullies, gulches, and ravines through the center of
which the river still flowed. This area not only provided some
of the world's most freakish scenery but also shelter of sorts
against the icy winds that swept the plains through winters
when the temperature dropped as low as sixty below zero.
The Badlands got their name from the French voyageurs who
had found them *mauvaises terres pour traverser*. For cattle,
the cuts and coulees in the Badlands not only held richer

grass than the level plateau on both sides of them but also offered protection against storms from any quarter of the compass.

Roosevelt was far from being the only, or even the most, incongruous newcomer who hoped to capitalize on the opportunities offered by the Badlands for turning an honest, safe, and reasonably rapid dollar. The whole area in fact was sprinkled with ambitious Easterners and enterprising Europeans of whom one, a canny Scot named Gregor Lang, was directly responsible for Roosevelt's debut in the cattle business. A man of wide education and unusual background, Lang had managed a whiskey distillery in Ireland until the wife of its proprietor developed teetotaling scruples. Soon afterward, the proprietor, Lord Pender, through a New York friend named Abraham Hewitt, had heard about Gorringe's cattle-ranching syndicate and sent Lang to Little Missouri to investigate the possibilities. Lang grew apprehensive about Gorringe's other associates and set up an independent ranch some forty miles upriver, where Roosevelt had visited him during his 1883 Buffalo hunt. As elucidated by Lang, cattle ranching seemed to be just as sound a venture as *Beef Bonanza* indicated. Since Lang himself was unavailable as a manager, Roosevelt entrusted the first installment of his investment to two experienced local cattle hands whom Lang recommended. These were former Canadian railroad workers named Bill Merrifield and Sylvane Ferris, to whom he handed a check for $14,000 as a down payment with which they were to start operations by buying a herd of between four and five hundred head.

While Roosevelt's approach to the cattle business was dashing and expansive, it was outdone on both counts by that employed by one of his near neighbors. This was a former French cavalry officer named Antoine-Amedée-Marie-

Vincent Manco de Vallambrosa, Marquis de Mores. Not content with mere cattle ranching—which, however, he proposed to conduct on a grand scale—de Mores planned to set up a whole series of packing plants along the Northern Pacific to enable him and his fellow ranchers to ship their beef after it had been butchered instead of on the hoof. This would not only furnish additional profits for the ranchers but also diminish the price of beef to retailers in the East. As the cornerstone of his packing empire, Little Missouri would become the Chicago of the Northwest thus providing the Marquis with the wherewithal needed in order to validate his claim to the throne of France, to which he stood in the line of succession. When Little Missouri proved unresponsive to the destiny he had planned for it, the imperturbable Marquis, who had already built himself a handsome twenty-five-room chateau and hunting lodge on a bluff above the town, was not seriously disconcerted. He founded another town directly across the river on the Eastern, or right, bank of the Little Missouri and, breaking a bottle of champagne over the first tent, christened the place Medora. His wife was the former Medora Von Hoffman, glamorous German-born daughter of the banker, Louis A. Von Hoffman, who had offices at 50 Wall Street and the ample means required to finance the far-flung activities of his enterprising son-in-law.

Roosevelt's appearance on the Badlands scene in 1883 occurred at a dramatic period in the region's history. On the very day before his first arrival in Little Missouri, a special train had passed through town carrying ex-President Grant, top-ranking officials of the Northern Pacific and kindred dignitaries to the golden-spike-driving ceremonies a few hundred miles further West. That autumn, Sitting Bull, the Sioux Indians' most famous chief, led a thousand of his braves on their last great buffalo hunt which disposed of nine of the remaining ten thousand head, and a few weeks later the first herd of Texas Longhorns was driven into the Badlands range country. It was during the following winter that the Marquis weighed Little Missouri in the balance and found it wanting. When Roosevelt returned in June of 1884, the station at which his train stopped was not Little Missouri but Medora where the chimney of the de Mores packing plant contributed a new and incongruous feature to the already astonishing skyline.

Roosevelt's relations with de Mores in the ensuing seasons were superficially amicable but basically unsympathetic. On the one hand he dined from time to time at the Marquis's chateau where champagne was served in crystal goblets and where their common interests proved to include not merely ranching but also riding to hounds with the Meadowbrook Hunt on Long Island—where the fences, according to the Marquis, were higher than any he had encountered in France. On the other hand, the Marquis's somewhat feudalistic approach to ranching proved disturbing on several occasions. One of these occurred during Roosevelt's absence when a de Mores foreman, who proposed to quarter some of his noble employer's cattle on Roosevelt's land without permission, had to be somewhat brusquely ordered off. On another, after the Marquis had offered to buy some of Roosevelt's steers, a misunderstanding about terms led to a cancellation of the deal. These difficulties finally culminated in what almost became the most important U.S. duel since Burr vs. Hamilton, and one which had equally noteworthy causes.

Medora and its environs were by no means exclusively populated by French noblemen, Scots philosophers and patrician New York politicians. Also much in evidence were more raffish characters like Bill Williams, who ran the town's

biggest saloon and disorderly house; "Hell Roaring" Bill
Jones, so nicknamed because his vocabulary was even less re-
fined than that of two other local "Bill Joneses"; and a "cold,
quiet old fellow" named E. G. Paddock who enjoyed the dual
distinction of being the most sinister figure in town and the
parent of the settlement's only minor. The latter, a prodigy,
had proved himself to be a chip off the old block by holding
up the local railroad paymaster with a pistol at the age of
fourteen. This peccadillo was a pale imitation of his father's
exploits of which the most recent was the shooting of a rene-
gade plainsman named Riley Luffsey in an ambush a few
miles west of town. Since Luffsey, while in his cups, had
been heard to threaten the life of the Marquis and since
Paddock was in the latter's employ, the Marquis himself was
suspected of being implicated in the misdeed which had taken
place shortly before Roosevelt's arrival in the neighborhood.
When de Mores was finally brought to trial at the nearby
county seat of Mandan two years later, one of the witnesses
for the prosecution was Joe Ferris, who had been Roosevelt's
guide on his 1883 buffalo hunt and was the brother of his
manager, Sylvane. Feeling, apparently, that Ferris's role as a
hostile witness implied unseemly bias on the part of a fellow
aristocrat, the Marquis wrote Roosevelt a letter which might
have been interpreted either as a rather plaintive plea for
more friendly treatment or as an outright challenge, using
for this purpose the stationery of his Northern Pacific Re-
frigerator Car Company:

> *Bismarck, Dak.*
> *September 3, 1885*

My dear Roosevelt:
>   My principle is to take the bull by the horns. Joe Ferris
> is very active against me and has been instrumental in getting
> me indicted by furnishing money to witnesses and hunting

them up. The papers also publish very stupid accounts of our quarrelling—I sent you the paper to New York. Is this done by your orders? I thought you were my friend. If you are my enemy, I want to know it. I am always on hand as you know and between gentlemen it is easy to settle matters of that sort directly.

Yours very truly,
Mores

I hear the people want to organize the county.
I am opposed to it for one year more at least.

To Roosevelt, this letter naturally provided something of a puzzle. On the one hand, the last thing he had any intention of doing was to back away from any sort of a fight. On the other, the letter was engagingly outspoken and the tone of the postscript certainly suggested that the Marquis was prepared to keep their relations on an amicable footing. He composed an answer that may have been equally puzzling to de Mores:

Medora, Dakota
September 6, 1885

Most emphatically I am not your enemy; if I were you would know it for I would be an open one, and would not have asked you to my house nor gone to yours. As your final words however seem to imply a threat it is due to myself to say that the statement is not made through any fear of possible consequences to me. I too, as you know, am always on hand, and ever ready to hold myself accountable in any way for anything I have said or done.

Yours very truly
Theodore Roosevelt

As things turned out, no duel occurred and the Marquis was in due course acquitted of the charge of murder. His logical but visionary plan to establish Medora as the Chicago of the Northwest, however, fell far short of accomplishment, as did his hopes of using the proceeds thereof to establish himself on the throne of France. He abandoned Medora, circumnavigated the globe and, in 1896, was himself ambushed and killed in North Africa by Touareg tribesmen while trying, some decades ahead of time, to arrange a Franco-Islamic alliance. The de Mores chateau, which still stands across the river from Medora, now belongs to the state of North Dakota to which it was presented in the 1930s by the Marquis's son, who inherited the family's senior title of Duc de Vallambrosa.

Roosevelt's first visit to the Badlands in September of 1883 had been a lighthearted holiday of which one major purpose was escape from a Catskill cure-hotel. He had spent his time searching for a shot at one of the region's last remaining buffalo while staying at the ranch where Gregor Lang lived with his sixteen-year-old son, Lincoln, named after the Great Emancipator. On his return in 1884, Roosevelt found Bill Merrifield and Sylvane Ferris established in a two-room cabin seven miles south of Medora on a ranch variously known as the Maltese Cross, after its brand, or the Chimney Butte, after its most conspicuous topographical feature. Of the four hundred and forty head which they had bought the autumn before, only twenty-five had been killed by wolves, exposure, or other causes and these had been more than replaced by a hundred and fifty-five new calves. Roosevelt moved into the Maltese Cross cabin and, with even more than his customary diligence, set about learning the cattle business from the ground up. Meanwhile, he gave his managers $26,000 more with which to expand his holdings by buying another thousand head.

Not content with enlarging his commitment to Merrifield

and Ferris, Roosevelt also decided to carry through a plan which he had been concocting since the previous winter. This was to bring Bill Sewall and his nephew, Wilmot Dow, from their camp in Island Falls to the Badlands and set them up in the cattle business also. This scheme too was by no means wholly impractical. Both men had raised cattle in Maine, both were used to primitive surroundings, and both were indefatigable workers. To be sure neither of them knew much about the West but then most of the residents of Medora were by definition newcomers also, and at least Sewall and Dow were honest which was more than could be said for many of the others. Moreover, they were Roosevelt's friends and this looked like a reasonable chance for them to make, or at least to improve, their fortunes. Roosevelt wrote to Sewall:

"Now a little plain talk, though I think it unnecessary for I know you too well. If you are afraid of hard work and privation, do not come West. If you expect to make a fortune in a year or two, do not come west. If you will give up under temporary discouragements, do not come west. If on the other hand, you are willing to work hard, especially the first year; if you realize that for a couple of years you cannot expect to make much more than you are now making; and if you also know at the end of that time you will be in receipt of about a thousand dollars for the third year, with an unlimited rise ahead of you and a future as bright as you yourself choose to make it, then come."

By autumn, Sewall and Dow were established at a second ranch, named the Elkhorn after a set of interlocking antlers Roosevelt had found on the site, which was some thirty miles north of, or downriver from, Medora. Here, assisted by Roosevelt, the two newcomers cut and split the timbers for a more capacious eight-room ranch house than the one at the Maltese Cross, moved into it, and settled down for the winter. The

next summer Dow returned to Maine to get married and
brought back with him his own bride, Mrs. Sewall, and the
latter's year-old daughter. Unlike the Maltese Cross cabin,
which was on the main trail south from Medora and an un-
official resthouse for passing ranchers, hunters, and tourists,
the Elkhorn was well off the beaten track and contained a
room available for Roosevelt's use as a study. In it, when not
riding herd on his cattle, breaking horses, or hunting big
game, he turned out the major portion of two books, his
Hunting Trips of a Ranchman and *Life of Thomas Hart
Benton.*

Roosevelt's falling out with the Marquis de Mores eventually helped to establish him in the community as a young
man who was quite capable of taking care of himself but this
altercation did not reach its denouement until after he had
been in residence for more than a year. In the meantime,
just as had been the case at Harvard, the Republican Club on
Fifty-ninth Street, and the Assembly at Albany, he was regarded as an amiable oddity, and fit game for hazing in an
environment where conventions for this pastime were
somewhat rougher than those observed in the East.

As pointed out by Roosevelt in his autobiography, adequate vision seemed an obvious prerequisite for the life of
the plains. Anyone who lacked this essential was likely to be
considered as a questionable character on any one of several
counts. The thick-lensed glasses, which earned Roosevelt
nicknames like "Four Eyes" and "Storm Windows," were
the most conspicuous thing about him, but thoroughly in
keeping with these, and equally out of keeping with his environment, was his Harvard accent and vocabulary. Once at a
roundup, when Roosevelt had occasion to tell one of his
hands to hurry, he shouted, "Hasten forward quickly there."
This command presently became a frontier catchword, es-

pecially popular among patrons of Medora's several saloons when requesting fresh supplies of stimulants.

As had been the case in Albany, those of Roosevelt's associates who were misled by his demeanor into underestimating his capabilities were subject to dramatic forms of enlightenment. One afternoon, on the way back to his ranch from a visit to Montana, Roosevelt found himself obliged to spend a night at the colorful small town of Mingusville, named, with delicate regard for euphony, after its leading citizens, Min Grisy and her husband, Gus. When Roosevelt, wearing his steel-rimmed spectacles, entered the hotel lobby which also served as a bar, one of its several patrons, far gone in his cups, was flourishing a pistol. "Four Eyes is going to treat," shouted this individual, and, as Roosevelt made his way to a table in the corner, pursued him and repeated his remark for the benefit of the entire company:

"Maybe you didn't hear me. Four Eyes is going to treat!"

Glancing modestly down beside his chair, Roosevelt observed that his self-appointed adversary was standing with his feet placed close together. He rose, as though to comply with instructions, and let go with a short right to the jaw. On the way to the floor, the recipient hit the back of his head against the bar. Totally unconscious, he was dragged outdoors to recover.

In overcoming the disadvantages of his upbringing and his physical liabilities, Roosevelt followed his usual procedure of learning the game thoroughly and playing it hard. In open-range cattle ranching on the Badlands, the hardest part of the year's work was the annual spring roundup when cowboys representing the various ranchers in the area gathered to take census of the herds, brand new calves, and get each rancher's cattle back onto his range. Starting in the South and working gradually northwards, the roundup lasted some six weeks, during which all hands who attended, owners or otherwise, got up before dawn every morning and stayed in the saddle until sunset unless there was a night stampede, in which case they worked through the darkness also. Since the roundup coincided with the longest days of the year, this meant long hours which Roosevelt naturally found no less congenial than the dangerous and difficult work upon which they were expended.

In his autobiography, Roosevelt describes one night when a heavy thunderstorm caused a large herd to stampede and plunge over a steep bank into the Little Missouri. Riding at breakneck speed to overtake and turn the leaders, Roosevelt's pony plunged into the river also but managed to swim to the other side where the pursuit continued. By dawn, the herd was sufficiently re-assembled to make possible a regular day's work which ended shortly after sunset. Roosevelt's account of this episode concludes characteristically:

> By this time I had been nearly forty hours in the saddle, changing horses five times, and my clothes had thoroughly dried on me, and I fell asleep as soon as I touched the bedding. . . . The above was the longest number of consecutive hours I ever had to be in the saddle. But, as I have said, I changed horses five times and it is a great lightening of labor for a rider to have a fresh horse. . . .

The longest time Roosevelt records spending in the saddle without changing mounts was twenty-four hours when he was on his way back from a grizzly bear hunt in the Big Horn Mountains near what is now Yellowstone Park. Bored with riding all day at the slow pace of the pack wagon on the way home, he and Merrifield left it behind after supper and galloped the last fifty miles of the journey by moonlight. Roosevelt's grizzly bear hunt was the high point of the big-game shooting career with which he relieved the ennui of his cow-punching and writing careers at the Elkhorn. It involved a thousand-mile overland journey from his home ranch and an arduous two days of tracking before he finally got a glimpse of "Old Ephraim, as the mountain men styled the grizzly." The final confrontation at a distance of ten yards in a mountain thicket provided material for another lively paragraph in *Hunting Trips of a Ranchman:*

He had heard us, but apparently hardly knew exactly where or what we were, for he reared up on his haunches sideways to us. Then he saw us, and dropped down again on all fours, the shaggy hair on his neck and shoulders seeming to bristle as he turned toward us. As he sank down on his forefeet I had raised the rifle; his head was bent slightly down, and when I saw the top of the white bead fairly between his small, glittering, evil eyes, I pulled the trigger. Half rising up, the huge beast fell over on his side in the death throes, the ball having gone into his brain, striking as fairly between the eyes as if the distance had been measured by carpenter's rule.

To his story of the shooting of his first grizzly, Roosevelt appended a handy rule of thumb for dealing with dangerous game in general:

A novice at this kind of sport will find it best and safest to keep in mind the old Norse Viking's advice in reference to a long sword: "If you go in close enough your sword will be long enough." If a poor shot goes in close enough he will find that he shoots straight enough.

Along with writing, ranching, and hunting, Roosevelt while in the Badlands devoted a substantial part of his attention to matters of law and order. At the time of his return to the Badlands in 1884, Medora was much exercised about an epidemic of horse-thievery which, there as elsewhere in the

West, where horses were a prime necessity, was considered
a capital offense. In the absence of enforcement officers, a
band of vigilantes was formed to find and punish the culprits.
Roosevelt offered to join it but, like that of the equally spirited Marquis de Mores, his application for membership was
rejected on the ground that the participation of such a conspicuous member of the community would be less help than
hindrance. In due course, however, Roosevelt took leadership
in starting the Little Missouri branch of the Montana Stockmen's Association, the function of which was to prevent over-
stocking of the ranges and to adjudicate disputes among the
ranchers. He became its first president.

Roosevelt's most spectacular contribution to the cause of
law enforcement was made during the late winter of 1886.
Through most of the year the Little Missouri was an aid to
transportation, as a bridle path in summer and an icy highway for sleighs in winter. From March to June, however,
during the flood season, the stream was frequently unford-
able and Roosevelt, whose Elkhorn range extended on both
sides of the river, kept a boat near his ranch house for emergency crossings. One morning in March of 1886, when Roosevelt and Sewall were planning to cross the river to shoot ante-
lope, Sewall found the boat missing and the painter severed
in a fashion that plainly indicated theft.

Being without another boat in which to pursue the thieves,
who already had a comfortable head start, Roosevelt was at
something of a disadvantage. He reasoned, however, that
since the thieves would be aware of his predicament and
therefore overconfident, it might be as well to give chase in
any case. First step in his plan was for Sewall to ride to
Medora to buy nails. The next was to use them in construct-
ing a makeshift raft. The third was for Sewall, Dow, and
himself to row and pole their way downstream on this in

pursuit of the robbers. These preparations took three days, but once on the river, the pursuers, all veterans of Maine's waterways under similar climatic conditions, made excellent time. Three days after leaving the ranch, they surprised the three boat thieves in their camp and succeeded in capturing them without bloodshed.

With the thieves in hand, the next problem was to bring them to justice. For six days, Dow, Sewall and Roosevelt took them downstream in the recovered boat until they came to a ranch house where it was possible to borrow a wagon. Then, leaving Dow and Sewall to continue downriver, Roosevelt set out overland for Mandan where he arrived with the thieves two days later. On the last forty-five mile leg of the trip, he was obliged to keep a constant watch over his captives who, though disarmed, could have overpowered him if he had dozed for a moment. Roosevelt was assisted in staying awake by reading *Anna Karenina,* recently published and a controversial best-seller. After describing the capture of the thieves in a letter to Elliott, he commented on the book in a letter to Corinne:

"I took *Anna Karenina* along on the trip and have read it through with very great interest. . . . Vronsky had some excellent points. I like poor Dolly—but she should have been less of a patient Griselda with her husband. You know how I abominate the Griselda type. Tolstoi is a great writer. . . . What day does Edith go abroad, and for how long does she intend staying? Could you not send her, when she goes, some flowers from me? . . ."

The last sentences of this letter referred to a new and important development not directly connected with either Tolstoi or the boat thieves. During the two years that he had devoted chiefly to ranching in the Badlands, Roosevelt had by no means lost all touch with the East. On the contrary, while a less constant commuter than the Marquis de Mores, who used a private car named the Montana for this purpose, Roosevelt made no fewer than half a dozen round trips to New York between June, 1884, and what proved to be his more or less permanent departure from Medora in the fall of 1886.

While in the East, his mode of existence was no less strenuous than it was on the Western plains and sometimes even more so. Roosevelt made a habit of following the Meadowbrook hounds on Long Island, where, after one especially severe fall, he remounted with a broken arm and rode on fast enough to be in at the death. Describing this mishap in a letter to Lodge, he set forth his reactions: "I am always willing to pay the piper when I have had a good dance, and every now and then I like to drink the wine of life with brandy in it."

Shortly before his first marriage Roosevelt had started to acquire some ninety-five acres of land in the Cove Neck section of Oyster Bay, Long Island, thirty odd miles East of New York. His plans to build there had gone forward after Alice's death and, by the fall of 1885, the house was ready to be lived in. Roosevelt made a convenient arrangement with his sister, Anna, then acting as guardian to little Alice. This was that she would use the Oyster Bay house during his absences in the West, and that he would put up at the house on Madison Avenue into which she had moved after their mother's death, when he was in New York. During his Eastern visit in the fall of 1885, a noteworthy codicil was added to this arrangement. This was that he be informed in advance whenever their old friend Edith Carow was likely to call, since he wished to avoid meeting her.

Roosevelt's anxiousness about meeting Edith Carow was an

indication of his state of mind after a year and a half of celibacy in the Badlands, where a complete change of scene, associates, and activities had helped take his mind off the tragic events of February, 1884. Shortly after his arrival in Medora, Merrifield, himself a widower, had tried to offer consolation by saying that time would help to dull the edge of his grief. Roosevelt had replied: "Time can never change me in that respect."

Roosevelt's determination to remain faithful to the memory of his first wife, while perhaps proof against new emotional attachments, was understandably powerless against those that had existed prior to his meeting with Alice. His attachment to Edith Carow had roots almost as deep as those of his devotion to his father. As his arrangement with his sister indicated, the roots were by no means lifeless and as might have been expected, the codicil in the arrangement with his sister proved ineffective. One winter afternoon Roosevelt entered the Madison Avenue house just as Edith was leaving it and they met on the stairs. Thereafter they made arrangements to see each other frequently.

According to subsequent family tradition, Roosevelt had proposed to Edith Carow before leaving for Cambridge in 1876. Nothing in his diary substantiates this but it was true that, during the years of his marriage to Alice Lee, Edith Carow was the only one of his New York friends whom she had never come to know well. In the winter of 1886, the Carow family, in straitened circumstances since the death of Edith's father, was planning to go to Europe where, then as now, a meager income could be stretched further than in the U.S. By the time Roosevelt returned to the Badlands in March, he and Edith had reached an understanding about the future but no one else was told of it. The request to his sister to send flowers to Edith on the occasion of her sailing was the only overt indication of his feeling—except for a card to go with the flowers which he enclosed in his next letter.

Roosevelt's good opinion of the Badlands as cattle country was not shared by Bill Sewall. The latter's observations indicated that, while steers could for a time be fattened on the range in summer and survive the winters in the open, the weather cycle could prove too rigorous over a long period. In the late summer of 1886, he and Dow informed Roosevelt that they were going back to Maine in the autumn. This was a fortunate decision on their part. Up to 1886, cattle ranchers in the Badlands, although unaware of it, had been favored by relatively mild winters during which the snow was not too deep to prevent the cattle from feeding on the stem-cured hay beneath it. In 1886, however, winter came early, with heavy snow in November followed by a thaw and later freezing that sealed off the hay with an unbreakable crust. Blizzards, high winds, and record low temperatures followed. Unlike buffalo, whose massive furry fronts enable them to face snow storms head first, the long-horn cattle headed away from them and "drifted," seeking nonexistent shelter. By spring more than half the herds had perished of cold or starvation.

Roosevelt himself in the summer of 1886 was as active as usual. After delivering a July Fourth oration at the nearby town of Dickenson, he spent a month in the East doing the final research for his Benton book and looking into the possibilities of an appointment which had been offered to him as President of the New York Board of Health. By August 7, he was back in Medora where he was re-elected President of the Stockmen's Association. Thence he wrote Lodge that in the event of war with Mexico he would like to raise some companies of volunteers from the Badlands cowboys, and departed on another hunting trip to the Big Horn mountains.

During this expedition, he wounded a mountain goat and finally killed it after a two-day chase in the course of which he fell off a forty-foot cliff into the top of a pine tree, "bounced down through it and brought up in a balsam with my rifle all right and myself unhurt except for the shaking."

Roosevelt's departure for the East again on October 3 marked the end of his life in the Badlands and started a new period in his career. When he arrived in New York, he was asked to accept the nomination for mayor on an Independent ticket. Knowing that it meant inevitable defeat, he nonetheless accepted and conducted an energetic campaign. Shortly after the election—in which Gorringe's friend, Abraham Hewitt, was elected and Roosevelt ran a creditable third—he took ship for London. On board he met a young Englishman named Cecil Spring Rice who proved to be a mutual friend of Cabot Lodge and who later became one of his own closest friends. Spring Rice was best man when, in a quiet ceremony at St. George's Church in Hanover Square on December 2, Theodore Roosevelt married Edith Kermit Carow.

V

BY THE TIME Roosevelt left
the Badlands in 1886, he had overcome his long-standing
tendency toward asthma and "cholera morbus." In their place
he was acquiring the thick trunk and look of robust health
that were to characterize him for the rest of his life. But the
changes made by the West went much deeper than physical
appearances.

Until 1884, Roosevelt's career in politics had been that of
a freak who was also a prodigy. He was a prodigy on account
of his age, which was more appropriate to a law apprentice
than to a political figure of national renown. He was a freak
because he came from an economic and social stratum which
rarely sent its representatives at any age whatever into the
political arena. Now, superimposed on marital tragedy and
the setback to his career at Chicago, the experience of living
and working on terms of equality with some of the nation's
roughest characters, in what were assuredly some of its

roughest conditions, had given him a new sort of knowledge and maturity.

Now he had begun to know at firsthand not merely a new and increasingly important section of his country, but, what was even more significant, the character of his compatriots in general. The traditional American success story starts at the base of the social pyramid but Roosevelt had done something even better than being born in a log cabin. Born in an urban mansion, he had built his own log cabin and lived in it during a period of development when, far more than might have been the case in infancy, he was capable of perceiving the true implications of such an environment.

Roosevelt himself well understood what his years in the West had meant to his emotional and intellectual, even more than to his physical, development. After the fall of 1886, he returned to the Badlands only rarely and then only for short periods, but thereafter he could always identify himself with the U.S. West and the U.S. workman as completely as with his native region and social background. Roosevelt's feeling is stated clearly in a fine passage in his autobiography:

> We knew toil and hardship and hunger and thirst; and we saw men die violent deaths as they worked among the horses and cattle, or fought in evil feuds with one another; but we felt the beat of hardy life in our veins, and ours was the glory of work and the joy of living.

Visiting the West years later, he said to a friend: "Here the romance of my life began." In 1900, when a Vice-Presidential campaign trip took him through the gently rolling plains between Bismarck and the Badlands, he seated himself alone on the observation platform and watched the tracks drawing together in the distance. To a member of the party who asked to see him, the colored porter in his car replied: "The Governor don't want to see nobody just now."

While Roosevelt's sojourn in the Badlands was to have far-reaching benefits, one immediate effect that was even more noticeable than the improvement in his health was the impairment in his finances. Roosevelt's views on monetary matters were, to put it mildly, unconventional. During his first winter in New York, he had invested twenty thousand dollars in a "silent partnership" in the publishing firm run by his father's old friend, George Haven Putnam, paying for it blithely with a check drawn on a bank account which contained less than half that amount. (The check was validated in due course but the partnership proved unworkable owing to the silent partner's temperamental incompatibility with such a role.) To a good friend and fellow Rough Rider, Major John C. Greenway, T.R. remarked in later years: "I have had an unusual life and have had most of the fine emotions that come to an American with the exception of one and I am a little ashamed that I have never experienced it. . . . I have never known that wonderful experience of being 'flat broke' and that emotion which comes to a man who doesn't know where the next meal, the next suit of clothes, are coming from." In the spring of 1887, however, he might well have felt that he was making rapid headway toward just such a predicament.

In a paragraph written in the fall of 1886 for his *Ranch Life and the Hunting Trail*, Roosevelt had made a shrewd observation on conditions in the Dakota ranges:

> Overstocking may cause little harm for two or three years but sooner or later there comes a winter which means ruin to the ranches that have too many cattle on them: and in our country, which is even now getting crowded, it is merely a question of time as to when a winter will come that will

understock the ranges by a summary process of killing off about half the cattle throughout the Northwest.

The winter of 1886–87, by far the worst in the memory of the region's white inhabitants, did a good deal more than that. Losses ranged from fifty to ninety percent, and the overall damage was about seventy-five. On his return from his honeymoon in Europe in the spring of 1887, Roosevelt went out to Medora in April to see for himself the effects that Merrifield and others had described in their letters. While less disastrous than for some other ranchers, whose herds had lacked even the partial protection of the broken country in the Badlands, these were even worse than he had imagined. Certainly the situation was bad enough to indicate that his career as a ranchman had failed even more dramatically and completely than his career as a politician. He summed up the situation in a letter to Lodge:

"Well, we have had a perfect smash-up all through the cattle country of the Northwest. The losses are crippling. For the first time, I have been utterly unable to enjoy a visit to my ranch. I shall be glad to get home."

According to his friend and biographer, Hermann Hagedorn, whose *Roosevelt in the Bad Lands* is the best source on the subject, Roosevelt's total investment in the West by the autumn of 1886 amounted to a little over eighty thousand dollars. After the departure of Sewall and Dow, management of both his ranches was in the hands of Merrifield and Sylvane Ferris. In subsequent years, they slowly rebuilt the herds so that by 1899 Roosevelt was able to dispose of his last holdings at an over-all loss, not counting interest, of only about twenty thousand dollars, or twenty-five percent. In the spring of 1887, however, his losses threatened to be much more serious than that. In a letter to Bamie, he said: "I wish I was sure I would lose no more than half the money I invested out here. I am planning how to get out of it."

Since Roosevelt had inherited an additional sixty-five thousand dollars after his mother's death, his ranches represented about forty percent of his available capital. Half of this now appeared to be lost and the rest frozen. This meant that—considering also his substantial investment in Sagamore Hill —he had about a hundred thousand dollars left on which to live. As shrewdly handled for him by his brother-in-law, Douglas Robinson, this might have provided an income of perhaps six thousand dollars a year. The payroll for half a dozen servants at Sagamore Hill, in days when unrestricted immigration provided an ample supply, was not much more than a hundred dollars a month. Nonetheless, this still left Roosevelt, to use his own metaphor, with barely enough bread and butter to get along on and certainly very little in the way of jam. Nor were his prospects, as he and his second bride set up housekeeping in Oyster Bay, especially promising.

With ranching and politics at least temporarily ruled out, the only congenial line of activity available to Roosevelt was writing. He plunged into it with his customary enthusiasm, embarking first on a biography of Gouverneur Morris, and then on the most ambitious project of his entire literary career, *The Winning of the West*. The latter, much in the manner of Francis Parkman to whom it was dedicated, was not concerned merely with the recent and spectacular expansion in which Roosevelt himself had been a participant and could therefore write with special authority. Its subject, to be developed in three massive volumes, was the entire Westward movement, first of the thirteen colonies and then of the United States as a nation. Roosevelt saw all this as the final and climactic stage of the expansion of the Anglo-Saxon race as a whole—since the Pacific coast of the United States represented the inherent limit of such progress.

Roosevelt's substantial virtues as a writer have been somewhat obscured by the fact that his work fell into two entirely separate categories, the distinction between which his critics have often found it convenient to ignore. Much of what Roosevelt wrote—and understandably the part that attracted most attention during his lifetime—were speeches, reports, and state papers of which the purpose was not merely to interest the reader but rather to produce a response in terms of specific action. In writing of this sort, Roosevelt was at no more pains to achieve eloquence *per se* than is an officer giving orders to his troops. As he himself expressed it in a conversation with a friend:

"I had to wake up the people and keep them awake. For many years, Wall Street and Big Business and their allies had 'doped' the people and got away with things while the masses slept. That is how I found them. If you want to wake up a hundred million people, you've got to make a big and resounding noise and you have got to keep that up for a while, lest they turn around and go to sleep again. Moreover, if you want any new notions and impressions to sink in and spread across a continent, you have got to iterate and reiterate and emphasize and drive home until you pretty well weary of the sound of your own voice."

In writings of a different sort—biographies, hunting sketches, memoirs, and essays—Roosevelt is quick, vivid and, above all, unfailingly interesting. If critics have claimed, not without some justice, that most of his work in these categories lacks "profundity," one reason may be that profundity is usually the last thing his subject called for. It is demanded of the author perhaps only because we feel it too modest in such a world-famous personage to be content merely to entertain

us. As a writer, Roosevelt was primarily, and altogether
properly, a brilliant raconteur. He could rise to heights of
poetry and quite often did so—most notably perhaps in his
descriptions of winter on the Western plains or in his eloquent essay on "History as Literature," which he delivered as
a lecture to the American Historical Association in 1912. But
the very essence of his talent as a writer is to be found in his
shortest and most casual pieces, especially the letters to his
family and, most of all, those to his children, many of them
embellished with his pencil sketches of the objects, animals,
and people he was telling about. His touch in such correspondence rarely deserts him, even when writing from the
White House—a name, incidentally, which he established in
place of the former stilted and pretentious name, "Executive
Mansion." A fair sample, chosen more or less at random from
the published collection, is this easy sketch of a Presidential
encounter with a kitten:

Darling Ethel:
     . . . Today as I was marching to church, with Sloane
some 25 yards behind, I suddenly saw two terriers racing to attack
a kitten which was walking down the sidewalk. I bounced forward with my umbrella, and after some active work put to
flight the dogs while Sloane captured the kitten which was a
friendly, helpless little thing, evidently too well accustomed to
being taken care of to know how to shift for itself. I en-
quired of all the by-standers and of people on the neighboring
porches to know if they knew who owned it; but as they all
disclaimed, with many grins, any knowledge of it, I marched
ahead with it in my arms for about half a block. Then I saw
a very nice colored woman and little colored girl looking out
of the window of a small house with on the door a dress-
maker's advertisement, and I turned and walked up the steps
and asked if they did not want the kitten. They said they did,

and the little girl welcomed it lovingly; so I felt I had gotten it a home and continued toward church. . . .

It was in the early years of his second marriage that Roosevelt established the patterns of life at Sagamore Hill which, when it became the summer White House, were to become world-famous. At Sagamore Hill—first named Leeholm, for his first wife, and re-christened after her death in honor of the Indian chief from whom its original white owner had obtained possession—Roosevelt's boundless physical energy, tireless aptitude for sport and love of the outdoors found multiple expression in a variety of pastimes and pursuits that sometimes drove visitors to the brink of distraction. These were perhaps most feelingly described by Eleanor A. Roosevelt, wife of his eldest son, Theodore, Jr.—who was later to fight in both World Wars and win the Medal of Honor which his father had once coveted but never received. Her account of her first Sagamore Hill picnic is memorable:

"Under the blazing sun we rowed and rowed. There was not a vestige of breeze; the Sound was as calm as glass. By and by, I began pointing out places where we might stop, but they were all declared quite unsuitable and far less attractive than the spot to which we were going. Some two hours later, we landed on a beach precisely like the one from which we had started except that it was farther from home. There was not the least shade. Because of the poison ivy we could not go near the trees. . . .

"When the clams were judged ready, my father-in-law selected one, opened it, sprinkled it with pepper and salt and handed it to me. It was very large and had a long neck. . . . At first, although gritty with sand, it was delicious; but that soon wore off and it became like a piece of old rubber hose."

When Eleanor Roosevelt tried to get rid of the clam by

slipping it under the log on which she was sitting, her father-in-law, who had observed this ruse, made a good-humored comment: " 'You're not as persistent as Archie was when he was small. The first time he ate a clam on a picnic, he chewed for a time, then ate three sandwiches, half a dozen cookies and an orange. About half an hour later he came to me and asked what he should do with the poor little dead clam. It was still in his mouth.' "

When the lunch ended and the party prepared to return, a head wind sprang up which made the outward two-hour row a four-hour row home. "Faces and necks were burned to a crisp; hands were blistered. My father-in-law had a difficult time in reaching shore at all as the boat in which he was rowing my mother-in-law began to leak badly. In spite of it all, everybody considered that the picnic had been a great and glorious success." By the end of the summer, Eleanor Roosevelt felt that she had "gained immeasurably in valuable experience. . . . It was splendid training, but, while it was going on, I lost twenty-six pounds."

Eleanor Roosevelt's experience at her first picnic barely scratched the rough surface of such outings. The basic ingredient of these were "scrambles"—a term borrowed from the mountaineer, Edward Whymper, who often refers to "My scrambles amongst the Alps," and applied by T.R. to comparably arduous point-to-point races on his native terrain. At Sagamore Hill scrambles were likely to include running down the almost perpendicular face of Cooper's Bluff, a two-hundred-foot sand precipice dividing the entrance to Oyster Bay from that of Cold Spring Harbor. Picnics that involved an all-night stay on some damp and pebbly beach, as many of them did, were climaxed by ghost stories toward the end of which T.R. was likely to pounce on whatever child happened to be nearest him, as a fitting climax for the terrifying narrative.

Sagamore Hill picnics represented the strenuous life only in its more juvenile or preliminary aspects. For adults, it also included more vigorous pursuits like polo, tennis, and fox hunting, all practiced with Rooseveltian abandon. Roosevelt played tennis in a unique style, holding his racket halfway up the handle in a pen-holder grip, his forefinger pointing to the throat. In the languorous days of his first marriage he had once distinguished himself by playing ninety-one games, or the equivalent of a dozen average sets, in the course of one otherwise normally active day. As he grew older, he found tennis less adequate as an outlet for his energies, especially when the weather or other conditions tended to impede the game.

At Sagamore Hill, one impediment to tennis was a certain ignorant chipmunk who often chose to scamper across the court in the middle of a rally. Roosevelt, of whom it was later said that he killed lions like mosquitoes and mosquitoes like lions, was pleased by the breath-taking temerity of this little creature. Under such circumstances, he always halted play and had the point played over. In later years at Washington, where the court had a canvas backstop that often helped the interior temperature to rise into the nineties, Roosevelt enjoyed the game in the summer but found it too tame in the winter or on rainy days. His military aide, Archie Butt, described one notably rainy match played on a court covered with water, with balls so wet they would not bounce. His friend, Laurence Murray, described another more typical one when the President stopped play, saying: "It is just the day and time for a long walk and run. We will go."

As they set off through Rock Creek Park without raincoats

or umbrellas, Roosevelt issued a note of caution: "Tie your shoes on extra tight or the muck will pull them off." That this warning proved to be entirely justified did not impair T.R.'s enjoyment of the outing. Presently he said: "From here it is exactly four miles to the White House. We will now run every step of the way back." On another rainy-day walk in Washington, Roosevelt and his companion, Maurice Francis Egan, got chatting about the best way to stab a wolf. Roosevelt hailed a hansom cab and, when it had stopped, drew a diagram on the horse's chest of the proper place to insert the knife.

Like tennis, polo was still something of a novelty in the United States during the eighties. This made it all the more exciting to Roosevelt who, in 1888, organized a team to play at Meadowbrook, later the capital of this pastime for its practitioners in the Western hemisphere. A letter to Bysie includes a description of a scratch game against "the Meadowbrooks" played with three men on a side instead of four, thus guaranteeing each more action: "We beat them six goals to one; a pretty bad beat. . . . At the very end of the game, when fortunately there was only a couple of minutes left I got a tumble and was knocked senseless."

Roosevelt's next letter to Bysie related the consequences of this mishap: "Edith has just had a miscarriage. . . . The mischief of course came from my infernal tumble at the polo match. The tumble was nothing in itself; I have had twenty worse; but it *looked* bad because I was knocked perfectly limp and senseless, and though I was all right in an hour, the mischief had been done to Edith though we did not know it for over a week."

Edith Carow Roosevelt's reaction to her husband's fall on the polo field was in sharp contrast to the remarkable composure which in later years she had learned to maintain under comparable or even more trying circumstances. It was her dignity, common sense, and calm that kept his often outrageous ebullience in some kind of check and provided a balance of sorts for his extravagantly impulsive behavior. Having known T.R. from his ailing infancy, she—like no one else except possibly his older sister—knew precisely what lay behind the magnificent façade and where the flood of fearless action had its original springs. A deeply sensitive and reticent but notably courageous wife and mother, she learned eventually just how best to cope with her amazing spouse under all the astonishing contingencies he created for himself from Cooper's Bluff to the Congo.

In dealing with T.R., one of Edith Roosevelt's most effective techniques was that of gentle ridicule. During their early days in Washington, Roosevelt wrote Lodge about a dinner the young couple had given for Spring Rice, by then attached to the British Embassy, and several other notables: "Bill of fare, crabs, chicken and rice, claret and tea. Springy nervous and fidgetty; I, with my best air of Oriental courtesy, and a tendency to orate held in check by memory of my wife's jeers."

The youthful quality of Roosevelt's response to life was dryly noted by Spring Rice who, in later years, was to say: "One thing you must always remember about Roosevelt is that he is about seven years old." The same characteristic was also perceived by many others including his official biographer, Joseph Bucklin Bishop, who said of Roosevelt as police commissioner: "The peculiarity about him is that he has what is essentially a boy's mind." Edith Roosevelt had summed up this trait even more aptly one day when, packing to leave the White House for Oyster Bay, she was asked by Mrs. Bellamy Storer, then a close friend, whether the President were going too. "For Heaven's sake, don't put it into

Theodore's head to go too," was the reply, "I should have another child to think of."

Edith Carow Roosevelt was understandably less than whole-heartedly sympathetic with her husband's frequent propensity for placing himself in the path of serious injury. Once when he appeared in the front hall at Sagamore Hill with a deep and gory cut on his scalp, sustained while trying to repair the barn windmill, her reaction was more crisp than sympathetic: "Theodore, I do wish you'd do your bleeding in the bathroom. You're spoiling every rug in the house." During the course of one Sagamore Hill picnic, Roosevelt encouraged the juvenile participants to go swimming with their clothes on. On their return, they were all sent to bed with doses of ginger syrup and in response to their pleas for intervention, T.R., then President, felt obliged to reply:

"I'm afraid there is nothing that I can do. I'm lucky that she did not give me a dose of ginger too."

When T.R. was making plans for his post-Presidential visit to Africa and Europe, the question of what clothes he should take with him came up for discussion at the White House. To Roosevelt's statement that he would not wear knickerbockers and silk stockings at court functions in Europe on the way home, Archie Butt replied that he was entitled to the dress uniform of a cavalry colonel. Roosevelt had always been enthusiastic about picturesque costumes and had once ridden fifty miles across the Badlands to get a buckskin cowboy outfit in which he had later had himself photographed in New York. Butt's suggestion delighted him and he immediately announced that he would order one and wear it with patent leather boots. Edith Roosevelt's response was characteristic. "If you insist on doing this," she said, "I will have a *vivandiere's* costume made and follow you throughout Europe."

When Roosevelt and his son Kermit sailed the following

March, Butt asked the latter how his mother was bearing up. "She was perfectly calm and self-possessed when we left home," Kermit replied, "but I had the feeling that her heart was broken." How right this diagnosis was, Butt learned when he called at Sagamore Hill to pay his respects a few weeks later. "It was a dreadful day," Edith Roosevelt told him, "I have never known but one like it—that day when Archie's fate was in doubt and we didn't know whether he would live or not."

Roosevelt's courtship of Edith Carow had lacked the turbulence of his pursuit of Alice Lee half a dozen years earlier. Their wedding was a quiet one at which the groom's sister, Anna, finding her brother and his best man "intensely occupied in a discussion over the population of an island in the Southern Pacific," became seriously worried lest they keep the bride waiting at the church. Nonetheless, based upon lifelong compatibility as well as deep and constant love, the marriage was a magnificent success. "This is the 32nd anniversary of Mother's and my engagement," he wrote to his youngest son, Quentin, on November 17, 1917, "and I really think I am just as much in love with her as I was then—she is so wise and good and pretty and charming."

Roosevelt's showing in the three-cornered mayorality election of 1886—60,000 votes compared with a normal Republican total of fifteen or twenty thousand more—had not been especially impressive. By the following spring, E. L. Godkin, editor of *The Nation* and spokesman for the "mugwump," or independent, voters, whose impractical approach to reform politics Roosevelt despised, felt justified in writing that it had been a mistake "ever to take him seriously as a politician. . . ." The magazine *Puck* went considerably further:

Be happy, Mr. Roosevelt, be happy while you may. . . . You have heard of Pitt, of Alexander Hamilton, of Randolph Churchill and of other men who were young and yet who, so to speak, got there just the same. Bright visions float before your eyes of what the party can and may do for you. We wish you a gradual and gentle awakening. We fear the party cannot do much for you. You are not the timber of which Presidents are made.

By the spring of 1888, Roosevelt was thoroughly bored with the inactivity of a life that included nothing much except the writing of a three-volume history combined with constant tennis, fox hunting, polo, and aquatic exercises along with the excitement of acquiring an heir, when Theodore, Jr., appeared on the scene in late 1887. That fall he took an active part in the campaign in which—after Blaine had declined it— General Benjamin Harrison accepted the nomination and handily defeated Grover Cleveland. As Secretary of State in Harrison's cabinet, Blaine was generous enough to suggest that Roosevelt receive some recognition for his efforts, as did his good friend Lodge. The following spring, their suggestions bore fruit when the President offered Roosevelt the minor but nonetheless, for an enthusiastic young reformer, wholly appropriate post of Civil Service Commissioner. Leaving his family—which by then also included Kermit—at Oyster Bay, he took office on May 13, 1889, a day which Matthew F. Halloran, Executive Secretary to the four-man Commission, later recalled clearly. First there was an extraordinary commotion in the outer office. Then Roosevelt burst in to exclaim:

"I am the new Civil Service Commissioner. Have you a telephone? Call up the Ebbitt House. I have an appointment with Archbishop Ireland. Say I will be there at ten o'clock."

Prior to Roosevelt's appointment, the Civil Service Commission had been a dignified bureaucratic edifice which provided an effectively protective front behind which political patronage could operate with a minimum of outside interference. With Roosevelt's appointment, its character underwent immediate and drastic change. The new Commissioner took the view that "offices are not the property of the politicians at all . . . on the contrary, they belong to the people and should be filled only with regard to the public service." Six weeks after taking office, he wrote to Lodge that "I have made this Commission a living force." His activities in this direction had by that time already been sufficient to cause anxious inquiries from the White House. To these, ". . . I answered militantly that as long as I was responsible the law should be enforced up to the handle everywhere, fearlessly and honestly."

A decade later, when Roosevelt was Governor of New York and under consideration for the Vice-Presidential nomination, Harrison voiced amiable recollections of his Civil Service Commissioner: "The only trouble I ever had with managing him was that . . . he wanted to put an end to all the evil in the world between sunrise and sunset. . . ." If Harrison had no trouble with Roosevelt, the same could certainly not be said of his diligent postmaster general, John Wanamaker, the renowned Philadelphia storekeeper.

Wanamaker owed his cabinet post to his substantial contributions to the party treasury in the 1888 campaign. While a staunch supporter of Sunday schools and of civic righteousness in general, he was also a stout proponent of the theory, often endorsed by Roosevelt himself when joining issue with the mugwumps, that political reform could best be achieved within the framework of the existing party system rather than by idealistic methods outside it. By November of 1889, Wanamaker had demonstrated his loyalty to the two-party system as then constituted in convincing fashion by dismissing no fewer than thirty thousand fourth-class postmasters and replacing them with deserving Republicans.

That Wanamaker and Roosevelt would presently collide head on was evident within a fortnight of the latter's arrival in Washington. With his fellow commissioner, Hugh S. Thompson, he set out on a nationwide tour of inspection starting, appropriately enough, at the New York Customs House which had been denied to his father through the workings of the spoils system in 1876. Roosevelt uncovered evidence that three of its employees had been appointed after fraudulent examinations and recommended their dismissal. The investigators then made a ten-day swing through the Midwest which uncovered further irregularities in Milwaukee, Indianapolis, and elsewhere. Roosevelt's debut as a commissioner was in fact energetic enough to cause not only concern at the White House but also, even less to his satisfaction, approval among the mugwumps. Roosevelt confided his feelings about this ironical development to Cabot Lodge: "I have been seriously annoyed at the mugwump praises for fear they would discredit me with well-meaning but narrow Republicans, and for the last week my party friends in Washington have evidently felt a little shaky."

The collision with Postmaster General Wanamaker occurred toward the end of 1890 upon disclosure by Charles Joseph Bonaparte—a distinguished Baltimore advocate of Civil Service and later Attorney General in the Roosevelt cabinet—of widespread corruption among the postal officials in his city. An investigation followed of which the result was a recommendation by the Commission that at least two dozen or so of the thirty thousand new Wanamaker appointees be summarily dismissed. When no dismissals followed, Roosevelt submitted his findings on both Baltimore and Wanamaker to the House Committee on Civil Service. By this time, the Democrats were again in control of the House and the Committee reported favorably on Roosevelt's charges. Whether or not the feud with Wanamaker would eventually have resulted in Roosevelt's removal, as he himself was inclined to believe, is a moot point but, as things turned out, it had an unexpectedly advantageous effect on his career. Cleveland, with whom Roosevelt had worked on behalf of Civil Service in New York during the former's term as Governor, was restored to the White House in 1892. Roosevelt's hostility toward spoilsmen in his own party made it all the easier for Cleveland to retain him on the Commission where he continued to serve until the spring of 1895.

Roosevelt's six-year stint as Civil Service Commissioner is a period of his career that many of his biographers have brushed aside as less important, as it was certainly less colorful, than his lively excursion to the Badlands, his precocious triumphs in the New York State Assembly, and his dramatic uphill fight to overcome his physical liabilities in childhood. In fact, his first half-dozen years in Washington may well have been especially meaningful ones. Up to that time, Roosevelt's life had been an almost uninterrupted series of crises, some of them triumphs and some disasters, some imposed by circumstance and some self-created. Now, for the first time, he found himself in circumstances of relative stability and at the same time in a congenial new environment in which he could put down roots.

Washington in the nineties was not, as it is now, a bustling metropolis of almost a million souls and one of the two major power centers of the globe. It was a cozy little city of some two hundred thousand, which was much less glittering socially and less significant politically than any of the half-dozen major capitals of Europe. Most of the thousand or so

people who counted for anything in terms of influence and
prestige soon came to know each other reasonably well. If the
Badlands had given Roosevelt an insight into the American
people, his years of apprenticeship in Washington gave him
an insight into American government, on the national as
distinguished from the state level. It was in these years that
he came to know many, and to know about most, of the men
and institutions with which his subsequent career was to be
involved. With Lodge and Spring Rice as mentors, the Roosevelts were soon on easy terms with a circle whose major
figures were Henry Adams and John Hay—who could remember meeting Roosevelt in the latter's nursery.

Along with politicians and diplomats, the Roosevelts'
group of close friends came to include numerous artists and
writers, among them John Singer Sargent, Augustus St.
Gaudens, Rudyard Kipling and Richard Harding Davis, who
later covered the Rough Riders' charge at San Juan Hill.
Kipling, whom Roosevelt disliked at first but later came to
admire, used to enjoy visits to the Cosmos Club where he was
likely to find Roosevelt holding forth in the lounge. "I curled
up on the seat opposite," the author said, "and listened and
wondered until the universe seemed to be spinning around
and Theodore was the spinner."

Under Cleveland, Roosevelt continued to plug away cheerfully at his job in the Commission, of which he had written
earlier: "I have pretty hard work and work of rather an
irritating kind; but I am delighted to be engaged in it. The
last few years politically have been for me largely a balancing
of evils, and I am delighted to go in on a side where I have
no doubts whatever. . . ." Some of Roosevelt's innovations
in the Civil Service regulations reflected his enthusiasm for
the strenuous life as well as for his job. At a Civil Service
dinner in Baltimore in 1892, he related with pride how he

had introduced marksmanship into the examination of customs guards on the Texas border, pointing out also that in
their work horsemanship counted more than arithmetic and
that the ability to read brands was more important than a
knowledge of conventional spelling. His ally Bonaparte, who
spoke next, suggested that Roosevelt had been remiss. "He
should have had the men shoot at each other and given the
jobs to the survivors."

Despite such friendly digs, Roosevelt's record in his job
was an impressive one. At the end of his six years in Washington, when he left to accept the post of Police Commissioner in New York, twenty-six thousand jobs had been
transferred from the category of political plums to that of
posts awarded on the basis of competitive examination. But
his accomplishment went far beyond this statistical summary.
He had helped to bring the principle of Civil Service to national attention and into national favor and had given the
Commission a new stature and importance. If his career had
ended there, he would have earned a small but secure niche
in history for his contribution to the evolution of sound government under a democracy.

VI

BEFORE accepting the post of Police Commissioner, Roosevelt had turned down that of Commissioner of Street Cleaning; for the latter, "I did not feel I had any particular fitness," while the former, "was in my line and I was glad to undertake it." There was a substantial basis for this view; Roosevelt's 1884 investigation had shown him most of the Police Department's shortcomings. He knew what the evils were and an effort on his part to put an end to them—between sunrise and sunset, or otherwise—seemed entirely suitable. There were, however, other and even more compelling reasons why he sensed at once that he would find the post congenial and rewarding.

One reason was the mere fact that it was completely new; like most men who have the capacity and the urge to grow, Roosevelt loved change for its own sake and always found it stimulating. Another was that it promised to provide occasions for direct and drastic action of a sort which had rarely arisen at the Civil Service Commission or even in the Assembly. Finally, the new post would bring him back into the limelight for the first time in more than a decade and presumably keep him there under favorable circumstances. The highly volatile essence of Roosevelt's temperament had been bottled up under pressure for half a dozen years; now the chance to blow off steam, or better, to apply it in a public and productive fashion, was precisely what he needed.

Like the Civil Service Board, the Police Commission was a bipartisan body composed of four members. At its first meeting, in the dingy old Police Headquarters on Mulberry Street, his fellow members promptly elected Roosevelt President. Friction with two of his three colleagues followed in due course but much more noticeable at the outset was wholehearted support not only from his fellow commissioners but from the forces of municipal reform in general and their chief spokesman, the eloquent Presbyterian clergyman, Charles H. Parkhurst, in particular. From his pulpit at the Madison Square Church, Parkhurst had since 1892 been preaching sensational and widely admired sermons to the effect that New York was a "hot-bed of knavery, debauchery and bestiality" where disorderly houses and gambling dens "flourish . . . almost as thick as the roses of Sharon." Parkhurst's denunciations had, indeed, been a major factor in the 1894 downfall of Tammany Hall and the election of Mayor William L. Strong, a businessman of high repute, on an Independent reform ticket. To the preacher and his adherents, Roosevelt's appointment to the key post of Chief Police Commissioner presaged the end of the vicious alliance between the agents of law enforcement and the wrongdoers they were supposed to combat. Most of the city's newspapers were equally enthusiastic and Arthur Brisbane, then headquarters correspondent for Joseph Pulitzer's *World,* wrote a glowing feature story:

"We have a real Police Commissioner . . . His teeth are big and white, his eyes are small and piercing, his voice is rasping. He makes our policemen feel as the little froggies did when the stork came to rule them. . . ."

Roosevelt's first item of business on taking office at Mulberry Street was to dismiss the then Superintendent of Police, an easygoing individual named Tom Byrnes, who had blandly explained his possession of a $300,000 fortune by saying that he had acquired it in Wall Street, with the assistance of Jay Gould. With Byrnes out of the way, the Chief Commissioner set about improving the caliber of the force by imposing sharp penalties for laxness or corruption and conferring prompt rewards for meritorious service. He made it clear to all, from seasoned captains to rookie "roundsmen," that he considered it their function to enforce the law without fear or favor and that anyone who neglected to fulfill it was liable to immediate dismissal.

One of the principal sources of collusion between New York's underworld and the police force was the law which forbade sales of all stimulants, including beer, on Sundays. In consequence of this edict an arrangement had long since developed, with the enthusiastic and well-paid cooperation of the force, whereby saloonkeepers merely closed their front doors on the Sabbath, leaving side or back doors open to all regular customers. The Sunday closing law did not by any means reflect Roosevelt's personal views on the sale of liquor. These views, as he had said earlier and would say more frequently later on, were that regulatory legislation was far better than any sort of absolute, and hence unworkable, prohibition. Nonetheless, he now took the position that, so long as the law was on the books, the morale of the police force if nothing else required him to enforce it. The shock to members of the force—who had understandably come to feel that the law had been expressly devised to enable them to pad out their salaries—was even greater than that to the general public. Upon the latter, however, the effect was also noteworthy.

Hardest hit among members of the tippling population were not the habitual guzzlers of whiskey and other spirits, who could, if need be, lay in a week-end supply or buy a surreptitious pint under the counter. Those who suffered most were rather the less dissolute citizens who enjoyed a sociable glass of beer on the way home from church or later in the day. Hardest hit of all were large numbers of recently transplanted Germans who traditionally spent their Sunday afternoons in beer gardens, accompanied by their wives and children. When the German element held a protest parade shortly before the 1895 elections, an invitation was sarcastically sent to Roosevelt who, much to the surprise of its despatchers, promptly accepted it. As the parade marched past the reviewing stand, carrying banners deriding "Roosevelt's Razzle-Dazzle Reform Racket" and "Roosevelt's Russian Rule," a marcher shouted loudly:

"Wo ist der Roosevelt?"

Grinning happily, Roosevelt leaned over the balustrade and shouted back:

"Hier bin ich!"

This brought a roar of laughter from the crowd and turned what had been intended as an attack on the Commissioner into a personal triumph.

Himself partly of Teutonic stock, Roosevelt later on in his term gave an even more dramatic display of his thereafter frequently proven aptitude for handling outbursts of German temperament, including those of Kaiser Wilhelm. As Police Commissioner, his opportunity was provided when an aggressively anti-Semitic German orator, the Rector Ahlwardt, arrived in New York to give a lecture and requested police protection. Jewish elements in the city promptly retaliated by demanding that the pastor, far from receiving protection, be refused permission to speak at all. How Roosevelt solved this dilemma with characteristic aplomb, and in a way that made headlines in Europe, is engagingly narrated in his autobiography: "The proper thing to do was to make him ridiculous. Accordingly I detailed for his protection a Jew sergeant and a score or two of Jewish policemen. He made his harangue against the Jews under the active protection of some forty policemen, every one of them a Jew!"

In trying to weed out or punish bad policemen and to promote or otherwise reward good ones, Roosevelt naturally chose the most strenuous means available. One of these was to fare forth late at night and prowl about the city to observe the conduct of patrolmen on duty without revealing his own identity. Such prowls often lasted until morning and, after a breakfast of ham and eggs and an hour's sleep, were followed by a day's work at his desk. They were also likely to result in dismaying experiences for patrolmen who were slow to adjust to the new order of things and who persisted in their previous convivial habits. On one occasion, encountering a roundsman who was enjoying a small hours chat with a young lady of the streets, Roosevelt paused to inquire as to the subject of their talk.

"What's that to you?" retorted the policeman, and then, turning to his companion, asked: "Shall I fan him, Mame?"

"Sure, fan him to death," was Mame's reply.

Roosevelt revealed his identity and the pair made off rapidly in opposite directions.

The new Commissioner's nocturnal prowls delighted the newspapers, which covered them with enthusiastic flourishes. The New York *Recorder* ran a cartoon showing a patrolman cowering at night before a building on which were hung a set of teeth advertising a dentist's office and a pair of spectacles advertising an optician's, in juxtaposition that caused them to resemble the Commissioner's celebrated countenance. Papers in Philadelphia, Baltimore, and elsewhere took favorable note of Roosevelt's exploits and the Chicago *Times-Herald* called him the biggest man in New York "if not the most interesting man in public life." The Ithaca *Daily News* went a step further by declaring Roosevelt to be its candidate for the 1896 Republican nomination for President. Cabot Lodge had by this time long since come to hold the position of personal adviser of which Roosevelt had felt such acute need on the death of his father. He, too, spoke in glowing terms of the Senate or even, eventually, the White House, writing, in 1895 from Paris: "The day is not far distant when you will come into a large kingdom."

The day was, in fact, by now a good deal closer than Lodge suspected but naturally not even Roosevelt himself could possibly have been aware of that. Roosevelt, indeed, never felt much more confident about his presidential prospects than he did at the time of his earliest recorded comment on the subject, made during a farewell talk with his shrewd friend Bill Sewall at Medora in the summer of 1886. When Roosevelt expressed doubts about his future, Sewall, according to his subsequent recollection, remarked:

"If you go into politics and live, your chance to be President is good."

This compliment, which later proved to be an astonishing confirmation of Maine's reliability as a political barometer, brought forth a diffident reply: "Bill, you have a good deal more faith in me than I have in myself. That looks a long ways ahead to me."

Sewall stuck to his point: "It may be a long ways ahead but

100]   T.R.—THE STORY OF THEODORE ROOSEVELT

it is not so far ahead of you as it has been of men who got there."

Roosevelt' opinion of his prospects—at least insofar as he expressed it to others—had not improved much when, one day in 1895, his good friends Jacob Riis and Lincoln Steffens called at his office and asked him point blank whether he was a possible candidate for President. According to Steffens, Roosevelt leapt to his feet and, red with an emotion which the reporter took to be rage, replied:

"Don't you dare ask me that! Don't you put such ideas into my head. . . . Never, never must . . . either of you remind a man . . . on a political job that he may be President. . . . He loses his nerve; he can't do his work; he gives up the very traits that are making him a possibility! . . . I must be wanting to be President. Every young man does. But I won't let myself think of it. . . . If I do . . . I'll be careful, calculating, cautious and so . . . I'll beat myself. See?"

To call Jacob Riis, Danish-born New York newspaper man and later author of *Theodore Roosevelt, the Citizen,* a good friend of Roosevelt is something of an understatement. Riis's famous 1890 best-seller, *How the Other Half Lives,* was among the influences that prompted Roosevelt to welcome his New York post in the first place. It was with Riis, then police reporter for the *Evening Sun* and already a trusted confidant, and with Steffens, then of the *Evening Post,* to whom Riis introduced him on the way, that he arrived at Mulberry Street on his first day in office. "What shall we do first?" Steffens recalled that Roosevelt asked them. Then ". . . We went out into the hall and there stood the other three Commissioners together, waiting for us to go so that they could see T.R."

During the next three years, the relationship between

Roosevelt and Riis grew closer. The latter often accompanied the Commissioner on his midnight inspection tours and he became a frequent visitor at Sagamore Hill. On leaving office, Roosevelt described him as "the most loyal and disinterested man I have ever known." Riis and Steffens were only two of a wide circle of writers and newspaper men whom Roosevelt came to know well during his two years in New York. Brander Matthews, the Columbia professor and pundit who for many years held unrivalled eminence as the dean of U.S. literary critics, became a good friend as did Hamlin Garland and, to a lesser extent, Stephen Crane, then a New York reporter and later a war correspondent in Cuba. Closest of all the Commissioner's literary friends was Owen Wister who had been a year behind him at Harvard and who based his book *The Virginian* in part on Roosevelt's experiences in the Badlands. In his *Theodore Roosevelt, the Story of a Friendship,* Wister relates what happened during one of his calls at Roosevelt's Mulberry Street headquarters when a job-seeking surgeon named Marvin Palmer entered and presented a letter of recommendation from the Surveyor of the Port.

"I entirely agree that a Republican appointment would be timely and I am quite sure, Dr. Palmer, that you are qualified for the position," said Roosevelt, and then added: "And here's the way you can get the position. . . . Stand first on the Civil Service list!"

Dr. Palmer departed briskly, only turning at the door to call back:

"You can go to hell!"

Roosevelt's years on the Police Commission were the central ones of the decade later to be known as the Gay Nineties. The great social event of the era was the famous Bradley Martin Ball, an elaborate divertissement which was reported to have cost a hundred thousand dollars and which, since it took place during a minor depression, created a storm of adverse comment. To Roosevelt, the doings of society, as such, had always seemed a considerable bore, in part no doubt because, having inherited as secure a social position as his environment afforded, he could find in them neither novelty nor challenge. His opinion of the decade's most publicized festivities was summed up in a letter to Bamie, then in London:

"At a dinner at the Bronsons' this week, Bradley Martin took Edith in; we are immensely amused by the intense seriousness with which they regard themselves and their ball."

At Oyster Bay, the summer routine went on much as usual. Commuting via the Long Island Railroad in the nineties was no less of a trial than it remained a generation or two later and involved the additional hazzard, prior to the construction of the East River tunnel, of a ferry ride from Manhattan to Queens. For Roosevelt, the journey also included three miles of dirt road between the Oyster Bay station, where the line ended, and Sagamore Hill, a distance which he habitually covered by bicycle as a means of getting in some exercise whenever possible. Picnics, scrambles, and miscellaneous other excursions of a strenuous nature proceeded according to custom. During the summer that Theodore, Jr., was nine, his father deemed him mature enough to become an apprentice shooting companion, and recognized this development by giving him his first lethal weapon, a Flobert rifle. The recipient later recalled the sequel to the presentation. It was too dark to shoot after supper, but Roosevelt slipped a cartridge into the chamber nonetheless. Then, saying to his namesake, "You must promise not to tell Mother," he pointed the gun at the ceiling and pulled the trigger. "The report was slight, the smoke hardly noticeable and the hole in the ceiling so small that our sin was not detected."

In 1895, the big sporting event of the summer was the

series of races for the America's Cup, in which the challenger was the temperamental Lord Dunraven who took sharp exception to several rulings made by race officials. Roosevelt watched one of the races from the police launch and was much amused when Ted, Jr., christened a new Sagamore pig "Sulky Dunraven." That fall Ted, Jr., entered the Cove School, a one-classroom institution near Sagamore Hill where most of his fellow students were the sons and daughters of the neighborhood servants and laborers. Archie, Kermit, and Quentin later attended the Cove School also, until they were old enough to be sent off to Groton—whose founder, Roosevelt's Harvard classmate Endicott Peabody, had somewhat naively offered the future President a teaching job in 1886.

In spare evenings and over week ends, Roosevelt went ahead with the last volume of *The Winning of the West* on which he was busy correcting proof by March of 1896. Meanwhile he also found time to write a letter to the Harvard *Crimson,* setting students and faculty straight about what was then the major squabble on the international calendar, i.e., the U.S. dispute with Britain over the latter's threat to occupy port cities in Venezuela as a means of extracting debt payments. Roosevelt was troubled less by the pressure of his high tempo schedule than by the bugbear of idleness. In December, 1895, his sister Anna married Captain William Sheffield Cowles, then naval attaché at the United States Embassy in London. The following March, Roosevelt wrote her that by May or June "I shall . . . have finished a year of as hard work and of as much worry and responsibility as a man could well have; yet I have enjoyed it extremely, and am in excellent health. I don't mind work; the only thing I am afraid of is that by and by I will have nothing to do, and I should hate to have the children grow up and see me having nothing to do. . . ."

The almost unanimous enthusiasm with which New York's press and public had greeted Roosevelt's debut at Mulberry Street began to disintegrate a few months later in the uproar caused by his enforcement of the Sunday Closing Law. Early in 1896 he was writing to Lodge that "At present I literally have not got a friend in this city of any note . . . and I am rather inclined to think that they will succeed in legislating me out of office; but they will not succeed in making me alter my position one handsbreadth." What had happened to cause this abrupt decline in T.R.'s popularity was a sequence of events as educational as it was disagreeable.

Roosevelt's abrupt dismissal of Police Chief Byrnes had naturally not gone unnoticed by that worthy's numerous friends and well-wishers. These included New York's seasoned and resourceful Republican Boss, Senator Thomas Collier Platt, who, some eighteen years before, had been instrumental in blocking Theodore Roosevelt, Sr.'s appointment as Collector of the Port. Platt was also aware of a painful dilemma concerning the Sunday Closing Law. On the one hand, strong dry sentiment among upstate Republicans made it seem injudicious to take a stand in favor of repealing the law. On the other hand, enforcement along the lines upon which Roosevelt insisted was sure not only to deprive deserving police officers of an accustomed source of revenue but also to cost the party thousands of votes among the city's harassed beer drinkers. Under these difficult circumstances, Platt's objective was to retain the law but impede enforcement by whatever means remained available, in the hopes of thus resorting the situation to its *status quo ante* Roosevelt's appearance on the scene.

In impeding Roosevelt's enforcement campaign, Platt found two ready allies among his fellow Commissioners. One of these was Frederick D. Grant, son of the Civil War General, who had been understandably distressed by statements in the papers to the effect that he compared with Roosevelt as "a freight train to a limited express." The other was Andrew D. Parker, a former Democratic Assistant District Attorney, who took Roosevelt to task for making speeches outside New York and began to work with Byrnes's successor to block the Chief Commissioner's appointments and promotions. Roosevelt's only supporter on the Board was its remaining member, Major Avery D. Andrews, an anti-Tammany Democrat and former West Pointer, who not only refused to be drawn into the hostile cabal but remained T.R.'s loyal ally.

Efforts to block Roosevelt's enforcement of the Sunday Closing Law took several ingenious forms. One, apparently instigated largely by Tammany, was to bring pressure upon the police to enforce with equal vigor various obsolete ordinances prohibiting the Sunday sales of harmless items such as soda water, ice and flowers. Another was passage by the State Assembly of an amendment known as the Raines Law making it legal for "hotels" to serve liquor and defining hotels, with noteworthy imprecision, as establishments that served meals and maintained at least eight bedrooms. The result of this, as might have been, and probably was, foreseen, was a rash of fake hotels like one in the Bowery that provided horse-stalls roofed over with wire as rooms, along with a sign over the bar that read: "Sleeping in this Hotel Positively Prohibited." In other hotels, the added rooms provided convenient facilities for prostitution not only on Sundays but during the week as well.

Under these circumstances, increasingly outspoken quarrels at meetings of the Commissioners became the rule rather than the exception. Presently the city comptroller, Ashbel P. Fitch became embroiled in these when he objected to the way in which certain police funds had been expended. Roosevelt defended the use of the funds and failed to conciliate his opponent by suggesting that he was a physical coward. The subsequent course of the discussion was quoted in the New York *Tribune:*

> Fitch: I would never run away from you.
> Roosevelt: You would not fight—
> Fitch: What shall it be, pistols or—
> Roosevelt: Pistols or anything you wish.
> Mayor Strong: Come, come. If this does not stop, I

will put you both under arrest.

The widely publicized squabbles among the Commissioners, coming on top of the scandal of the Raines Law hotels and the consequent increase in commercialized vice, created an impression that things were likely soon to go from bad to worse. Dr. Parkhurst was presently heard to say from his pulpit that "the Board, by the indignity of its demeanor, . . . is doing more to depress than to elevate the tone of the force." The alarm caused to the reformers and the general public eventually helped to alienate even Mayor Strong who took to making increasingly sharp comments about his head Police Commissioner. At a public banquet, he related that, when an upstate citizen had asked to borrow one of the Commissioners to help clean up a local crime wave, he had felt obliged to reply that "All four were busy watching the girls who sold flowers and the poor devils who sold ice on Sundays." He presently added: "I found that the Dutchman whom I had appointed meant to turn all New Yorkers into puritans."

In the course of upgrading the personnel of the police force, Roosevelt had instituted examinations of the Civil Service type for positions which had previously been awarded in return for political services or sold outright, often to applicants with few qualifications or none at all. In due course this long overdue reform also came under attack from one of Platt's henchmen who asserted that the questions on the examinations were frequently unfair, improper or both. Roosevelt's reply to this accusation took the form of a long and explicit letter to William Cary Sanger, then a member of the Assembly and later Roosevelt's Assistant Secretary of State for War. This letter, published in the New York *Sun* of February 6, 1897, was a communication noteworthy no less for its style than for its substance:

(My Dear Sir:) I have read with interest the four pages of questions quoted from the Police Civil Service examinations, under the heading "The Reign of Roosevelt," and apparently gathered by or for Mr. Abraham Gruber. He refers to these questions as if they were in some way improper, and not such as should be asked candidates for the position of patrolman.

It may be well at the outset to state that patrolmen receive ultimately $1,400 a year, and that from their ranks are developed a chief, a deputy chief, five inspectors, thirty-seven captains, nearly 200 sergeants and nearly 200 roundsmen, with salaries ranging from $6,000 to $1,500. The highest among these men occupy positions of trust as important as there are in the city, and even the ordinary patrolman is an exceptionally well-paid public official in a position of exceptional responsibility. To many of our poorer fellow citizens he is the embodiment of government itself, and it is to him that they must look for law and justice. Such an officer, therefore, should not only be brave, honest and physically powerful, but also possessed of intelligence distinctly above the average.

This intelligence is excellently tested by our mental examinations, which include five subjects—spelling, penmanship, letter writing, simple arithmetic and a rudimentary acquaintance with the history, government and geography of the United States.

Mr. Gruber does not take the position that patrolmen should be unable to spell or write, and therefore I need not touch upon these features of the examination. He seems to regard with hostility, however, all the other kinds of questions which are asked. . . .

The part of the examination to which Mr. Gruber seems to object most strenuously is that embracing geography, history and government. During the year when we asked the questions which he quotes the United States District Court for the Southern District of New York examined some thousands of aliens seeking naturalization. The clerk of the court required them to answer certain questions in United States history and government which are almost precisely such as those we have asked: (1) "How long do Senators hold office?" (2) "How long does the President hold office?" (5) "Who elects the United States Senate?" (6) "When was the Declaration of Independence signed?" (7) "Where is the capital of the United States?" (8) "Who was the first President of the United States?" (9) "What are the duties of the President?" (10) "Who makes the laws of the United States?"

Mr. Gruber's contention apparently is that questions which it is proper to ask a man before he becomes a citizen are improper when asked him upon his seeking to become the official representative of all citizens and, in a peculiar sense, the guardian of the laws and the upholder of the Government.

Perhaps by quoting the answers to some of the questions we asked it may be possible to give a clearer idea of the mental development of the candidates who failed. For example, one question we asked was to name five of the States that seceded from the Union in 1861. One answer was "New York, Albany, Pennsylvania, Philadelphia and Delaware."

Another question was, "Name five of the New England States." One answer to this question was, "England, Ireland, Scotland, Whales and Cork." Another answer was, "London, Africa and New England." Another question was, "In what

State and on what body of water is Chicago?" One competitor answered, "New York State, on the Atlantic Ocean," and another, "California, on the Pacific Ocean." Another question was to name five of the States bordering on the Great Lakes, to which one competitor answered, "New Jersey, Georgia, Florida and Alabama." Another question was, "Name four of the Executive departments of this Government?" Among the answers was one of two words, "Exzctiv Commite." Another question was, "Upon what written instrument is the Government of the United States founded?" The conclusion one bright competitor reached was expressed in the brief word "Paper." Yet another question was "Into what three branches is the Government of the United States divided?" Rather a common answer to this during the heat of the last campaign was "Democrats, Republicans and Populists." Another question on this line recently asked was: "What is the highest branch of the Judiciary Department of the United States?" This drew out a fine crop of replies, which included "Fiar Department," "Sir Pream Coart," "Senitar," "Exzegitive," "General Secession," "The Postmaster" and "The Juryman." Yet another question was: "Why were July 4th and Feb. 22d made legal holidays?" One answer read, "The day of George Washington landing and crossing the Delaware"; another, "On them days the country was freed"; another, "The President takes his seat," and yet another "Julu Forth was the end of the ware." Another question was, "In case of the absence or disability of the Mayor, who would perform his duties?" One man, evidently puzzled by the spelling, simply wrote "Mair." Another, with deft flattery, names President Roosevelt, while the opinions of others varied from "Board of Encumbrances" to "Any police captain he wants to. . . ."

The final test to which Mr. Gruber takes exception is that of letter writing. . . .

A request for a letter about Abraham Lincoln brought out the information from a number of candidates that he was the

President of the Southern Confederacy. One man had him assassinated by Thomas Jefferson, another by Garfield, and yet another by Ballington Booth. . . . As a final answer I will give the following: "Kind gentleman in reference to the life of Abraham Lincoln would say that I am not pearsonaly acuanted with him. He was clurc in a grocery store and could lick any of the village boys. He at one time had a very bad friend who at the end killed him." With this gem, I think I will close the collection.

Roosevelt's letter defending the questions asked in the police force examinations was one of his parting shots in his battle to clean up his home town. By the time it appeared, William McKinley had defeated William Jennings Bryan in the closely contested Presidential election of 1896 and Roosevelt, who had found time among his other activities to campaign vigorously and effectively on his behalf, was clearly in line for a new and bigger job in Washington. His close friend Cabot Lodge and McKinley's Ohio neighbor and financial benefactor, Bellamy Storer, pushed him for the post of Assistant Secretary of the Navy under former Governor Long of Connecticut. Long, who had led the convention fight for Edmunds in 1884, had good reason to remember Roosevelt and also favored him for the post, against the opposition of Platt and others who had more docile candidates to propose. After mature deliberation, the President submitted Roosevelt's appointment to the Senate on April 5 and Roosevelt sent Mayor Strong his resignation as Police Commissioner a few days later.

By the time Roosevelt resigned, Parker, his chief adversary on the Board, had been publicly charged with neglect of duty and—after a hearing at which Roosevelt was the major witness for the prosecution—dismissed from his post by the Mayor. However, since the Governor had refused to enforce the order of dismissal, Parker had remained in office; and to him, Roosevelt's Washington appointment appeared to be merely "a glorious retreat." Since Roosevelt was effectively prevented from making much further headway in New York, the new appointment did in fact provide a convenient means of turning a difficult corner in his career. However, far from being a retreat—a type of action of which T.R. was congenitally incapable—it could perhaps more accurately have been regarded as an application of the rules that governed Roose-veltian "scrambles" and which permitted going over obstacles as well as through them, so long as one never detoured or was stopped by them.

Despite Roosevelt's difficulties with his colleagues on the Commission, his record in the job had again been impressive. Reforms introduced during his tenure included not only the new examinations but also more effective methods of training, the introduction of telephone communications and the formation of a "bicycle squad," forerunner of later-day traffic and highway patrols. Even more important were lasting improvements in the morale and the status of the force as a whole. When he took office, political influence or bribery were not only the accepted methods of getting on the force but the methods accepted by the public for dealing with it. When he left, the character as well as the technical efficiency of the police of the nation's biggest city had begun to set a new pattern for the nation as a whole, just as Roosevelt had set a new pattern for his successors on the Commission. Steffens quoted a patrolman on his resignation: "It's tough on the force, for he was dead square, was Roosevelt, and we needed him in the business."

Perhaps even more to the point, in view of later developments was what his two years on the Police Commission had done for Roosevelt. In the first place, it had brought him

into close, if not altogether agreeable, contact with the state
political machinery, with which he was to be connected
through the rest of his career, on a new and more significant
basis. Secondly, it had given him a chance to administer a
major executive job under testing conditions of intense personal and political pressure. And finally it had helped to
make him a national or even an international figure—since
some of his exploits in New York had attracted comment in
the British and European as well as in the domestic press. By
the time he returned to Washington a few months before his
thirty-ninth birthday, Roosevelt was a tried and tempered
young veteran of the democratic rough-and-tumble, well-
versed in all the intricacies of the game and able to hold his
own against all comers.

At the same time, Roosevelt was now no longer, as he had
been ten or twelve years earlier, in any sense a political
prodigy. The eminence of his new post was by no means disproportionate to his age; and the sudden subsequent rise that
was to put him in the White House less than four and a half
years later was in no way the consequence of a conscious
drive to reach that goal as rapidly as possible. Certainly there
is nothing about the office of Assistant Secretary of the Navy
that makes it especially appropriate as a stepping-stone to the
White House. Indeed only one other President ever held the
office and in the case of that one—Franklin Delano Roosevelt
—even with the aid of family tradition, the time lag between
the two jobs was sixteen years. However, if T.R., as he had
expostulated to Riis and Steffens, made a point of not even
letting his thoughts dwell on Presidential possibilities, it is
at least fair to say that he made full use of all the unforesee-
able circumstances that were so soon afterward to put it unexpectedly within his reach.

VII

FOR MANY YEARS it has been considered fashionable to deride the Spanish-American War as a sort of comic opera contretemps, promoted by William Randolph Hearst as a circulation stunt and fought by T.R. and a handful of cowboys, chiefly for motives of personal vanity. The much graver hostilities that followed a few years later may provide some excuse for this view. Nonetheless, Cuba's more recent history suggests that political developments in that area are not necessarily wholly inconsequential for the United States and also that armed invasions of the Cuban coast are not necessarily child's play. In long range retrospect, the United States performance in Cuba in 1898 may seem by no means either trifling or discreditable.

Like those now confronting the United States in the same area in at least one respect, the issues of 1898 were readily discernible. Cuba, together with the Philippines on the other side of the world, represented the last remnants of the great Spanish Empire of the sixteenth and seventeenth centuries.

Both were no less jealously preserved than they were badly administered. When the Cubans, last of the Latin Americans to rebel, launched a belated war for independence in 1895, United States sympathy was all on their side. Advocates of direct intervention could, moreover, find a ready rationale for such a policy in the Monroe Doctrine. When the U.S. battleship *Maine,* sent to Havana on a "courtesy visit," blew up accidentally or otherwise, on February 15, 1898, U.S. enthusiasm for helping the rebels on both humanitarian and political grounds increased rapidly. That this sentiment was undoubtedly fanned by the bellicose tone in which newspapers reported the crisis—as widely noted by later historians —scarcely disproves its existence or invalidates its motives.

So far as T.R. was concerned, he rarely made the mistake of exaggerating the significance of the war with Spain. While not yet able then to compare it with the First World War, he could and did compare it with the Civil War, many of whose survivors were still on hand to point out the discrepancies in dimension. This lead him to a view of his own participation analogous to that of the legendary gambler who, reproached for his foolishness in playing poker with cardsharps, excused himself on the ground that it was the only game in town. It was true that Roosevelt wrote a book about the war which he called *The Rough Riders* and of which Peter Finley Dunne had his famous Mr. Dooley say that it might more appropriately have been entitled, "Alone in Cubia" or "Th' Darin' Exploits iv a Brave Man be an Actual Eye-Witness." Nonetheless, the fact was that the book was quite candidly intended as a personal memoir and as such there was no way to write it except in the first person. Actually, indeed, the narrative erred on the side of modesty if only by confining itself solely to the insular campaign. The war with Spain was really even more of a one-man show

than T.R. made it seem. The biggest of his three major contributions to the rapid and resplendent U.S. victory was
made, not during the famous charge at San Juan Hill, but
while he was still at his desk in the Navy Department at
Washington.

So far as Cuba was concerned Roosevelt had naturally been
a convinced interventionist from the outset of the uprising
in 1895. In addition, he was of course a lifelong advocate of
preparedness in general and his *Naval War of 1812* had been
written expressly to document his thesis that the best way not
only to win but also to avoid war was to be always prepared
to fight one. In Washington, accordingly, he saw his new job
as primarily a priceless opportunity to get the Navy ready for
the action that he felt sure would not be long in coming. In
this endeavor, he was vastly, albeit unintentionally, aided
by his immediate superior who formed the habit of absenting
himself from his office and allowing his Assistant to fulfill
the role of Acting Secretary.

The first instance of Roosevelt's characteristically broad
interpretation of his responsibilities in this capacity concerned the selection of a Commander for the Asiatic Fleet
who, if war with Spain broke out, would have the major assignment of attacking the Philippines. Ranking candidate for
the post was an admiral named John Adams Howell who, in
addition to seniority, had important political backing and
the support of the Bureau of Navigation. Roosevelt had quite
a different man in mind for the job. This was an enterprising
young captain who, several years before, when off Argentina
during a period of possible trouble with Chile in 1892, had
attracted his attention by coaling his ship on his own responsibility in order to be ready to steam around Cape Horn
promptly in case the need arose. As Assistant Secretary, Roosevelt made it his business to get in touch with this young

officer, whose name was George Dewey, and to advise him
to muster whatever political assistance he could in order to
reinforce his claim to the post in the Far East. Dewey, it
turned out, had a strong ally in the person of President
McKinley's good friend Senator Proctor of Vermont. Proctor's support proved to be just what was needed to get the
appointment, and Dewey sailed for Hong Kong in early
December of 1897.

A message from Secretary Long to Dewey on February 18
contained the news of the sinking of the *Maine,* which made
the subsequent declaration of war more or less inevitable.
However, the cable that really alerted the Asiatic squadron
—and which, incidentally, provides an interesting contrast
with the instructions sent from Washington to the Far East
commanders in December of 1941—was one that came a week
later and read as follows:

> Dewey, Hong Kong:
>   Order the squadron, except the *Monocacy,* to Hong
> Kong. Keep full of coal. In the event of declaration of war
> Spain, your duty will be to see that Spanish Squadron does
> not leave the Asiatic Coast and then offensive operations in
> Philippine Islands. Keep *Olympia* until further orders.
>   Roosevelt.

This message, sent on a Saturday afternoon when Long was
absent from the office and Roosevelt was throwing himself
enthusiastically into his consequent role of Acting Secretary,
later became the subject of controversial comment between
his superior and its recipient. Long, when he returned to his
office, took a poor view of it. He noted in his diary that
Roosevelt had "gone at things like a bull in a China closet"
and lacked "a cool head and discrimination." Dewey was
more favorably impressed. In his autobiography, the hero of

Manila assigns to Roosevelt full credit not only for giving him command of the fleet in the first place but also, having done so, for enabling him to make the preparations that ensured a resounding victory in the biggest naval battle fought by the United States in the first hundred and fifty years of its existence.

In addition to ensuring the subsequent victory at Manila, the cable to Dewey precluded any likelihood that Secretary Long would again entrust his assistant with the role of Acting Secretary. However, what chagrin Roosevelt might otherwise have felt on this score was speedily assuaged by something even more exciting than an occasional chance to run the war at a distance: an opportunity to take direct and full-time part himself, under the most favorable circumstances imaginable. These were provided by Congressional authorization, soon after the declaration of war on April 25, for the raising of three national volunteer Cavalry Regiments. These would supplement the elements of the regular army which were to demolish Spanish resistance in Cuba—unless the Navy contrived to accomplish this feat beforehand.

Offered the Colonelcy of one of the three volunteer regiments by Secretary of War Russell A. Alger, Roosevelt modestly declined, on the grounds that his inexperience of military matters was so complete that it might take him a full month to rectify it. This month, he pointed out, might be just enough to prevent his regiment from reaching the scene of action in time to take part. As an alternative, he proposed that he be made Lieutenant-Colonel and that his good friend, Leonard Wood, an Army surgeon who had won a Medal of Honor for leading troops in pursuit of the Apache chief, Geronimo, be given the top command. This proposal proved acceptable and within days the First United States Volunteer Cavalry, christened by the press "the Rough

Riders" since most of its personnel was recruited from the cowboy population of the Far West, went into training at San Antonio, Texas.

The modesty of Roosevelt's estimate of his soldierly qualifications was, in point of plain fact, more than amply justified by the facts in the matter. At the outbreak of hostilities, his service record consisted of three years with the New York National Guard, with which he had drilled from time to time in odd moments, and in which he held a reserve commission as Captain. How little he knew of even rudimentary military usage was well illustrated one afternoon soon after his arrival in San Antonio when, after a hard day's drill, he and his troop passed an inviting beer hall on the way back to camp. In a moment of indulgence, Roosevelt dismounted, led the troops inside and offered to stand treat. That evening, Colonel Wood tactfully explained to him that the responsibilities of an officer in the field did not normally include those of acting as host upon such occasions. Roosevelt thought the matter over and returned to report:

"Sir, I consider myself the damnedest ass within ten miles of this camp."

Four weeks after assembling at San Antonio, the Rough Riders were deemed sufficiently well disciplined to go into action and entrained for Tampa, whence they would embark for Cuba. The embarkation involved even more confusion than that which ordinarily attends such procedures. At one point it looked as though only four troops of the Rough Riders would actually get away on the first transport and that the other eight, including Roosevelt's, would stay in Florida. When this dreadful possibility was averted and eight troops—Roosevelt's with them—received orders to embark, some logistical oversight caused the transport to which they were assigned to be designated also for two other units, one volunteer and one regular. How T.R. and his commanding officer solved this dilemma in characteristic style, while the transport was tying up at the Tampa pier, was engagingly recalled by Roosevelt in his *Autobiography:*

> . . . As it was evident that not more than half the men assigned to her could possibly get on, I was determined that we should not be among the men left off. The volunteer regiment offered a comparatively easy problem. I simply marched my men past them to the allotted place and held the gangway. With the regular I had to be a little more diplomatic, because their commander, a lieutenant-colonel, was my superior in rank, and also doubtless knew his rights. He sent word to me to make way. . . . I played for time. . . . I sent respectful requests . . . entered into parleys, and made protestations . . . I was under the orders of my superior and . . . —to my great regret, etc. etc.—I could not give way as they desired. As soon as the transport was fast, we put our men aboard at the double. Half of the Regular regiment got on, and the other half and the volunteer regiment went somewhere else.

The voyage to Cuba, preceded by a six-day delay in weighing anchor, occupied another six days and was attended by further confusions. The landing, at a point on the Coast a few miles east of Santiago, was apparently the scene of the climactic disorder. Finally the eight troops of Rough Riders got more or less safely ashore and by June 22 the stage was set for the action that gave Roosevelt's career the jet propulsion needed to carry him to the White House.

T.R.'s decision to enlist had been, as was understandable, opposed by all his closest friends and relatives. Lodge, Robinson, and the New York *Sun* were all against it. Edith Roosevelt was still only in the last stages of convalescence after a major operation which had followed the difficult birth of her fifth child, Quentin. Theodore, Jr., was suffering from a persistent minor infirmity and his doctor, Alexander Lambert, had also demurred. To all such remonstrances, Roosevelt replied that his work in the Navy Department, essentially one of preparation, would end when war was declared. He felt that his usefulness as a public servant would be finished forever unless in time of war he practiced what he had preached in time of peace. When Roosevelt sent in his resignation, Secretary of the Navy Long's comment in his diary was that his assistant's job would be to "ride a horse and . . . brush mosquitoes from his neck in the Florida sands." Years later, he re-read the passage and scribbled across it:

"Roosevelt was right . . . His going into the Army led straight to the Presidency."

Partly because of T.R.'s own buoyant descriptions and partly because of its peculiarly happy consequences for him, the Santiago campaign in particular, like the Spanish-American War in general, has acquired a historical character which bears a dubious relationship to the truth. The picture usually conveyed is that of Roosevelt, handsomely mounted, resplendently uniformed, and waving a saber as he leads his men in a parade-ground charge up San Juan Hill against an abject group of cringing Spaniards on the summit. The event itself had little in common with this cliché. The action at Santiago was in fact a dangerous and difficult affair, costly in casualties, appallingly mismanaged and much less picturesque than it was painful for most of those who survived it. That it was described in the high-flown idiom favored by the writers of the period rather than in the tone of terse disparagement employed by chroniclers of more recent holocausts does not alter the character of the actual fighting. This seems to have been more or less of the same pattern as World War II operations in the jungles of New Guinea or

Burma, with certain salient differences. Two of these were that the defenders were securely entrenched on high ground and that the invaders lacked adequate artillery and air power —with the dubious exception of one observation balloon whose sole contribution was to reveal its own position at a critical moment.

So far from being mounted, all six hundred of the Rough Riders who had embarked at Tampa, excepting officers, had left their horses there. Many of the latters' steeds, including one of Roosevelt's two, were drowned in the course of the landing operations, when they were tossed overboard in the hope that they could swim to shore. To other elements of the army of some six thousand that eventually reached the beach a few miles east of Santiago, the proud cavalrymen speedily became known by the more appropriate nickname of "Wood's Weary Walkers." The sixty-year-old Major General W. R. Shafter, in command of the expedition as a whole, was, to be sure, equipped with a quadruped to get him to the front but in his case it made little difference. Weighing three hundred pounds and suffering severely from gout and heat prostration, he remained on board the transport through the earlier and most crucial period of operations. When he did get ashore, as he himself plaintively recalled, he had to have a platform built to enable him to climb on his horse, and wore gunny sack instead of a boot on his gouty extremity.

Roosevelt, to be sure, was indeed mounted, on an undersized cow pony named Texas, during the early part of the assault on the San Juan forts. Far from affording him any personal advantage, this merely served to make him a more conspicuous target. He had worn his sword in an earlier battle fought on foot a few days before but had no chance to flourish it in the air. He found, on the contrary, that it impeded his progress through the underbrush by getting between his legs and tripping him up. Thereafter he was careful not to wear it when in action.

After the helter-skelter landing operations at Daiquiri on June 22, Cuban scouts reported that the Spaniards had withdrawn toward Santiago. Pursuit started the next day and the Rough Riders encamped that night seven miles to the West at the coast hamlet of Siboney. Here new information indicated that a force of Spaniards were entrenched at Las Guasimas, four miles inland. Brigadier General S. D. M. Young, commanding the cavalry brigade which included the Rough Riders, decided upon a dawn attack in which he would lead two regiments of regular cavalry along a valley road on the right while Wood and Roosevelt took their volunteers along a hill trail to the left. After not much more than an hour's fast march along this jungle track, the volunteers halted because of, or immediately before receiving, a volley of rifle fire from an enemy concealed in the jungle. There followed a sharp skirmish about which considerable controversy developed among later commentators.

Richard Harding Davis, in his first dispatch to the New York *Herald,* stated that the Rough Riders had been "ambushed by receding Spaniards. . . ." In a later account, written in 1910, he stated that "far from anyone running into an ambush, every one of the officers had full knowledge of where he would find the enemy." Ambush or otherwise, the encounter resulted in an impressive casualty list of sixteen dead and fifty wounded. Included among the former were Sergeant Hamilton Fish and Captain Allyn Capron, who had been leading the forward troop and who, together with Captain "Bucky" O'Neill, who was killed the next day, were later singled out by Roosevelt for special praise.

Roosevelt's own account of the action and its result are by far the best available. From *The Rough Riders:*

As we advanced, the cover became a little thicker and I lost touch of the main body under Wood; so I halted and we fired industriously at the ranch buildings ahead of us, some five hundred yards off. Then we heard cheering on the right, and I supposed that this meant a charge on the part of Wood's men, so I sprang up and ordered the men to rush the buildings ahead of us. They came forward with a will. There was a moment's heavy firing from the Spaniards, which all went over our heads, and then it ceased entirely. When we arrived at the buildings, panting and entirely out of breath, they contained nothing but heaps of empty cartridge-shells and two dead Spaniards, shot through the head.

And from the much later *Autobiography:*

By the time I had taken possession of these buildings all firing had ceased everywhere. I had not the faintest idea what had happened: whether the fight was over; or whether this was merely a lull in the fight; or where the Spaniards were; or whether we might be attacked again; or whether we ought ourselves to attack somebody somewhere else. . . . I . . . proceeded to where Generals Wheeler, Lawton and Chaffee, who had just come up, in company with Wood, were seated on a bank. . . . They expressed appreciation of the way that I had handled my troops. . . . As I was quite prepared to find I had committed some awful sin, I did my best to receive this in a nonchalant manner, and not to look as relieved as I felt. . . .

For Roosevelt, the importance of the brush at Las Guasimas was that "we wanted the first whack at the Spaniards and we got it." For the next five days, the regiment waited for further orders while the Spaniards dug in for a last stand on the hills outside Santiago. Meanwhile, the illness of General Young caused Wood to be given command of the brigade, thus making room for Roosevelt's promotion to Colonelcy of the regiment. He spent the ensuing days visiting the wounded in field hospitals and trying to remedy the breakdown of the supply system which had left his troops with short rations. His method of accomplishing the latter was to authorize foraging parties to buy food. For this purpose he provided them with some four hundred dollars of which three hundred came from his own pocket and the rest was borrowed from a friend. "He worked," wrote Stephen Crane, "like a cider press . . . let him be a politician if he likes, he was a gentleman down here." Finally, on June 30, orders came for a general advance on Santiago. The troops marched through the jungle all that day and slept that night in the open, at a place called El Poso.

Early the next morning, U.S. artillery began firing from the hill ahead of the spot where Roosevelt and his men were encamped. The return fire from the Spanish reached the encampment and a lump of shrapnel fell on Roosevelt's wrist, "hardly breaking the skin but raising a bump about as big as a hickory nut." Presently the firing ceased and, on Wood's orders, the troops began the move toward Santiago. Roosevelt's account of the start of what was doubtless the most exciting single day of his life, like his *post mortem* on Las Guasimas, has a little of Crane's capacity for conveying the nervous and sometimes inert confusion of battle:

> . . . We were marched down from the hill on a muddy road through thick jungle toward Santiago. The heat was great and we strolled into the fight with no definite idea on the part of anyone as to what we were to do or what would happen. There was no plan that our left wing was to make a serious fight that day; and as there were no plans, it was naturally exceedingly hard to get orders and each of us had to act largely on his own responsibility.

In the plan for the battle as a whole, an infantry division under General H. W. Lawton was expected to assault and take the village of El Caney some miles to the right, while the left wing detained the main Spanish Army in Santiago. This assignment took Lawton most of the day; and when Roosevelt and Wood were ordered to cross and then follow along a little stream in order to connect with Lawton, they found themselves "within fair range of the Spanish entrenchments along the line of hills which we called the San Juan Hills, because on one of them was the San Juan block house." It was at this point, too, that the observation balloon, which had already betrayed the brigade's position, was to everyone's horror seen to be descending toward the ford, where it later collapsed.

Under these difficult circumstances, Roosevelt hurried his men across the stream, moved along toward the right for a mile or so and then sent back for orders, meanwhile halting behind the Ninth, Sixth, and Third Cavalry brigades which were deployed from right to left in front of him. In front of the latter were two hills—the closer of the two being the one on the right called Kettle Hill, because of the presence there of a large sugar kettle, on the summits of which the Spaniards were sheltered by ranch buildings or haciendas as well as trenches.

The fight was now on in good earnest, and the Spaniards on the hills were engaged in heavy volley firing. The Mauser bullets drove in sheets through the trees and the tall jungle grass, making a peculiar whirring or rustling sound. . . .

Roosevelt was just making up his mind

that in the absence of orders I had better "march toward the guns" when Lieutenant-Colonel Dorst came riding up through the storm of bullets with the welcome command "to move forward and support the regulars in the assault on the hills in

front." . . . The instant I received the order I sprang on my
horse and then my "crowded hour" began.

I started in the rear of the regiment, the position in which
the colonel should theoretically stay. . . . I had intended to
go into action on foot as at Las Guasimas, but the heat was so
oppressive that I found I should be quite unable to run up
and down the line and superintend matters unless I was
mounted; and moreover, when on horse-back, I could see
the men better and they could see me better. . . . I soon
found that I could get that line behind which I personally
was, faster forward than the one immediately in front of it,
with the result that the two rear-most lines began to crowd
together; so I rode through them both, the better to move on
the one in front. This happened with every line in succession
until I found myself at the head of the regiment. . . .

By the time he reached the head of the regiment, the regiment itself had caught up with the Ninth and some of the
First Regulars, whose men were lying down and firing at the
Kettle Hill fortifications from under the cover of trees and
jungle.

I spoke to the captain in command of the rear platoons, saying that I had been ordered to support the regulars in the
attack upon the hills and that in my judgment we could not
take these hills by firing at them, and that we must rush them.

When the captain replied that he could not charge without
orders, Roosevelt asked for his colonel who was not in sight
and then,

as he was not in sight, said, "Then I am the ranking officer
here and I give the order to charge"—for I did not want to
keep the men in the open suffering under a fire which they
could not effectively return. Naturally the captain hesitated
to obey this order when no word had been received from his
own colonel. So I said, "Then let my men through, sir," and

rode on through the lines, followed by the grinning Rough
Riders, whose attention had been completely taken off the
Spanish bullets, partly by my dialogue with the regulars, and
partly by the language I had been using to themselves as I
got the lines forward. . . .

As Roosevelt and his Rough Riders passed through the
Ninth

it proved too much for the regulars and they jumped up and
came along, their officers and men mingling with mine, all
being delighted at the chance. When I got to where the head
of the left wing of the Ninth was lying, . . . I was enabled
to get back into the lane, at the same time waving my hat
and giving the order to charge the hill on our right front.

At the same time, either inspired by the intermittent
glimpses of the Rough Riders's charge or simply because their
officers had reached the same decision as Roosevelt at about
the same time, other elements of the Ninth and also members
of the Third, Sixth and Tenth joined the rush up Kettle Hill.

By this time we were all in the spirit of the thing and greatly
excited by the charge, the men cheering and running forward
between shots. . . . Being on horseback I was, of course, able
to get ahead of the men on foot, excepting my orderly, Henry
Bardshar, who had run ahead very fast in order to get better
shots at the Spaniards who were now running out of the ranch
buildings. Some forty yards from the top I ran into a wire
fence and jumped off little Texas, turned him loose. . . .
Almost immediately afterward the hill was covered by the
troops, both Rough Riders and the colored troops of the
Ninth, and some men of the First. There was the usual confusion and afterward there was much discussion as to exactly
who had been on the hill first.

From the top of Kettle Hill, Roosevelt and his men had a

splendid view of the charge on the San Juan block-house to our left, where the infantry of Kent, lead by Hawkins, were climbing the hill. Obviously the proper thing to do was to help them, and I got the men together and started them volley-firing against the Spaniards in the San Juan blockhouse and in the trenches around it. . . . We kept up a brisk fire for some five or ten minutes; meanwhile we were much cut up ourselves. . . .

The punishing fire from which Roosevelt's men were suffering on the summit of Kettle Hill came not from the San Juan forts on their left but from another line of entrenchments directly in front. When, aided by four Gatling guns brought into action on the left, the infantry gained the San Juan summit, Roosevelt turned his attention to the hill in front. His first effort to lead a new charge toward them proved abortive when, in the uproar and confusion, only four men heard his command and followed him into the open. Roosevelt dashed back,

filled with anger against the troopers, and especially those of my own regiment, for not having accompanied me. They, of course, were quite innocent of wrong-doing; and even while I taunted them bitterly for not having followed me, it was all I could do not to smile at the look of injury and surprise that came over their faces while they cried out: "We didn't hear you, we didn't see you go, Colonel; lead on now, we'll sure follow you." I wanted the other regiments to come too, so I ran down to where General Sumner was and asked him if I might make the charge; and he told me to go and that he would see that the men followed.

By this time everybody had his attention attracted, and when I lept over the fence again . . . the men of the various regiments which were already on the hill came with a rush and we started across the wide valley which lay between us and the Spanish entrenchments. . . . Long before we got near them, the Spaniards ran. . . .

It was during this second charge that Roosevelt, using a revolver salvaged from the wreck of the *Maine* that had been given to him by his brother-in-law, Captain Cowles, shot and killed a Spaniard at ten yards' range. Not content even with gaining the new line of trenches, Roosevelt and his men finally pushed on further, "driving the Spaniards through a line of palm-trees, and over the crest of a chain of hills. When we reached these crests we found ourselves overlooking Santiago."

Later that afternoon there were sporadic counterattacks consisting mostly of rifle fire; and that night rumors were circulated about an impending order to withdraw. Nothing came of the latter. The men made a good supper of the beans that they found already cooking on the Spaniards' stoves; and three days later the Spanish fleet ventured out of the harbor to its complete destruction. Roosevelt's experience of the war was over after a week's campaign and one hard day of fighting, but that had been ample to have a considerable effect on the course of the coming century.

Meanwhile, it was still ten days before William Jennings Bryan became Colonel of the Third Nebraska Volunteers, a regiment which he thought might go down into history "called 'The Silver Battalion' because so many of my personal friends are in the ranks." This unit eventually got as far as Florida.

For Roosevelt himself the battle at the San Juan hills had an interior significance which, derived from that which it had for the nation, was even more intense. For him that single day's fighting was the culmination of a lifetime of endeavor. It answered the deepest of dreams and wishes dating back to his earliest childhood and nourished thereafter through years of tragedy and hardship, of humdrum toil in offices in Washington and reckless adventure in the western wilderness. The wonder was not that he remembered every detail of the event for the rest of his life and had no difficulty in recalling them all in sharp focus when writing his autobiography nearly twenty years later. Rather it was that, instead of accepting his exploit as the ultimate fulfillment of his destiny, he took it in stride and went on to others in comparison with which later historians found this one so relatively insignificant that his own satisfaction in it seemel incongruous.

That the capture of the San Juan hills had broken the back of the Spanish resistance became apparent rather gradually. Throughout the next day, Roosevelt and his men endured heavy fire and were obliged to repel repeated counterattacks. A truce went into effect at noon on the third of July ending active hostilities until the tenth when they were again subjected to bombardment which, however, grew progressively more feeble until the city surrendered on the seventeenth. Roosevelt and his men were then moved from the trenches to a camp within the city where the problem of health soon became an increasingly acute one. Four weeks of tropical warfare with a minimum of hygiene, rest, and even food had lead to a widespread outbreak of malaria from which only Roosevelt and one other officer in his regiment escaped. Even more serious was the threat of an epidemic of yellow fever which threatened to decimate the entire force. Roosevelt's role in averting this threat and getting the Army safely back to the United States was his third major contribution to the conduct of the war and in some respects perhaps the most important one.

What happened was that, with hostilities still in progress and with the prospect in view of a possible land battle for Havana or in Puerto Rico, the War Department in Washington had found it convenient to leave the Cuban force where it was until the future became clearer. To Roosevelt and the officers in command it seemed little less than criminal to reward the troops for their bravery and efficiency in action by letting them die wholesale of illness during the peak fever months of August and September. At a staff meeting near the end of July, some of the other officers suggested that—in view of his special influence as a public figure and the fact that he was immune to the career considerations that affected his colleagues—Roosevelt write a letter to the commanding general which the latter could then make public, setting forth the situation as strongly as possible. Roosevelt agreed to do so; and emboldened by his agreement, the other officers then decided to subscribe to a round robin to General Shafter along the same lines, which Roosevelt signed also. The net import of both letters was summed up in the penultimate paragraph of the second:

"This army must be moved at once, or perish. As the army can be safely moved now, the persons responsible for preventing such a move will be responsible for the unnecessary loss of many thousands of lives."

Roosevelt's letter and the round robin, published in United States papers on August 5, caused a national uproar. The order to embark the troops arrived three days later and the transport *Miami* landed them at Montauk, Long Island, on August 15. By this time, peace was being discussed and on September 4, the Colonel—he had been brevetted while on the way to Montauk—bade farewell to his troops. The tenor of his remarks perhaps expresses in part his own attitude to the experience they had all shared:

"I feel, and I feel that you all feel, that we are knit together by ties that can only be severed by death. I care much for the officers; I care even more for the men who make up the rank and file. . . . What we have done only calls us to renewed exertion in the future. . . . The world will be kind to you for about ten days; until then everything you do will be considered right. After that you will be judged by a stricter code; and if you prove worthless you will be deemed to have been spoiled by the war. . . ."

The ties that bound Roosevelt to his Rough Riders were indeed to prove durable; and any forebodings as to their future conduct implied in his farewell were by no means misplaced. The efforts which he later felt himself obliged to make to keep them more or less congenially employed and, at least when possible, out of jail, would have been enough to provide a full time career for many men. By 1901, even Roosevelt admitted that "they have driven me nearly wild"; and Mrs. Roosevelt, he said, had described their sensations as those of "the parents of a thousand very large and bad children." Nonetheless, his loyalty to the troopers never wavered. Even in the White House he remained as concerned for their welfare as he had been the week before the charge at San Juan Hill.

Looking back from the vantage point of an era when the United States is one of the world's two superpowers, it is easy enough to smile at the excitement caused by victory over a handful of colonial troops representing a decadent and impoverished European nation of eighteen million souls. To do so, however, is to ignore the point that it was, in large part, precisely this victory, and the complex results that stemmed from it, that first gave the United States its standing, and then its awareness of itself, as a great power. Before the war against Spain was declared, Easterners had foreseen a bombardment by the Spanish fleet of United States coastal cities and even shuddered at the possibility of an invasion. Rents in Newport and resorts along the Jersey coast dropped to unheard of lows for the summer of 1898 and prudent Boston bankers moved the contents of their vaults to Worcester or Springfield. The victory, one-sided as it was, brought feelings of relief as well as of jubilation; and the opportune triumph over the Spanish fleet that ended the resistance at Santiago on July 3 made welcome United States headlines on Independence Day.

Roosevelt's Cuban military venture had taken a total of under four months, from the date of his resignation as Assistant Secretary of the Navy. He had left as a promising, but perhaps already slightly *passé*, political sensation. Now he was a national hero and a strong candidate for the Republican nomination for Governor of New York—about which, indeed, party chiefs had been in communication with him while his regiment was still encamped at Santiago.

VIII

D<small>URING</small> the campaign in Cuba, Roosevelt had been receiving letters from Cabot Lodge to the effect that, on his return as a national hero, almost any political position would be within reach. Even more specific were communications from Lemuel Ely Quigg, spokesman for New York's boss and Senator Thomas Collier Platt, which began to arrive as soon as he reached Montauk. These indicated that the Republican nomination for Governor was readily available, subject to certain qualifications.

What had happened was that the incumbent Republican Governor, Frank S. Black, had offended Platt by insufficient docility in obeying his instructions and at the same time lost favor with the public because of scandalously high prices expended for repairs on the Erie Canal. Platt considered it essential to replace Black. He also considered Roosevelt the only available replacement who would be a likely winner. Moreover, he suspected that, failing to receive the Republican nomination, Roosevelt would accept an Independent one which might well mean a Republican defeat. Under these circumstances, Platt was prepared to swallow his personal dissatisfaction with the hero, who, only two years before, had been such a constant source of annoyance as Police Commissioner.

While for Roosevelt the appeal of renewed association with Platt was severely limited, that of the available alternatives was even more so. To run for Governor on an Independent Reform Ticket might well mean wasting the unique chance to achieve major political office now suddenly provided by his war renown. His hopes that President McKinley might oust Secretary of War Alger and turn the post over to him were, it soon became painfully clear, by no means to be gratified. Thus, while the factors in his equation were different from those in Platt's, the results were substantially the same. At a breakfast meeting in Platt's hotel, an agreement was worked out whereby, in return for the nomination, Roosevelt would, if elected, consult with Platt as to his subsequent political appointments. At the same time he made it clear to Platt that he proposed to retain complete freedom to act as he saw fit.

To many members of New York's reform element, Roosevelt's apparent readiness to effect reconciliation with the boss of the Republican machine seemed a sorry betrayal of the high principles they had hoped that he exemplified. Meanwhile, he remained anathema not only to Tammany Hall but even to the Big Business wing of his own party. In the campaign that followed, his opponent was Augustus Van Wyck, whose brother was the Tammany Mayor of New York. Roosevelt wore a soft black hat modeled after the one he had worn in Cuba, had himself introduced to cheering crowds by the notes of a bugle, and was often accompanied onto the platform by seven Rough Riders in uniform.

Scheduling speeches in characteristically strenuous style, T.R. on at least one occasion overreached himself with painful results. Booked for an evening talk in New York, to what promised to be a large Negro audience, he was summoned also, at the last moment, to a daytime appearance at a county fair near Troy. Unfortunately, by the time he reached Troy, he found that newspapers there had announced that he could not appear owing to his evening engagement in New York. After speaking to the handful who turned up despite this error, he rushed back to New York for his evening speech only to find that the audience there consisted of a single aged Negro. The city newspapers, it developed, had announced that, owing to his daytime appearance in Troy, the evening speech had been cancelled.

His sister Corinne's account of the incident in her book *My Brother Theodore Roosevelt* was revealing:

> My brother, in spite of distinct distress of mind, turned laughingly to me as we walked rapidly away and said, quoting from Maria Edgeworth's immortal pages, "Little Rosamund's day of misfortunes!" . . . From that day on, through the strenuous campaign, my brother was known by the family entirely as "Little Rosamund"!

The incident that decided the election was a speech by Tammany's celebrated Boss Croker in which he made the tactical error of explaining Tammany's failure to renominate a State Supreme Court Justice on the grounds that Tammany Hall had "a right to expect proper consideration at his hands." Roosevelt and his skillful ally, Elihu Root, pounced on this blunder to divert attention from the Erie Canal scandal and squeak through to victory by a margin of less than eighteen thousand votes. In late November, Roosevelt summed up his feelings in a letter to Spring Rice: ". . . I knew you would be pleased with my success. I have played it in bull luck this summer. First to get into war; then to get out of it; then to get elected. I have worked hard all my life, and have never been particularly lucky, but this summer I *was* lucky, and am enjoying it to the full. I know perfectly well that the luck will not continue and it is not necessary that it should. . . ."

As Governor of New York in the closing years of the nineteenth century, Roosevelt had, in fact, the further good luck to encounter no problems that threatened seriously to impair his new stature as a national hero. At the same time, the job served him, as it had served, and would serve, others, both as a means of staying in the public eye and of taking a sort of post-graduate course in top-level public administration —a diploma for which should perhaps be made a required qualification for the United States Presidency. Roosevelt, needless to say, enjoyed both aspects of the post to the utmost, meanwhile keeping himself in condition to do so by, among other things, taking up the sport of wrestling, in which he received lessons from the United States middleweight champion several times a week.

In 1898, the main issue in the state was the question of whether, and if so, how, to tax corporation franchises, most especially those then being awarded to private companies for the electric streetcar lines that were replacing horsecars in urban and suburban districts. This was a matter on which the views of Roosevelt and Senator Platt were sharply at variance. When, at Roosevelt's instigation, a bill to provide for such taxation was rather abruptly brought out of committee for a vote in the spring of 1899, Platt was understandably horrified. The result was an exchange of letters that served to define the progress of the rift between Roosevelt and the right wing of his party that, starting years before with his attack on Judge

Westbrook, was to continue growing wider until it culminated in the open break of the 1912 campaign. Wrote the
urbane Senator:

"I had heard from a good many sources that you were a
little loose on the relations of capital and labor, on trusts and
combination, and, indeed, on those numerous questions
which have recently arisen in politics affecting the security of
earnings and the right of a man to run his own business in his
own way, with due respect, of course, to the Ten Command-
ments and the Penal Code. . . . You have just adjourned a
legislature which created a good opinion throughout the
State. I congratulate you heartily. . . . But at the last moment, and to my very great surprise, you did a thing which
has caused the business community of New York to wonder
how far the notions of Populism, as laid down in Kansas and
Nebraska, have taken hold on the Republican party of the
State of New York."

Roosevelt's reply met the question head on: "I knew that
you had just the feelings that you describe; that is, apart
from my 'impulsiveness,' you felt that there was a justifiable
anxiety among men of means, and especially men representing large corporate interests, lest I might feel too strongly on
what you term the 'altruistic' side in matters of labor and
capital and as regards the relations of the State to great
corporations. . . . I do not believe that it is wise or safe for
us as a party to take refuge in mere negation and to say that
there are no evils to be corrected. It seems to me that our
attitude should be one of correcting the evils and thereby
showing that, whereas the Populists, Socialists and others
really do not correct the evils at all, or else only do so at the
expense of producing others in aggravated form; on the
contrary we Republicans hold the just balance and set ourselves as resolutely against improper corporate influence on

the one hand as against demagogy and mob rule on the other. . . ."

Roosevelt's strategy in securing passage of a Franchise Tax Bill showed that his mastery of tactics had advanced considerably. First, he pushed for passage of a bill which, only partially satisfactory to himself, contained certain features which were especially obnoxious to his opponents. Then he called a special session of the legislature to provide an amended and stronger version that removed these latter features. Finally, he secured passage of the amended version on the threat of signing the earlier one if it were defeated. The second version, which was in due course signed by Roosevelt, contained a clause which was subsequently attacked as unconstitutional by the very corporations that had caused it to be inserted, hoping thus to kill the law as a whole. When the State Supreme Court eventually denied their claim, the bill became law; and Roosevelt, along with most historians, considered it the most important single legislative achievement of his years in Albany.

At Albany, T.R. and his family enjoyed living in the roomy, albeit antiquated and elaborate, executive mansion the ornate grandeur of which its occupant likened to that of "a really swell Chicago Hotel" of the period, or "to a railroad directors' boardroom." Ted, Jr., and Kermit found it an appropriate locale for a miniature guinea pig ranch, in which their father took a lively and approving interest. During the summers the family went to Sagamore Hill to which the Governor commuted for week ends of the customary commotion. The stream of guests arriving at one or the other establishment included, in addition to local political and journalistic notables, more exotic figures ranging in social stature from Lord and Lady Mingo, who ventured down from the Viceroy's Palace in Ottawa to Oyster Bay for a week end to attend a new series of international yacht races, to a former Rough Rider known as Happy Jack, who came all the way from Arizona to offer his services as bouncer at the executive mansion in Albany. The latter made his first appearance unannounced at Corinne Roosevelt Robinson's house at 422 Madison Avenue, where Roosevelt often stopped off en route between Oyster Bay and the State Capital.

One of the reasons the Robinson house on Madison Avenue was so convenient was that it represented a central point of comparatively neutral ground where the Governor could meet Senator Platt and other political associates for breakfast conferences on Saturday mornings. When, at such meetings Platt asked for a few minutes in private, T.R., according to his hostess, was likely to reply: "We shall be quite private except for my sister. I always like to have her present. . . . She takes so much interest in what I am doing." Social doings at 422, however, were by no means confined to political shoptalk and also included numerous luncheon or dinner parties which, usually organized on the spur of the moment, sometimes occasioned minor consternation on the part of the Governor's devoted sister.

On one occasion, when her brother had asked if she would be able to accommodate ten guests for lunch, Mrs. Robinson, having foresightedly had the table set for its maximum of fourteen, was mildly disconcerted when, after thirteen were assembled in the drawing room, she saw two latecomers ascending the steps. Firmly insisting that her brother tell at least one of the two that he would have to have lunch elsewhere, she saw him go glumly into the front hall to do so. A moment later, she recalled, he returned with a Rough Rider and "an air of triumph. 'The other,' he whispered, 'was the President of the University of ———. I told them they had to toss up and the Rough Rider won.' "

On another occasion, during the spring of 1900, the guest of honor was a young Englishman named Winston Churchill, whom Roosevelt had met once before at a dinner party where Churchill, already a confirmed cigar smoker, had incurred his disfavor by lighting up without asking his hostess's permission. On this occasion they got along well because, or in spite of, Roosevelt's victory in a dispute about a battle in the Boer War from which Churchill had just effected a triumphant return by his celebrated escape from a prison camp.

When the former British war correspondent mentioned an incident as having taken place at Bloemfontein, Roosevelt interrupted him to say it had actually occurred at Magersfontein. Flabbergasted by such temerity on the part of the Governor of the largest U.S. state, young Churchill reiterated that it had occurred at Bloemfontein adding that—as he had already given his listeners ample reason to be fully aware—he had been present at the time. "I think Mr. Churchill," reiterated Roosevelt, "that if you will stop and think for a moment, you will remember that I am right in this instance and that that incident took place at Magersfontein." The visitor paused, frowned and then, according to Mrs. Robinson's recollection of the conversation, replied: "You are right, Governor, and I am mistaken."

Similarity of interests and temperament between the twentieth century's two greatest practitioners in the combined fields of politics and literature gave rise to little amiability. Annoyed by the young Englishman's assertive manner, Roosevelt expressed his feelings most clearly once when, in referring to the well-known American novelist of the same name, he identified him as "Winston Churchill, the gentleman." The meeting at the Robinson house marked a peak of Rooseveltian cordiality only exceeded by one attained in August, 1914.

Then, impressed by Churchill's display of the cardinal virtue of preparedness in his job of First Lord of the Admiralty, Roosevelt, recalling his own performance under closely analogous circumstances, felt justified in sending him a message of congratulation through Viscount Lee: "I have never liked Winston Churchill, but in view of what you tell me about his admirable conduct and nerve in mobilizing the fleet, I do wish that if it comes your way, you would extend him my congratulations on his action."

After Roosevelt's first winter in office, his sister felt emboldened to ask a leading question:

"Theodore, are you not going to take a complete rest some time this summer? You certainly need it. It has been year after year, one thing after another, more and more pressing all the time—Civil Service Commissioner, Police Commissioner, Assistant Secretary of the Navy, Lieutenant Colonel, then Colonel of the Rough Riders, and all that the campaign meant and now Governor of New York State. Surely you must take some rest this summer."

"Yes, of course, you are right," Roosevelt replied. I do mean to take a rest of one whole month this summer. . . . I don't mean to do one single thing during that month—except write a life of Oliver Cromwell." As things turned out, Roosevelt failed to meet his self-imposed deadline. He got so interested in Cromwell that he kept on writing about him until the book had to compete for his attention not only with his gubernatorial duties but also with his campaign to avoid being nominated for the Vice-Presidency of the United States. Now bound together with *The Rough Riders* to make a single fat volume in his collected works, *Oliver Cromwell* rivals that unique memoir in vigor and assurance. In his graceful introduction, Viscount Lee quotes an anonymous friendly critic, who sounds exactly like Elihu Root, to the effect that the book amounts to a "fine imaginative study of Cromwell's qualifications for the governorship of New York."

As time drew near for the Republican National Convention in Philadelphia in June, 1900, Roosevelt found himself in a curious position. On the one hand, many of his good friends, including Henry Cabot Lodge, wanted him to run for the Vice-Presidency vacated by the death in late 1899 of the incumbent, Garret A. Hobart. On the other hand, Roosevelt himself felt that it would be preferable to stand for a second term as Governor especially since, running in a Presidential year with a strong national ticket, he would have a good chance of re-election. Nonetheless, the decision was by no means an easy one. While the Vice-Presidency was too inactive to suit him, it was a major office in the national arena. Moreover, even if he won another term in Albany, this would leave him at loose ends in 1902.

Meanwhile, the plans and objectives of other influential personages had a strong bearing on the question. Senator Platt, who had been urging Roosevelt to run for another term as Governor, rather suddenly changed his position in favor of the Vice-Presidency after passage of the Franchise Bill. Platt's strategy was, it appeared, much what it had been three years before when Roosevelt had become a problem on the Police Commission—that of kicking him upstairs. But the difficulty here was another major Republican boss who, if often less devious than Platt, was even more powerful. This was the illustrious Senator Marcus Alonzo Hanna of Ohio whose attitude was presently to be summed up in his remark: "Don't any of you realize that there's only one life between this madman and the White House?"

Finally, there was one more element to be considered, in the form of popular opinion. Roosevelt by this time was

enough of a national figure to have received in New York a
letter mailed from Arizona with no address except a drawing
on the envelope of a set of teeth and a pair of spectacles. In
June of 1899, his reception at a New Mexico Rough Riders'
reunion had been so enthusiastic that he felt it tactful to
make a speech setting forth his loyalty to McKinley. Now in
the West, where the threat of Bryanism was strongest, there
was considerable sentiment to the effect that Roosevelt's name
on the national ticket might mean the difference between
victory and defeat.

The quandary in which Roosevelt found himself was engagingly, if somewhat imprecisely, described by his sister
Corinne, who at his invitation also attended the Convention.
Arriving at the hotel where he was staying, she went to his
room and, receiving no answer to her knock, opened it and
entered. Her brother was sitting at an open window with his
back to the door and a huge book on his knees. "I tiptoed up
behind him and leaned over his shoulder and saw that the
great volume spread out before him was the 'History by
Josephus'! I could not but laugh aloud, for it seemed too
quaint to think that he, the centre of all the political ani-
mosity, should be quietly apart, perfectly absorbed in the
history of the Jews of a long-past day. As I laughed, he turned
and jumped to his feet, and in a moment . . . had sketched
the situation for me. 'Yes, Platt and Odell did want to eject
him but it wasn't only that. The West felt strongly, and the
Middle West as strongly, that his name was needed on the
presidential ticket. No, he didn't want to give up a second
term as Governor of New York State; he hated the thought of
a vice-presidential burial party, but what was he to do? He
didn't really know himself.' "

What actually happened in due course was that Roosevelt
informed Platt that he wanted the New York Governorship

and was prepared to make a fight for it. This forced Platt to give the New York delegation's support for Vice-President to another candidate. Roosevelt issued a statement to the effect that, while sensible of the great honor represented by the Vice-Presidential nomination, he felt that he could be of more use to the ticket and to the country as Governor of New York. These two moves, however, left the door open to a nomination springing not from Platt's sincere desire to eject him from New York but from the equally sincere but considerably more gratifying eagerness of the Far West to have him on the national ticket. On this basis, Roosevelt was quite prepared to accept and did so with his usual exuberance, as expressed in a letter to Cabot Lodge:

"I should be a conceited fool if I was discontented with the nomination when it came in such a fashion. . . . It certainly is odd to look back sixteen years when you and I sat in the Blaine convention on the beaten side while the mugwumps foretold our utter ruin and then in this convention, over which you presided, to think how you recognized me to second McKinley's nomination and afterwards declared me myself nominated in the second place on the ticket." To his good friend and later biographer, Joseph Bucklin Bishop, he added with jaunty assurance: "If I have been put on the shelf, my enemies will find that I can make it a cheerful place of abode."

In the campaign that followed, Hanna, making the best of a distasteful situation, informed Roosevelt that he would have to do the brunt of the speaking while McKinley, renowned as the most dignified personage who ever occupied the White House, made one or two pronouncements from his residence in Canton, Ohio. This suited Roosevelt perfectly. "I wish in this campaign to do whatever you think wise and advisable— whatever is likely to produce the best results for the Republi-

T.R.—THE STORY OF THEODORE ROOSEVELT

can ticket," he wrote to Hanna. "I am as strong as a bull moose and you can use me up to the limit taking heed of but one thing and that is my throat. Two years ago in the New York campaign I only managed to hold out just barely to the end and could not have spoken for three days longer. Of course then I had to make some three hundred speeches in four weeks and carry the whole campaign on my own shoulders, so the case is not quite the same now. Still, I do not want my throat to give out. . . ."

For a time in 1899 it had looked as though the Democratic nominee might be none other than the redoubtable Admiral Dewey, hero of Manila Bay, who had indeed gone so far as to indicate that he might not mind running with Roosevelt as *his* Vice-Presidential candidate. Dewey, however, had impaired the confidence of even his most ardent admirers by asserting that he would run for either party that chose to nominate him, that he had no particular policies in mind and no intention of forming any and that he was "convinced that the office of President is not such a very difficult one to fill." The eventual candidate was again William Jennings Bryan who chose to stand once more on the same free silver platform on which he had been beaten four years before. For the Republicans, the issues were the Full Dinner Pail and Manifest Destiny, two topics which, in an era of marked prosperity and national expansion, had more immediate appeal. When the ballots were counted on November 6, McKinley and Roosevelt had won by 292 electoral votes to 150 and a plurality of 850,000.

Roosevelt's contribution to this result had been a substantial one. Starting in late June at a second Rough Riders' reunion, he had criss-crossed the country so thoroughly that by the time the campaign ended, the New York *Times* estimated that he had covered 21,209 miles and addressed a total of

3,000,000 people—perhaps a record for the era that preceded TV, radio, or even platform-amplifiers. On one single speaking trip toward the end of the campaign, he had visited twenty-four states and 567 towns and cities for a total of 673 speeches. On his return from this excursion to make a final address at Madison Square Garden, Roosevelt spent the night at his sister's house at 422 Madison Avenue, having wired her in advance to have a throat specialist ready to treat him on arrival. The specialist provided the treatment and then ordered his patient to stay quiet for the rest of the evening. Roosevelt, however, started to tell his sister and her husband "a few of the very funny incidents that happened on my trip." Her recollection of what happened thereafter was significant:

"And with that he began—my husband and I feeling very conscience-stricken, but so fascinated that we had not the strength of mind to stop him. Suddenly, to our perfect surprise, the early morning light crept in through the windows, the milk-wagons began to rattle in the streets, and we realized that the dawn of another day had come. . . ." Far from doing him any harm, the total disregard of his doctor's orders had a stimulating effect. The following night Roosevelt was in the best of form and voice for his climactic appearance.

Roosevelt's duties as Governor ended with the turn of the year and the inauguration of his successor, Platt's right-hand man, Benjamin Odell. His duties as Vice-President, however, did not start until March 4 and to fill in the interim, Roosevelt hit upon a characteristic scheme. This was a Colorado cougar-and-lynx hunt in the dead of winter in which the technique used was riding to a pack of savage hounds on cow ponies over the most difficult terrain imaginable. From Keystone Ranch, owned by the professional hunter, John B. Goff ("a fine quiet, hardy fellow, who knows his business thoroughly") his guest of honor wrote a vivid description of the sport to his eldest son and namesake: "We walked our ponies up and down steep, rock-strewn, and tree-clad slopes, where it did not seem possible a horse could climb, and on the level places we got one or two smart gallops. At last the lynx went up a tree. Then I saw a really funny sight. . . . The dogs proceeded literally to *climb the tree,* which was a many-forked pinon. . . . I shot the lynx low, so as not to hurt his skin."

Shooting wildcats under these conditions soon came to seem somewhat tame but Roosevelt discovered means of providing additional spice. This consisted of ending the hunt, on occasions when the pack intercepted their quarry on the ground, by wading into the melee on foot and stabbing the cougar to death barehanded with a hunting knife. This stage of the proceedings he described in detail to the acquaintance best equipped to appreciate it, the South African big-game hunter and naturalist, Frederick C. Selous, with whom for several months he had been carrying on a lively correspondence about the Boer War:

"We hunted on horseback and the great interest (aside from the delight of the long rides through the brilliant winter weather over the snow-clad plains and among the mountains) was to see the dogs work. My part was wholly insignificant. If the animal was treed, I shot it. If, as four times happened, the dogs got it on the ground, there was a savage worry and I ended the struggle with the knife as soon as possible to save the pack. They were quite competent to kill the cougar by themselves, but always received a good deal of damage. . . . There were eight hounds and four fighters, two of the latter being killed. . . ."

In arranging to make his Vice-Presidential shelf as cheerful an abode as possible, T.R. made intensive preparations.

Most characteristic of these was a plan to resume studying law (with weekly quizzes by Supreme Court Justice E. D. White every Saturday afternoon) while functioning as an apprentice in a Washington law office so that, at the end of his term, he could qualify for the Bar in New York State. There he would in 1904 revert to the career interrupted eighteen years earlier by his departure for the State Assembly. How serious he was about this scheme and his reasons for undertaking it were set forth in a letter to Leonard Wood, by now a Brigadier General and Governor of Cuba, where Edith Roosevelt had visited him a year before:

"I intend studying law with a view to seeing if I cannot go into practice as a lawyer when my term as Vice-President comes to an end. Of course, I may go on in public life, but equally of course it is unlikely, and what I have seen of the careers of public men has given me an absolute horror of the condition of the politician whose day has passed; and who, by some turn of the kaleidoscope is thrown into the background; and who then haunts the fields of his former activity as a pale shadow of what he once was; or else who finds himself adrift in the hopeless position of the man who says he can do anything but who therefore can do nothing."

Roosevelt got back from his cougar-and-lynx hunt in time for a week at Oyster Bay before the inauguration—at which, since the President was already a familiar figure, he and his family were the main focus of attention. He then presided for five days over a special session of the Senate which ended on March 9. That, as it turned out, was the total extent of his performance of the duties of his new office; nor was it necessary for him to resume poring over law books in order to keep busy during his term and to ensure a livelihood for his family thereafter.

The spring and summer of 1901 went by rapidly at Oyster

Bay, with minor illnesses for several of the children added to the normal sequence of rides, picnics, rows, scrambles, and races down Cooper's Bluff. Roosevelt, already restless under the strain of his comparative inactivity, paid a second two-week visit to Colorado for a major speech and a few days of hunting and fishing in August. Later that month he went west again to attend a dinner in Springfield, Illinois, and deliver a speech at the opening of the State Fair at Minneapolis, then stopping off at Rutland, Vermont, for another speech on the way back. He was enjoying the annual outing of the Fish and Game League, at nearby Isle la Motte in Lake Champlain, when a telephone message from Buffalo reached him at the home of former Governor Nelson W. Fisk where he was attending a reception. The message was that, while giving a speech at the Pan-American Exposition at Buffalo, President McKinley had been shot twice by an anarchist named Leon Czolgosz and that his condition was serious.

Roosevelt hurried back across the lake and at Burlington took a special train to Buffalo, where he arrived the next afternoon. There, the news was reassuring. At the private house to which he had been taken from the Hall, the President had rallied well from the shock of his injuries. By the evening of that same day, his doctors were so confident that Roosevelt wrote his sister Anna that "I can now say definitely that I will be at your house for October fourth, fifth and sixth." By the tenth, the President was so far advanced on the road to recovery that it was felt permissible—and even advisable, as a means of reassurance for the nation—for Roosevelt to return to Oyster Bay. From there, the next day, he left for the Adirondacks where Edith Roosevelt had taken the children to stay at a residential club near Mount Tahawus in the hope that drier, cooler air would speed their recovery from their various ills. On the morning of the thirteenth, the family party went for a tramp in the mountain woods and in the afternoon Roosevelt ascended to the summit of Mt. Marcy. He was on his way down, at the edge of Lake Tear in the clouds, when he saw a messenger ascending the trail. This time, it was a telegram from Elihu Root, now Secretary of War:

"The President appears to be dying and members of the Cabinet in Buffalo think you should lose no time in coming."

By the time Roosevelt reached the clubhouse at the foot of the mountain, darkness had fallen. A courier was sent six miles to the nearest telephone to arrange for a buckboard to take him to North Creek, the nearest railroad station, fifty miles away. Roosevelt and the driver of the buckboard set out at eleven that evening. After three changes of horses and a wild drive along precipitous mountain lanes in the pitch dark, he arrived at North Creek, where a special train was ready to take him to Buffalo, at 5:30 in the morning. There Roosevelt's secretary, William Loeb, waiting to board the train with him, revealed that McKinley had died at 2:00 A.M.

In Buffalo, where he arrived at 1:30 the next afternoon, Roosevelt paid his respects to the deceased President's widow and then went to the house of Ansley Wilcox where he had stayed three nights the week before. There he found most of the members of the McKinley Cabinet, to whom he said: ". . . I wish to say that it shall be my aim to continue, absolutely unbroken, the policy of President McKinley . . . for the honor of our beloved country. . . ." Then, not yet quite forty-three, Roosevelt took the oath of office as the 26th President of the United States. After the ceremony, he and Elihu Root went for a short walk. Soon after they returned, Mark Hanna got out of his carriage at the Wilcox house. Before he could reach the door, Roosevelt had come out to meet him and to repeat the assurances that he had already given the members of the Cabinet. Hanna removed his hat and said:

"Mr. President, I wish you success and a prosperous administration. I trust that you will command me if I can be of service."

From Buffalo Roosevelt went to Washington where he called his first official meeting of the McKinley Cabinet, which he retained unchanged. Secretary of State was the now aging John Hay to whom Roosevelt at the age of ten had been introduced by his father, and whom he had come to know well during his earlier sojourn in the capital. As an older man, Hay, like his close friend and contemporary, Henry Adams, had often been more than a little amused by Roosevelt's rapid and strenuous rise. Now, a few weeks after the death of his own son, he sent his new chief a moving message:

"From the depths of sorrow where I sit, with the grief for the President mingled and confused with that for my own boy, so that I scarcely know, from hour to hour, the true source of my tears—I do still congratulate you. . . . With your youth, your ability, your health and strength, the courage God has given you to do right, there are no bounds to the good you can accomplish. . . .

"My official life is at an end—my natural life will not be long extended; and so, in the dawn of what I am sure will be a great and splendid future, I venture to give you the heartfelt benediction of the past. God bless you."

Roosevelt summed up his own feelings in a brief letter to Cabot Lodge: ". . . It is a dreadful thing to come into the Presidency this way; but it would be a far worse thing to be morbid about it. Here is the task and I have got to do it to the best of my ability; and that is all there is about it. . . ."

A few nights later, after attending the late President's funeral at Canton, Roosevelt took up residence at the White House. There, on the twenty-second of September, while Edith Roosevelt was packing up at Sagamore Hill, he invited his two sisters and their husbands to join him at a quiet family dinner. Corinne Robinson described the occasion:

"As we sat around the table he turned and said: 'Do you realize that this is the birthday of our father, September 22nd . . . I feel that it is a good omen that I begin my duties in this house on this day. I feel as if my father's hand were on my shoulder, and as if there were a special blessing over the life I am to lead here.' Almost as he finished this sentence, the coffee was passed to us, and at that time it was the habit at the White House to pass with the coffee a little boutonniere to each gentleman. As the flowers were passed to the President, the one given to him was a yellow saffronia rose. His face flushed, and he turned again and said: 'Is it not strange! This is the rose we all connect with my father. . . .'"

IX

Roosevelt's feeling that it was "a dreadful thing" to acquire the Presidency through the assassination of the incumbent was understandable enough. At the same time, it had certain advantages in enabling him to avoid many burdensome political obligations and enmities that would necessarily have accompanied it otherwise. More significant, however, than either the assets or the liabilities connected with the manner of his reaching the White House was the time at which he did so.

The turn of the century marked with convenient precision the coming of age of the United States both industrially and as a major power in world affairs. Viewed in perspective from more than a half-century later, this double coincidence seems almost majestically apparent. At the time, without benefit of hindsight, it was considerably less obvious. Much more perceptible then were the peculiar stresses and strains which marked this sudden maturation and which made the period seem—even more perhaps than any period must to those who live in it—one of change, uncertainty, and alarm.

Marking the start both of a new century and of a new era, the Roosevelt Presidency would almost necessarily have been a noteworthy one—and all the more since those of the three decades that preceded it had been so uniformly commonplace. What made it more than merely noteworthy was the way in which Roosevelt proved able to respond to, enhance, and embody the period as though it had been his personal creation. In a sense, indeed, this was exactly what it became.

One thing that helped T.R. to dominate his time was that he understood it so thoroughly and from so many aspects. Intimately acquainted with all sections of the country, either at first hand or by inheritance, he was equally familiar with its people on every level of wealth, education, and social status, having worked, played, and fought beside them from Island Falls to Tampa Bay and from Yellowstone to Santiago. Where he differed from the vast majority of his compatriots whom he knew so well was mainly in that he perceived more clearly than they the import of the era in which they were all living, along with its implications for the future.

Even more helpful perhaps than his perception of the forces that were at work in U.S. society and the world was Roosevelt's capacity for stating his perceptions with a clarity, emphasis, and insistence that made them, if not equally apparent, at least comprehensible to his countrymen and the world. To criticize his writings for lack of depth, subtlety, or delicate nuance is usually to miss their whole point and purpose. The function of a fire bell or a bugle call differs vastly from that of a symphony; the aim is not art but audibility.

Finally, and even more important, T.R.'s perceptions were presented not in terms of dire problems crying for solution so much as in those of glorious possibilities clamoring to be realized. His view of himself, his nation, and the period was one of highhearted assurance as opposed to gloomy foreboding. His message was one of courage and confidence, never of doubts and disabilities. In the bright morning of the new century, America as a whole responded in much the same way that Roosevelt's Rough Riders had done on the slopes of San Juan Hill.

One good example of Roosevelt's ability to distinguish between the major and the minor issues of his time, and to wrestle the former to a rapid fall, was the vexing question of labor vs. capital. What the United States industrial coming-of-age meant most of all in 1900 was simply a full-speed head-on collision between the interests of the workers who made the industry go, and the capitalists who paid their wages. During the thirties, when it became fashionable to interpret history in general and the labor movement in particular in terms of rudimentary Marxist economics, it was naturally deemed appropriate to deride T.R.'s approach since this came from a totally different direction. T.R.'s comprehension of the matter emphasized the element of basic morality, which even his contemporaries were often likely to ignore. His statements on the subject have accordingly gained rather than lost impact and relevance in the interim. When, in 1902, a Western mining executive wrote to rebuke him for having invited some miners to lunch at the White House, Roosevelt lost no time in setting him straight:

"While I am President, I wish the labor man to feel that he has the same right of access to me that the capitalist has; that the doors swing open as easily to the wageworker as to the head of a big corporation—*and no easier.* Anything else seems to me not only un-American, but symptomatic of an attitude which will cause grave trouble if persisted in. . . .

In my judgment the only safe attitude for a private citizen, and still more for a public servant, to assume is that he will draw the line on conduct, discriminating against neither corporation nor union as such. . . ."

In 1904, Roosevelt's Attorney General Philander C. Knox, having initiated T.R.'s seven-year seige against "malefactors of great wealth" by tossing a few block-busters in the direction of J. P. Morgan & Co., resigned to become a senator. Roosevelt seized this opportunity to write the one-time Philadelphia corporation lawyer some advice about his future career which sheds further light on his view of the struggle:

"So far as organized capital is concerned, I have not even a suggestion to make to you. You know far too much for any hint of mine to be of any service to you. But I do most earnestly hope that you will make the problem of labor as thoroughly yours as you have made the problem of capital. More and more, the labor movement in this country will become a factor of vital importance, not merely in our social but in our political development. If the attitude of the New York *Sun* toward labor, as toward the trusts, becomes the attitude of the Republican party, we shall some day go down before a radical and extreme democracy with a crash which will be disastrous to the Nation. . . . It would be a dreadful calamity if we saw this country divided into two parties, one containing the bulk of the property owners and conservative people, the other the bulk of the wageworkers and less prosperous people generally. . . . Here in this republic it is peculiarly incumbent upon the man with whom things have prospered to be in a certain sense the keeper of his brother with whom life has gone hard."

Only more impressive than Roosevelt's grasp of the moral issues at stake in the U.S. economy was his insight into what are now called geopolitics and how the U.S. fitted into the global future. That he foresaw both the Russian revolution and the rise of Russia as a world power, not to mention Germany's role in both World Wars, the development of Japan, and the imminent decline of the British Empire can be documented readily enough from the wide web of correspondence between the White House, when he occupied it, and all corners of the globe. More to the point, he foresaw also the vast responsibilities to which the U.S. would presently be called upon to rise and did his far from inconsiderable best to reveal the vision to his less clairvoyant countrymen.

T.R.'s thorough understanding of sea power—the best authority on that subject was his close friend, Captain Alfred Thayer Mahan—illuminates his 1904 letter to Ohio's Congressman Theodore E. Burton, a benighted inlander, who opposed building up the Navy:

"I respect your character and ability so highly. . . . and I am so confident in your good judgment, that I write you a word in reference to your speech on the Navy. . . . The one unforgivable crime is to put oneself in a position in which strength and courage are needed, and then to show lack of strength and courage. This is precisely the crime committed by those who advocate or have acquiesced in the acquisition of the Philippines, the establishment of naval stations in Cuba, the negotiation of the treaty for building the Panama Canal, the taking of Puerto Rico and Hawaii, and the assertion of the Monroe Doctrine, and who nevertheless decline to advocate the building of a navy such as will alone warrant our attitude in any one, not to say all, of these matters. . . .

"It is perfectly allowable, although I think rather ignoble, to take the attitude that this country is to occupy a position in the New World analogous to that of China in the Old World, to stay entirely within her borders, not to endeavor to assert the Monroe Doctrine, incidentally to leave the Philippines, to abandon the care of the Panama Canal, to give up Hawaii and Puerto Rico, etc., etc., and therefore to refuse to build up any Navy. . . . To my mind it is to inflict a great wrong on the generations who come after us if we persevere in these policies and do not back them up. . . . To be rich, aggressive, and yet helpless in war, is to invite destruction. . . ."

Denounced in his time and afterward as a "Jingo" and an "Imperialist," Roosevelt stuck to the simple thesis that he had worked out for himself after the encounter on his way to Moosehead Lake, that in keeping peace, strength and preparedness were much more of a help than a hindrance to a man or a nation. Twenty odd years after his death, considerable uproar was aroused by a magazine article that stated the thesis of an "American Century." Roosevelt had summed up the idea more briefly forty years before in *The Strenuous Life:* "We, here in America, hold in our hands the hope of the world, the fate of the coming years; and shame and disgrace will be ours if in our eyes the light of high resolve is dimmed, if we trail in the dust the golden hopes of men. . . ."

In one of his illuminating letters to Cecil Spring Rice, he enlarged upon the theme:

"I do not wonder that you sometimes feel depressed over the future both of our race and of our civilization. There are many reasons why one should be, although I think there are also many reasons why one should not be. I have been so busy and my own life has been so full and varied, and the interest in the struggle so great, and my home life is so very happy, that I do not have much time for pessimistic thoughts. . . . I think the twentieth century will still be the century of the men who speak English. . . ."

Roosevelt's insights into the challenge of his times, his

ability to define them and his exuberant response to them were enough in themselves to make him a memorable teacher and the ablest American political theorist of his time. They were not, however, by any manner of means what made him a great President. His claim to pre-eminence as such resides not in what he thought, said, or felt about the problems of his time nearly so much as in what he did about them.

Other Presidents may have had greater challenges forced upon them—though surely one reason Roosevelt's crises seemed so manageable was that he disposed of them before they had time to grow. What is indubitable is that T.R. not only bested every challenge that confronted him but sought out others on his own account and disposed of them summarily also. The impressive volume of Roosevelt's own works— some twenty volumes, not counting letters which would fill twenty more—is a mere trifle compared to what has been written about him in the forty-two years since his death—incomparably more than about any other President except Lincoln. Any one of more than a score of his individual projects as President deserves, and has received, at least one and, in some cases, several volumes of its own. Even a mere catalogue of his accomplishments in less than eight years in the White House has an epic ring as it calls the roll of the states, ranges the seven seas and splits the Western hemisphere.

Of all T.R.'s great projects, the Canal at Panama—"the Continents Divided, a World United"—was perhaps the most dramatic; certainly it was the one that started soonest and caused the most lasting controversy. Roosevelt's own ties with the Isthmus went back a long time, half-way to when Columbus started Westward, looking for a passage to the Indies. In 1698, the William Patterson who later founded the Bank of England guessed that a canal would be dug some day, thought

England should own the site, and tried to found a colony at Darien. Among those who set out to join it were the Reverend Archibald Stobo with his wife and their daughter, Jean. By the time the Stobo family arrived, the colony had been dispersed by Indians, the sun, and fever. Their ship turned back, stopping en route at Charleston, South Carolina, where Archibald Stobo found a vacant pulpit and where Jean presently married James Stephens Bulloch with whom she settled down at Roswell, Georgia. It was there that T.R.'s father had married her great-great-granddaughter, Martha, on December 22, 1853.

For T.R. himself, as for Mahan, the building of the Canal was an integral part of the development of United States sea power—since the ability to move warships speedily from one ocean to the other would, in effect, double the size of the Navy. That was, of course, if the U.S. fortified and guarded the Canal on its own responsibility while maintaining it for the commerce of other nations. The proposed Hay-Pauncefort Treaty—as drafted in 1898 by the Secretary of State—would have permitted England a partnership in the venture. While still Governor of New York, Roosevelt, with what seemed to some an outrageous presumption, had denounced the Treaty as effectively defeating the essential purpose of the enterprise. Congress, however, shared his view; and when he reached the White House the situation was ripe for action. T.R., naturally, took it.

First step was a new treaty with England, giving the United States sole responsibility for policing the Isthmus and adjacent seas. The next was to take over the assets of the bankrupt de Lesseps company that had spent two decades trying to make Panama into a second Suez. The third was to get the government of Colombia to turn over the land. That was where things stuck for a time. Offered ten million dollars outright and a quarter of a million a year rent, the Colombians first agreed and then held out for more until it began to look as though a costly cut through Nicaragua might be the only alternative. Then, suddenly, on November 3, 1903, there was a secessionist revolution in Panama—bloodless except for one bystander and a donkey—and the little country's new government gladly accepted the price that what T.R. termed the "homicidal corruptionists" in Bogota had turned down. All that remained to do about the Canal then was to build it.

Like a good many other things that T.R. did, the Canal aroused ample curiosity, by no means all of it friendly. One thing that gave rise to questions was the role played by an energetic Frenchman named Philippe Jean Bunau-Varilla who had been de Lesseps' chief engineer at twenty-five and who had indubitably encouraged the revolution in Panama. He turned up in Washington two days after it was over as Panama's plenipotentiary envoy, ready to sign the new treaty. Another was the contribution effected by a New York lawyer named William Nelson Cromwell (to whose law firm of Sullivan and Cromwell U.S. diplomacy was later on to be indebted for the Dulles brothers). Aided by the best of Wall Street connections, Cromwell helped persuade Congress to pay forty million dollars for the assets of the defunct French company, charged the latter a whopping fee of $800,000, and later made understandably handsome contributions to Republican campaign funds. Finally, the most obscure point of all seemed to be T.R.'s own connection with the revolution: Had he helped start it, or at least let it be known that it would have his blessing?

Roosevelt answered the question many times—best perhaps in a chat with a shipboard acquaintance when returning from Europe in the spring of 1914: "People say that I fomented insurrection in Panama prior to the time I became President.

While I was President I kept my foot down on these revolutions so that when the revolution referred to did occur, I did not have to foment it; I simply lifted my foot."

Before that, speaking at the University of California in 1911, he put the matter in another way: "I am interested in the Panama Canal because I started it. If I had followed conventional, conservative methods, I should have submitted a dignified state paper of approximately two hundred pages to the Congress and the debate would have been going on yet, but I took the canal zone and let Congress debate, and while the debate goes on the Canal does also."

The head-on collision between labor and capital was characterized by much less intrigue and mystery than the Canal but certainly by no less excitement. It began with a strike by Pennsylvania's anthracite coal miners which started on May 12, 1902, and which T.R. ended on October 15, having, in the interim, composed a considerable page of U.S. history.

In the nineteen-sixties, when company and union bosses meet on very different terms, to discuss very different matters, it may be instructive to recall the issues sixty years ago. Anthracite was the fuel that kept the Eastern seaboard warm in the long winters before oil burners and thermostats—the coal that baked the bread and boiled the coffee before gas and electricity took over the job. The miners dug it out of the ground with picks and shovels, until they died young of consumption or pneumonia—or, like 441 of them in 1901, of routine mishaps on the job. The pay had doubled since 1886, to the princely average of $560 a year. It was still based on how many tons a man could dig in a ten- or twelve-hour day; and the company weighed the coal. The miners who struck— 140,000 of them—were, it might seem nowadays, not making unreasonable demands. There was no talk of washrooms, coffee-breaks, golden-time or featherbedding. What John

Mitchell, the young President of the United Mine Workers of America, politely requested was a modest increase in pay, a slightly shorter day, and some assurance that the scales in which the coal was weighed were reasonably honest.

George F. Baer of the Philadelphia and Reading Coal and Iron Company spoke for the coal producers. Anthracite mining, he explained, was "a business . . . not a religious, sentimental or academic proposition." Baer was, nonetheless, a devout man, who did not exclude the Deity completely from industrial affairs. He made this clear when, in July, having received a letter telling him that it was his religious duty to end the strike, he turned to theology in his reply: "I beg of you not to be discouraged. The rights and interests of the laboring man will be protected and cared for—not by the labor agitators but by the Christian men to whom God in His infinite wisdom has given control of the property interests of this country . . ."

In view of the divergence of viewpoint and objective, it was not surprising that the strike—with national sentiment almost unanimously for the miners—outlasted the summer. By the end of September, coal on the retail market had jumped to $35 a ton and the question that confronted the President, a year after he had inherited his job, was essentially what that job was. According to some interpretations, the government generally, and the President in particular, were elected to do just what the constitution prescribed for them and any duties not set forth there were excluded. According to another, the President, when you came right down to it, could do anything not expressly forbidden to him. Roosevelt chose to apply the latter concept, before people began to starve or freeze. "The Constitution was made for the people," he explained, "and not the people for the Constitution."

The interesting thing was the way he did it. One way

might have been to send in troops to protect the property rights of the operators and enable them to hire strikebreakers. Another might have been to send the Army in to take away the mines and run them for the Government. Roosevelt did neither. He summoned operators and union officials to a meeting at which, according to his own account of the proceedings, "Mitchell behaved with great dignity and moderation. The operators on the contrary showed extraordinary stupidity and bad temper . . . and were insolent to me." The upshot of it all was an agreement, which he forced the operators to accept against their stubborn protests, to abide by the decision of an impartial commission. The men went back to work and five months later the commission gave them most of what they asked for.

Like most of his compatriots, John Pierpont Morgan made it clear throughout the coal strike that he had little sympathy for Baer. Two of his partners, indeed—Robert Bacon, T.R.'s Harvard classmate (and after Hay's death his Secretary of State) and George Perkins, later a backer of his Progressive party—helped the President throughout the trickiest part of the negotiations, which was getting the operators to accept a commission not packed in their favor. But Roosevelt's readiness to make good use of the most powerful financial figure in the country—the man who really ran it, a lot of people thought—did not argue any undue reverence on his part. That was something he had already made clear in the matter of the Northwest Securities suit, which he had started in the preceding February.

Northwest Securities, the first of the great U.S. holding companies, had been organized without undue fanfare the year before and incorporated at Trenton, N.J., with capital of some $400,000,000. What it amounted to was a tremendous railroad merger comprising James J. Hill's Great Northern and Edward H. Harriman's Union Pacific, along with the Chicago, Burlington and Quincy and the Northern Pacific. The consequence would be a monopoly on transportation through the whole of the U.S. Northwest with financial backing from the two great banking firms of Kuhn, Loeb and Company, acting for Harriman, and J. P. Morgan, representing Hill. Having just got through setting up the United States Steel Company, Morgan was especially pleased at a step which promised to bring the same sort of dimension and discipline to the railroad industry. Wall Street had been rudely disturbed by the fight between Hill and Harriman for control of the Great Northern in the spring of 1901; henceforth these two would be partners rather than rivals.

Unlike many reformers in the early nineteen-hundreds, notably Louis A. Brandeis, Roosevelt was never himself in any particular awe of the "curse of bigness," the threat of mere size as such. On the contrary, he was disposed to let corporations grow as large as they wanted—so long as they did not outgrow the law. In this case, however, there seemed to be considerable doubt on the latter point. A railroad monopoly affecting a quarter of the nation could obviously charge rates to suit its convenience and become a law unto itself, more powerful than the governments of the states through which it passed, of which it would become the master rather than the servant. Roosevelt turned for advice to his Attorney General, Philander Knox, who studied the subject and came up with the answer. This was that Northern Securities Company was vulnerable under the Sherman Anti-Trust Law. On the late afternoon of February 19, 1902, Knox announced that suit to compel the company to dissolve would shortly be filed, probably in Minnesota.

To Wall Street generally, and to Morgan in particular, this news was profoundly shocking on two counts. One was that a previous Supreme Court decision, concerning the American Sugar Refining Company, had seemingly provided a legal basis for just such a merger. The other was that the government had planned the suit without giving them warning. Of the two, the latter was the more significant. For three decades big business had regarded Washington as a sort of partner in charge of public relations. Hence the government's failure to advertise its intentions seemed to betoken stealth and the suit to be a stab in the back. Morgan, who received the news while entertaining guests at dinner, expressed surprise that Roosevelt had not done the gentlemanly thing. A few days later he paid a call at the White House accompanied by one of Roosevelt's father's friends, New York's patrician Senator Chauncey Depew. The meeting, at which the Attorney General was also present, was reliably reported for posterity by Roosevelt's official biographer, Joseph Bucklin Bishop:

> Mr. Morgan protested against the President's conduct in acting without letting him know of his purpose in advance. The President replied: "That is just what we did not want to do." "If we have done anything wrong," said Mr. Morgan, "send your man (meaning the Attorney-General) to my man (naming one of his lawyers) and they can fix it up." "That can't be done," said the President. "We don't want to fix it up," added Mr. Knox, "we want to stop it." Then Mr. Morgan asked: "Are you going to attack my other interests, the Steel Trust and the others?" "Certainly not," replied the President, "unless we find out that in any case they have done something that we regard as wrong.

The Great Northern suit was filed at St. Paul on March 10. Two years later, almost to the day, the Supreme Court on March 10, 1904, decided, five to four, that formation of the Northern Securities Company was in violation of the Anti-

Trust Law. As to its previous decision, by the same margin, in favor of the Sugar Trust, "This decision," wrote Roosevelt later, "I caused to be annulled by the court that had rendered it."

The suit against Northern Securities Company, the settlement of the coal strike and the start of the Panama Canal were by no means the only major moves of Roosevelt's first term. A few other matters also came up, including appointments of all sorts, from postmasterships to a vacancy on the Supreme Court; meeting or mending the wants or wishes of members of both houses of Congress and most especially of the great Republican bosses like Platt, Penrose, Quay, and Hanna; and various minor but potentially troublesome differences involving foreign lands, like England, the Philippines, and Venezuela.

The Venezuela matter was simple enough to handle. Its government, under President Cipriano Castro, had repudiated certain private debts and Germany, blockading her ports to dun for payment, was threatening to go further. Roosevelt called in the German Ambassador and informed him that the matter should be settled by arbitration. He added that, unless the Kaiser concurred within a week, Admiral Dewey, by that time in command of a fleet in the Caribbean, would be instructed to proceed to the scene of the blockade with orders to shoot if necessary. Presently Roosevelt was congratulating the Kaiser on a rapid and wise decision to refer the matter to the Hague Tribunal. Soon after that, he was welcoming the new German Ambassador who he had indicated would be the best possible choice—his old friend, Baron Hermann Speck von Sternburg.

The trouble in the Philippines was that, even after the daring young rebel leader, Emilio Aguinaldo, had been tracked down and pacified, dissident elements continued to resist their benefactors. Not only that, but many misguided and influential liberals at home—including, for example, President Charles Eliot of Harvard—seemed to feel that the United States should drop the White Man's burden like a hot potato. Roosevelt worked hard on the liberals at home and his increasingly good friend, the huge, genial William Howard Taft, whom McKinley had sent as Governor to Manila, worked hard in the Islands. Eventually the islanders were persuaded to defer hopes of premature independence and to accept the benevolent trusteeship that was to last until after World War II.

The brush with the British, perhaps the most satisfactory of the three, concerned the border between Canada and the panhandle of Alaska, a line which, after the discovery of gold in the Yukon, had suddenly acquired new importance. According to the maps made at the time of the U.S. purchase of Alaska, the line ran well behind the bays and inlets in the deeply indented coast. According to the new claim advanced by Canada, it took short cuts across the bays, thus in many cases giving Canada title to the harbors. Under pressure from Canada, England requested arbitration of the dispute. Roosevelt pointed out politely that even English maps showed the line running behind the bays and that to arbitrate was as absurd as it would be to arbitrate a U.S. claim to Nova Scotia. Nonetheless, to save England's face with her colony, he agreed to do it. His appointees to the commission were Elihu Root, his Secretary of War, Senator Cabot Lodge, and former Senator George Turner of Washington—all of whom he knew could be trusted not to give away a pebble. T.R.'s view of the question was completely justified when, with the two Canadians voting against the three Americans, the argument was settled in favor of the latter by Britain's Lord Chief Justice. Said he, when Canada remonstrated: "If . . .

they don't want a decision based on the law and the evidence, they must not put a British judge on the commission."

The Alaska boundary dispute, the peace in the Philippines and the Venezuela arbitration would in themselves have been enough to make T.R.'s inherited term memorable. Still, it was the anti-trust suit, the strike settlement and the Canal that confirmed its major claim on history. With the Canal, the United States became the colossus of the Western hemisphere that she has remained ever since. The strike settlement introduced and established the lasting principle, governing all subsequent battles between capital and labor, that the government represented an all-important third party, i.e., the public, and would not hesitate to intervene on its behalf. The battle with the trusts had only just begun with the Northern Security case, which lead to the establishment of the Department of Commerce, but the meaning was clear enough. T.R. had committed the United States to the belief that he expressed later in his memoirs: "Of all forms of tyranny the least attractive and the most vulgar is the tyranny of mere wealth, the tyranny of a plutocracy."

"I don't think that any family has ever enjoyed the White House more than we have. I was thinking about it just this morning when Mother and I took breakfast on the portico and afterwards walked about the lovely grounds and looked at the stately historic old house. It is a wonderful privilege to have been here and to have been given the chance to do this work, and I should regard myself as having a small and mean mind if in the event of defeat I felt soured at not having had more instead of being thankful for having had so much."

This excerpt from one of T.R.'s letters to Kermit, then at Groton, in June of 1904, may be something of an understatement. According to all accounts, including their own, the Roosevelt family not only enjoyed their official domicile, but revelled in it so enthusiastically that some observers wondered whether "the stately historic old house" would be able to stand the strain. Most of its previous occupants, coming to it from humbler surroundings and awed by its atmosphere of history and tradition, took a long time to get used to it and never felt entirely at home there. The Roosevelts, accustomed to spacious surroundings of their own and never awed by anything and least of all by history—which was in more ways than one merely the family business—settled in as though the place had been built for them. Their influence started with the very name of their new home. Considering the term "Executive Mansion" to be both grandiloquent and commonplace, since every state capital had such an establishment, T.R. replaced it officially by putting "The White House," previously a mere nickname, on his letter paper.

On the same premise, T.R. later insisted, sometimes with considerable acerbity, on being addressed as "Mr. President" rather than, as then tended to be customary especially for foreign diplomats, as "Your Excellency." His reasons were stated more gently than usual in a letter to his English friend, Sir George Otto Trevelyan, who had fallen into this error: "I would rather not be called Excellency, and this partly because the title does not belong to me and partly from vanity! The President of the United States ought to have no title; and if he did have a title it ought to be a bigger one. Whenever an important prince comes here he is apt to bring a shoal of "Excellencies" in his train. Just as I should object to having the simple dignity of the White House exchanged for such attractions as might lie in a second rate palace, so I feel that the President of a great democratic republic should have no title but President. He could not have a title that

would not be either too much or too little. Let him be called
the President and nothing more."

At the White House, Edith Roosevelt' first problem was to
find room for the six children, their French governess, their
nurse "Mame" and their assortment of house pets which included dogs, cats, guinea pigs, snakes, and lizards. The upstairs portion of the house, above public rooms and offices,
contained only five bedrooms of which two were small ones.
Arriving with Kermit and Ethel a few days after her husband
had installed himself, she spent several arduous weeks re-
organizing furniture so that by mid-October there was room
for Archie and Quentin to rejoin the menage. "Theodore
does long for them so," she wrote to Bamie with whom they
were visiting in New York where Alice stayed on for a few
weeks longer. Soon being referred to in the press as "Princess
Alice," the latter arrived in ample time to become the live-
liest figure in the Capital's active younger set, for whom her
White House coming-out party was Washington's main social
event in the winter of 1902. Later that year, when the Kaiser
sent his brother Prince Henry across the Atlantic to take
delivery of his new yacht, it was Alice who christened it
"*Meteor.*" To commemorate the occasion, she received
from the Emperor a diamond bracelet embellished with his
portrait—first item in what presently became a formidable
collection which she proudly described as her "loot."

While Alice was well suited by age and temperament to
derive maximum benefit from her new status, her younger
half brothers did their best to compete on their respective age
levels, as did small Ethel. On dinner party nights, she liked
to snoop downstairs in her nightgown to filch candy and
salted nuts from the dinner table. Caught in the act by James
Amos, the new colored butler who remained with T.R. as
valet and bodyguard until the end of his life, she squeaked

so indignantly that he felt obliged to escort her to her father. T.R. overruled his daughter's protests and deputized Amos to spank her or any of the other small fry whose misdeeds required it.

Kermit had only one winter in the White House before being packed off to Groton to join his brother Ted but he made the most of it, specializing in such contributions to its social life as bringing his live kangaroo-rat to the breakfast table. Strenuous life for Archie and Quentin was still in its nursery phase, comprising pillow fights and bedtime romps in which their father participated as enthusiastically as they did, usually in the role of a ferocious parent bear. "I play bear with the children almost every night, and some child is invariably fearfully damaged," he says in one letter, and in another: "The other night before the diplomatic dinner, having about fifteen minutes to spare, I went into the nursery, where the two small persons in pink tommies instantly raced for the bed and threw themselves on it with ecstatic conviction that a romp was going to begin. I did not have the heart to disappoint them, and the result was that my shirt got so mussed that I had to change it."

T.R.'s shirts were by no means the only things that got mussed from time to time. Along with the bedtime romps— which Edith Roosevelt presently tried to schedule before the children's dinner, so as to prevent their staying awake into the small hours—their father's catalogue of pastimes had now come to include, in addition to the customary gamut of tennis, boxing, scrambles, and horseback rides that included jumping over the highest hurdles available, lessons in judo and play at single sticks or broadswords.

The two latter pastimes, T.R.'s proficiency in which had been recently acquired, were reserved for days when unusually inclement weather or the pressure of appointments for-

bade more energetic pursuits outdoors. His teacher and most
frequent opponent was Leonard Wood, later assigned to the
Philippines where his promotion from Brigadier to Major
General occasioned a prolonged squabble in the Senate.

As the family settled into the routine of White House life,
T.R.'s avid enthusiasm for exertion in various forms led to
the formation of the celebrated "tennis cabinet" whose members included a cross-section of close friends in his official
cabinet, the Congress, and the *corps diplomatique*. Membership in the tennis cabinet was not indispensable to a place
in the President's affections but it was a considerable help,
as was competence in scrambles through Rock Creek Park
which might have taxed the endurance of the originator of the
term. T.R. reported to Ted, Jr., that on his first scramble the
new British Ambassador, Sir Mortimer Durand, had proved
to be "a bad walker and wholly unable to climb. He could
not go up or over even the simpler rocks, and got all done out
before the walk was through." A few months later, a letter to
Henry White in the U.S. Embassy at London, whom T.R.
considered the ablest man in the U.S. foreign service, contains
another revealing comment on the subject: "I do not know
whether it is my fault or Sir Mortimer's but our minds do
not meet."

The advantages of physical fitness to an Ambassador were
perhaps best exemplified on the positive side by Jules J.
Jusserand of France who was not only a charter member of
the tennis cabinet but a regular participant in scrambles and
one whose savoir faire went far beyond mere walking and
climbing. Rules for such excursions, based on the analogy
with mountaineering, were that when obstacles were encountered it was obligatory to go over or through them. On arriving at Rock Creek one winter afternoon, the members of the
party, in obedience to this convention, dutifully removed their

clothes and, holding them above their heads, prepared to wade across through lumps of ice. One of the group then noticed that Jusserand had kept his gloves on and asked him why.

"Because," replied the urbane Frenchman, "I thought we might meet ladies."

Indicative of the breadth of Roosevelt's cosmopolitan sympathies was the fact that, next to Jusserand, the closest of his ambassadorial tennis cabinet cronies was Speck von Sternburg, who owed his appointment as Germany's envoy largely to Presidential influence. Less astonishing, however, than the unusual range of T.R.'s close friendships among high-level diplomats was the wide assortment of contacts which he maintained with old friends in divergent fields including pugilism, literature, science, ranching, and most of the many other pursuits which he himself had practiced, studied or read about. Roosevelt not only liked many different kinds of people himself but liked to have them like each other and made strenuous efforts to mix them up together as thoroughly as possible, preferably at White House lunches. Among the New Englanders with whom he kept in more or less close contact, for example, were President Charles W. Eliot of Harvard, Bill Sewall, the Maine guide and lumberman whom he had tried to turn into a cowboy, and John L. Sullivan, the renowned Boston Strong Boy, who gave him a rabbit foot which he later carried on his trip through Africa. Once, when Sullivan called at the White House together with the most famous of his former opponents, Jake Kilrain, T.R. introduced both to John J. Pershing, then attached to the Tokyo Embassy, whom he described as "one of our *military* fighting men." Later he gave Sullivan, whom he revered as a "fair fighter," a letter of introduction to Charles Evans Hughes, some years before the latter was chosen to epitomize fairness as Chief Justice of the Supreme Court.

As to President Eliot of Harvard, his intimacy with T.R. enabled him to reveal that, while perhaps not quite as quick a draw as some of his former associates in the Badlands or even on the New York police force, T.R. as President often carried a six-shooter, hoping thus to get the drop on anyone who started gunplay. This secret formed an interesting footnote to Eliot's account of Harvard's 1902 Commencement Exercises.

"Theodore Roosevelt . . . reached my house on the morning of the Commencement, shortly before the Academic procession was to form in the College Yard. When I asked him what I could do for him, he replied: 'I must clean up before I go down to Massachusetts Hall.' I showed him to a chamber and followed him in, that I might tell him where the bathroom was. He hastily threw his coat and waistcoat on the bed, and drew from his hip-pocket a good-sized pistol which he laid on the dressing table. President McKinley had been assassinated in the previous September. When I asked if he habitually carried a revolver, he replied: 'Yes, when I am going into public places. I should have some chance of shooting the assassin before he could shoot me, if he were near me.' "

While T.R. was never called upon to defend himself against an assassin until long after he had left the White House and had ceased to carry side-arms, his strenuous life therein, as might have been expected, exacted a mounting toll of physical injuries. Early in 1904 he was writing Ted about "a rap on the back of my right hand . . . kept sore by the number of people with whom I had to shake hands." That autumn his horse put a foot through a rotten plank in a bridge and turned a somersault causing the President to land upside down and skin his forehead. "Most fortunately," he wrote Lodge, "the papers have not seemed to get hold of it—

which, as the mark was about the size of a small saucer and the skin came completely off, was remarkable." More serious and more widely publicized was the accident in Pittsfield, Massachusetts, where a trolley hit the automobile in which Roosevelt was riding on his way to make a speech. One member of his Secret Service escort—W. L. Craig, "an excellent fellow with a prizefighting past"—was killed. The President was thrown to the sidewalk in such fashion as to cause severe bruises which later turned into an abscess on his thigh. The President, as was his habit, so far as possible ignored his injuries. They did not keep him away from the meeting between John Mitchell and the coal mine operators, at which he presided in a wheel chair.

Most serious of all was the injury which eventually cost him the sight of his already defective left eye, inflicted accidentally by his military aide during the course of a friendly sparring match. With characteristic gallantry and good manners, Roosevelt concealed the fact that this eye had become completely blind until he had left the White House, lest news of the incident reveal the identity of the young officer—Captain Dan Tyler Moore, a distant cousin of the First Lady —and thus perhaps impair *his* professional advancement. As to his own loss, T.R. pointed out, after his return from Africa that this could be viewed as a stroke of good luck; the jab might just as well have gone into his right eye, which he employed for sighting a rifle, and thus have ended his shooting career before the best big-game hunt of his lifetime.

Like most people who enjoy outdoor activities, Roosevelt was averse to night life and preferred to discharge his social obligations in the daytime. Much White House entertaining, accordingly, was done at the lunch table where Edith Roosevelt's exceptional talents as a hostess were often tested to the utmost. By the time T.R. reached the Presidency, the wide range of his past activities and his present interests often combined to create incongruities in the guest list whose members were likely to include cowboys and cabinet ministers, New York socialites and ex-Rough Riders, erudite professors and polished diplomats, all mixed together with a fine disdain for protocol.

Table talk at such gatherings was usually fresh and uninhibited, like that recalled by Senator Leroy Percy of Mississippi on one occasion when, ". . . in order to get a rise out of the President I remarked: 'I notice that Mr. Carnegie in his dedication of his Temple of Peace at Pittsburgh last night said that there is no righteousness without peace. What do you think of that statement?' In his emphatic manner the President replied: 'I am just as strong for peace as Andrew Carnegie or any other man. That is the reason why I don't send any long-haired men or short-haired women to represent this country at The Hague. But I believe the best guarantee of peace for this nation is a strong navy.' Turning to the newly appointed Ambassador to Germany he said: 'Tell the Kaiser what I say about this. He will agree with me.' And then added: 'By George, there is a man for you. If you would drop him down in Chicago in less than a week he would be the boss of his ward but,' with a laugh, 'the Czar would not; he would be the President of a Mugwump Society.' "

Roosevelt's White House luncheons came in handy as a means of keeping up with doings in the literary world in a fashion later recalled by William Howard Taft—long after his break with T.R., their reconciliation and T.R.'s death—when he was Chief Justice: "When the President found a book he liked he would telegraph the author to any part of the country and invite him to lunch the next week, and the author would usually come. The President would garnish the table with a couple of his Cabinet officers and some others. The Cabinet officers not familiar with the new books were presented to the author. After the lunch was well on, the President would turn to him, after complimenting him on his book, and would say: 'I particularly liked that character whose traits you brought out so clearly in the tenth chapter.' The Cabinet officers knowing neither the author nor the book were left without power to add much to that part of the conversation; but the author thoroughly enjoyed himself . . . I remember Mr. Root, being invited to one of these lunches, hesitated as to whether he could accept or not. The President said, 'I understand you, Elihu; what you mean is that you will come if you have no subsequent engagement.' "

The best example of the effect of T.R.'s interest in U.S. writing was the case of the poet Edwin Arlington Robinson, a remote cousin of his brother-in-law. When Kermit Roosevelt, a frequent contributor of verse to the monthly *Grotonian,* had his attention called to Robinson's first book, *Children of the Night,* by one of his masters, who had met the poet in Gardiner, Me., he liked it and sent copies to both his mother and father. The President was also favorably impressed and soon wrote to Robinson:

"I have enjoyed your poems, especially *The Children of the Night* so much that I must write to tell you so. Will you permit me to ask what you are doing and how you are getting along? I wish I could see you. Sincerely yours. . . ."

Further inquiry indicated that Robinson was getting along as a timekeeper for construction workers on the New York subway and having a hard time making ends meet. T.R. collaborated with Kermit on a review of his book for the *Outlook* and got him a job in New York as a special agent of the United States Treasury, thus launching one of the most distinguished careers in U.S. letters. In later correspondence

Roosevelt admitted that, while he liked Robinson's verses, he was not always sure just what they meant and explained why he had gotten him a humdrum position in the United States instead of helping him to go to Europe:

"You know I believe that our literary men are always hurt by going abroad. If Bret Harte had stayed in the West, if he had not even come East, he might have gone on doing productive work. . . . In the same way, I think Joel Chandler Harris has continued to do good work because he has remained in Atlanta. . . ."

From a political viewpoint, the most controversial of all Roosevelt's White House guests was no doubt his good friend and adviser on racial matters, the famous colored educator, Booker T. Washington, head of Tuskegee Institute who turned up for a quiet family dinner on October 16, 1901, less than two months after his host had been in residence. Far in advance of all integration standards for the period, this informal gathering touched off an indignant uproar among Southern Democrats which continued to echo throughout both terms of his administration. The President ignored the commotion, explaining his action only in private letters to friends. In one he gave an account of his own feelings on the subject:

"I have consulted so much with him it seemed to me that it was natural to ask him to dinner to talk over this work, and the very fact that I felt a moment's qualm on inviting him because of his color made me ashamed of myself and made me hasten to send the invitation. . . . As things have turned out, I am very glad that I asked him, for the clamor aroused by the act makes me feel as if the act was necessary."

By the spring of 1903, when he had been in the White House for a year and a half, the limits which Washington placed upon physical exertion were beginning to be irksome.

This, along with the advisability of maintaining direct contact with his sources of political support in the Far West, caused Roosevelt to take a two-month Western swing in which he visited Wisconsin, North and South Dakota, Wyoming, Montana, Nebraska, Iowa, Illinois, Missouri, Kansas, Colorado, New Mexico, California, Oregon, Washington, Idaho and Utah, some of them several times, as well as several Eastern states en route. This excursion included visits to Medora and the Little Missouri country where he had done his ranching twenty years before; a fortnight stay in Yellowstone Park with John Burroughs, where he re-encountered his old friend "Hell-Roaring Bill Jones" after the latter had been arduously sobered up enough to rise to the occasion; and a sojourn in Muir Woods, near San Francisco, with John Muir.

Roosevelt's interest in natural fauna which had been touched off so many years before by the spectacle of the dead seal in the fishmonger's window on Broadway, had, by this time, proliferated widely. Main branches were his intense concern about animals of all sorts in the major categories of quarry, household pets and objects of scientific curiosity. On his Western trip, as happened frequently, the three categories tended to get somewhat confused. Tame creatures presented to Roosevelt in the course of the journey included, as he later explained in a long descriptive letter to John Hay, not only a "badger but two bears, a lizard, a horned toad and a horse." The badger, donated by a small girl in a Kansas cow-town who stated that the animal had recently been caught by her brother, Josiah, was named for the latter and speedily became part of the Presidential entourage, as did Bill the lizard. In a letter to Alice, the President reported on his traveling menagerie:

"I have been literally loaded down with gifts of every kind

and description. I fear there are only a very few of them to which mother will consent to give house room, though I shall have to preserve most. . . . There are a number of minor ones, however, which can be distributed among my offspring. I rather think you will like Josiah the badger. So far he is very good-tempered and waddles around everywhere like a little bear submitting with perfect equanimity to being picked up, and spending much of his time in worrying the ends of anybody's trousers. . . ."

Bears, whether real or simulated, always aroused T.R.'s particular interest. On this trip to Yellowstone he was more concerned about the elk, which he thought were multiplying rather too rapidly, but a year later he was writing about the poor Grizzlies who gave the rangers a hard time by getting their paws stuck in tin cans. A year before, on a Mississippi hunting trip, several members of the party caught a small bear and tied it up near the camp. The President insisted not only that the animal remain unharmed but that it later be turned loose. Reporters got wind of this event and a Washington cartoonist, amused by their stories, made an imaginative drawing of the bear. This resulted presently in the manufacture of stuffed toys nicknamed "Teddy Bears" which have remained important denizens of nursery menageries ever since.

A long letter from T.R. to John Hay about his Western trip is one of the high points of his regional writings which, for humor, authentic detail, and rapid action, invites comparison with Mark Twain's memoirs of nearby terrain a few years earlier. Of interest for additional reasons is its description of the proceedings at the copper-mining capital of Butte, Montana, where—after detouring back to St. Louis to open its World's Fair—T.R. stopped off for a few hours to make a speech and attend a banquet:

"My address was felt to be honor enough for one hotel, and the dinner was given in the other. When the dinner was announced the mayor led me in—or to speak more accurately, tucked me under one arm and lifted me partially off the ground, so that I felt as if I looked like one of those limp dolls with dangling legs carried around by small children. . . . As soon as we got in the banquet hall and sat at the head of the table the mayor hammered lustily with the handle of his knife and announced 'Waiter, bring on the feed!' . . . The dinner was soon in full swing and it was interesting in many regards. Beside my own party . . . there were fifty men from each of the Butte factions. In Butte every prominent man is a millionaire, a professional gambler, or a labor leader; and generally he has been all three. Of the hundred men who were my hosts I suppose at least half had killed their man in private war, or had striven to compass the assassination of an enemy. They had fought one another with reckless ferocity. They had been allies and enemies in every kind of business scheme, and companions in brutal revelry. . . . The millionaires had been laboring men once; the labor leaders intended to be millionaires in their turn or else pull down all who were. They had made money in mines; they had spent it on the races, in other mines, or in gambling and every form of vicious luxury. But they were strong men for all that. They had worked and striven and pushed and trampled, and had always been ready, and were ready now, to fight to the death in many different kinds of conflict. They had built up their part of the West. They were men with whom one had to reckon if thrown in contact with them. There was Senator Clark with his Iscariot face; goat-bearded Carter with his cold grey eyes; Heinze, heavy-jowled, his cheeks flushed, his eyes glittering—he regarded the dinner as a triumph for him because the mayor was his man, and in pure joy he had lost twenty thousand dollars in reckless betting on horse races that afternoon. In Butte proper at the moment he was the wealthiest and most powerful man. There were plenty of those at the table who would stop at no measure to injure him in fortune, in limb or in life; and as he looked at them he would lean over and tell me the evil things he intended in turn to do to them. But though most of them hated each other, they were accustomed to taking their pleasure when they could get it, and they took it fast and hard with the meats and wines."

In T.R.'s enjoyment of the White House, resumed on his return to Washington early in June, the only serious flaw was the remote possibility that it might come to an end on March 4, 1905. The trip west was one step to insure against this possibility but he took another even more important one soon after his return. Between T.R. and the Republican nomination the following year, the only important obstacle was Ohio's formidable boss and senator, Marcus Alonzo Hanna, with whom his relations had altered considerably since their meeting in Buffalo two years earlier. By now Hanna had long since ceased to regard Roosevelt as the "madman" he had considered him when the matter of the Vice-Presidential nomination had been up for discussion at Philadelphia; and the President—despite a widely quoted reference to himself as "that cowboy in the White House"—had since then found Hanna often a sage and trustworthy counsellor. Now, however, there were rumors, by no means necessarily ill-founded, that—unlike his senior senatorial colleague and rival, Joseph B. Foraker, who had already come out for Roosevelt—Hanna was preparing either to try to get the nomination for himself or at least to put himself in a position to decide who should receive it. The matter came to a head at the Ohio State Republican Convention of 1903 to which

Foraker was offering a resolution endorsing Roosevelt's nomination in 1904. On May 23, Hanna wired to T.R. that the resolution "has come in a way which makes it necessary for me to oppose" and added that, "When you know all the facts I am sure you will approve my course."

What this really meant was that T.R. was abruptly confronted with the question of whether he or Hanna was top dog in the party. He gave the matter thought for twenty-four hours and then wired back:

"Your telegram received. I have not asked any man for his support. I have had nothing whatever to do with raising the issue. Inasmuch as it has been raised of course those who favor my administration and my nomination will favor endorsing both and those who do not will oppose."

Now it was Hanna's turn to worry, about whether to come out into the open as a rival or lower his colors. He chose the latter course in a wire the next day:

". . . In view of the sentiment expressed, I shall not oppose the endorsement of your administration and candidacy by our State Convention. . . ."

Roosevelt's reply was gracious:

"I thank you for your telegram and appreciate your action."

That settled the matter of the nomination; and the peak excitement at Chicago the following June was not the roll-call for Roosevelt but something that was happening halfway across the world, in Morocco. There a well-to-do retired American named Ion Perdicaris who dabbled in painting at his villa, the Place of Nightingales, near Tangier, was kidnapped by a local chieftain named Rassouli as part of the latter's scheme to harass and embarrass Morocco's Sultan. Actually, there was nothing very dreadful about the abduction; Perdicaris found Rassouli an engaging host and was returned unharmed a few days later. Nonetheless, it occasioned a State Department cable to the U.S. Consul General at Tangier which, actually composed by John Hay with the help of a congenial newspaper man named E. M. ("Eddie") Hood, had the authentic Roosevelt note.

"We want," said the cable, "either Perdicaris alive or Rassouli dead."

The resounding message was read to the convention hall in Chicago causing prolonged cheers. It became a part of the imperishable Roosevelt legend and of the history of his era.

X

DEAR CABOT: You were right about the election, and I was mistaken. I had no idea that there would be such a sweep. Think of Missouri having gone with us! . . . I am particularly pleased that you approved of my utterance about the third term being made just when it was. How much I have to talk over with you!"

T.R.'s exuberance over the election was thoroughly understandable. Along with Missouri, he and his Vice-Presidential partner, Charles W. Fairbanks, had carried thirty-two states to thirteen for Judge Alton B. Parker. The final result, 336 electoral votes to 140; 7,628,785 popular votes to 5,084,442, was one of the most one-sided elections on record. The "utterance about the third term" had been made on election night, as part of his victory statement:

"I am deeply sensible of the honor done me by the American people in thus expressing their confidence in what I have done and have tried to do. . . . On the fourth of March next I shall have served three and a half years, and this three and a half years constitutes my first term. The wise custom which limits the President to two terms regards the substance and not the form. Under no circumstances will I be a candidate for or accept another nomination."

Characteristically forthright, this statement was also carefully considered and precisely phrased. It expressed T.R.'s basic beliefs about tenure of the Presidency which he summed up in a later letter to Lodge: ". . . the President should be a very strong man who uses without hesitation every power that the position yields; but because of this very fact I believe that he should be sharply watched by the people, held to strict accountability by them, and that he should not keep the office too long." Two other aspects of T.R.'s statement that deserve consideration were its applicability to unforeseen conditions in the future and its timing.

By renouncing a third term on election night, T.R. was boldly inviting a handicap for the whole of his second term comparable to that which had unavoidably accompanied his incomplete first one. Then he had held the job without having been elected; now, by his election night statement, he forfeited the leverage which a chief executive could derive from uncertainty about the time of his departure. As to his statement's applicability to the future, T.R. later had occasion to explain that his opposition to a third term applied only to a third *consecutive* term. His line of reasoning here was that any President while in office can usually control party machinery so completely as to be able to command renomination as often as he wants, whereas, once out of the office, a former President is, if anything, handicapped by having held it. With equal cogence he pointed out, however, that to have included this qualification in his election night statement would have reversed its meaning. To have said then that he would not be a candidate for a third consecutive term, would have been to imply that he *would* be a candidate again as soon as someone else had broken the succession—thus defeating his purpose so completely that it would have been better not to have made any statement at all.

This time the inauguration was a unique fiesta, with Rough Riders on horseback roping good-natured passers-by, brass bands playing "There'll be a Hot Time in the Old Town Tonight," and a bright sun shining in crisp spring weather as the President recited the oath of office to the white-haired Chief Justice Fuller. A few days later, T.R. went to New York to attend the St. Patrick's Day Parade and, later in the afternoon, to give away the bride at a fashionable wedding. She was his niece Eleanor, daughter of his brother Elliott who, long an incurable alcoholic, had died some ten years before. The groom was her distant Roosevelt cousin, Franklin Delano. No less avid for attention than most young ladies on such occasions, the bride felt understandably hurt when, after the ceremony, guests clustered around the President in the room where the refreshments were being served, leaving herself and the handsome groom comparatively unattended.

Looking back now at 1905, when the Civil War was not so far distant in the past as World War I is in the 1960's, it seems a time of wondrous calm and charming simplicity. Automobiles, telephones, and electric lights still claimed the character of novelties; the movies were to be seen only in nickelodeons or, on rare occasions in the homes of the well-to-do, as a form of entertainment appropriate for children's birthday parties. Edward VII had recently been crowned King of England; Lenin was preparing to occupy a walk-up flat in Zurich and the Wright brothers were struggling to get their motor-kite off the beach at Kittyhawk. And yet somehow there was a chill and a warning of storm in the warm autumn that followed the world's long Victorian sum-mer. Tensions were increasing and tempers growing sharper between classes at home, between nations abroad. T.R. sensed the coming of dark and tremendous changes and took steps to meet them.

If Roosevelt's first term had an epic ring, his second, when he became President in his own right, rang even truer from the very start. First of all, there was the matter of the war in the Far East. Japan, locked away from the rest of the world since the early 1600's, had suddenly opened her doors in 1860. Astoundingly, in the next forty years, she had covered the ground that it had taken Europe three hundred years to gain, becoming a great modern industrial nation without pausing even to change her feudal social structure. Now she was at grips with Czarist Russia, an archaic mammoth which, in the same three hundred years, had retained a feudal society with-out bothering to update her government, her economy, or her methods of waging war. At immediate issue were Russia's claims in Manchuria and Japan's in Korea but for Europe and the United States there was more at stake than that. For the United States, only recently become a Pacific power, com-plete victory for either side might mean a dangerous rival on the opposite shore of that ocean. For Europe, it meant pos-sible permanent changes in continental power relationships; and also, for the time being at least, it took Russia out of play as an active ally of France.

Japan won the first battle at Chemulpo before declaring the war. T.R. wrote Kermit that he was shocked at Russia's unreadiness for the attack. Then, with the world watching—and with General Arthur MacArthur and his son Douglas present as official U.S. observers—the Japanese won again, on land, at Mukden. This set the stage for the grand climax, when Admiral Rodjestvensky took a huge fleet of thirty-two warships lumbering down the Baltic, through the British Channel, along the coast of Europe and Africa, around the Cape of Good Hope, across the Indian Ocean, through the straits at Singapore, up the China coast and into the Japan Sea. It was an impossible voyage, beset by every kind of mishap; by the time the fleet reached the Strait of Tsushima, the antiquated ships were barely in shape to move, let alone to fight a major battle. Japan's Admiral Togo proved that in short order in a victory of which T.R. wrote to his friend and Harvard contemporary, Baron Kentaro Kaneko: "No wonder you are happy! Neither Trafalgar nor the defeat of the Spanish Armada was as complete. . . ."

Not long afterward, Japan's Minister to Washington, Kogoro Takahira, indicated that Japan had won all she wanted and was ready to conclude a conqueror's peace. Russia was ready to quit too, if she could do so with any show of pride and dignity; and both sides thought that T.R. was the right man to bring them together. A more ticklish job could scarcely have been imagined. Even choosing the right spot to talk was difficult. Europe was out of the question for Japan but Washington in midsummer was too hot. Finally, all agreed on the quiet old New Hampshire town of Portsmouth. Roosevelt invited the emissaries—Count Witte and Baron Rosen for Russia, Baron Komura and Minister Takahira for Japan—to lunch on board the Presidential yacht, *Mayflower*, anchored in Oyster Bay. Matters of protocol and precedence threatened to end the conference before it started. Who should sit on the President's right? Whose ruler should be toasted first? T.R. took his guests in to a buffet layed out at a round table. When all were served, he proposed a toast ". . . to which there will be no answer and which I ask you to drink in silence, standing . . . to the welfare and prosperity of the sovereigns and the peoples of the two great nations, whose representatives have met one another on this ship."

The conference at Portsmouth came to turn eventually on the matter of an indemnity which Russia refused to pay. Nonetheless, both sides wanted peace, Russia because continuing the war would mean a vast humiliating loss of territory and Japan because it would mean wrecking the national economy to win land she did not want. T.R. proposed a face-saving formula: that, in addition to the Korean protectorate, Japan get all of Sakalin Island but sell half of it back to Russia for a price which would be the equivalent of an indemnity but have a different name. When even this was rejected, he was drafting a letter to the Kaiser, requesting him to use his influence on his cousin "Nicky," when the telephone on his desk rang to announce that the envoys were ready to sign a treaty. By it, Japan gave Russia half of Sakalin—without requiring any payment at all.

The conference at Portsmouth initiated a new and astounding U.S. role in world affairs—that of a sort of stern and prestigious parent to the squabbling children on the other side of the globe. What confirmed it soon afterward was the Algeciras Conference to settle the vexed problem of Morocco which threatened to set off a general European war. The potential *casus belli,* as usual in such affairs, looks trifling in retrospect —even more so than the assassination of an Austrian archduke at Sarajevo nine years later. This time the trouble started when, dividing up North Africa with touching disregard for its denizens, England and France agreed that in exchange for endorsing the former's right to a free hand in Egypt, the latter should have one in unruly Morocco. To the Kaiser, a latecomer to the colonial game, this sounded a bit presumptuous. During a Mediterranean cruise, he stopped off at Tangier to make a belligerent-sounding speech in which he said that, in his view, the Sultan of Morocco was an independent monarch, beholden to no one. He then proposed an international conference on the subject, with the U.S. as a disinterested, and therefore especially welcome, participant.

On the face of it, nothing could have looked more like direct flouting of the classic Washingtonian policy of non-involvement in foreign affairs than participation in a conference about European interests in Morocco. Where the difference lay was that now, instead of being forced to take sides in a dangerous quarrel between combatants much bigger and more powerful than herself, the U.S. was being in effect invited to put a stop to a European quarrel just because of her status as an impartial, and powerful, outsider. Through Speck von Sternburg, T.R. got this point firmly established in the form of an agreement by the Kaiser to abide by any outcome which the U.S. considered "the most fair and the most practical."

What the Kaiser said he wanted was merely the familiar principle of the Open Door as applied in China, whereby trade with Morocco would be free to one and all. The conference at Algeciras proposed a Moroccan police force jointly administered by Spain and France, which might, more or less provide it. When the Kaiser demurred, Roosevelt tactfully reminded him of his promise and at the same time gave him full, and world-wide, credit for calling the conference that had been able to agree on such a satisfactory solution. As anticipated, this bait to Imperial vanity proved to be irresistible; nonetheless, when the Nobel Prize committee met to award the prize for 1906 the recipient they chose, for his good offices at Morocco as well as at Portsmouth, was not the Emperor but the President.

Preventing a major European war and stopping a major

Asian one was a totally new sort of work for a United States President. Roosevelt was a new sort of President, however, and he made that unmistakably evident on the home front as well. In his rewarding book, *The Era of Theodore Roosevelt*, George E. Mowry summed up the way he went about it:

> Three of the most cherished powers of private business had been the right to set its own prices for services, the right to maintain its books and records in secrecy, and the right to negotiate with labor without interference by a third party. The President's 1905 message challenged . . . all these rights. . . .

T.R.'s views on labor were hardly a surprise, after his settlement of the coal strike in 1902. His views on the responsibility of the government to keep big business in line had also been stated before but now he was stating them as an elected President, which made them something else again. The rostrum from which he set forth the domestic agenda for his second term was chosen with typical boldness: the Union League Club of Philadelphia, home town of Boies Penrose and the Pennsylvania Railroad. The message was simple: "The great development of industrialism means that there must be an increase in the supervision exercised by the Government over business-enterprise." In his inaugural address a few weeks later, he spelled it out again: "We do not intend that this Republic shall ever fail as those republics of olden times failed, in which there finally came to be a government by classes, which resulted either in the poor plundering the rich or in the rich . . . exploiting the poor."

Arch offenders in the first decade of the century were the railroads which fixed rates as they chose; a system of rebates to favored customers made the roads in effect a government within a government. Roosevelt wanted legislation giving the Interstate Commerce Commission power to fix rates that would be immediately effective, subject to limited court review but not subject to impeding or nullifying litigation. The Hepburn Bill, embodying what he considered the essential changes, came before Congress in the winter of 1906 and the fight over it in both houses showed how deep the issue went. When Progressives like Wisconsin's Robert La Follette opposed the Bill as not going far enough, Roosevelt's answer was that a stronger one had no chance of passing. To conservatives like Rhode Island's Nelson Aldrich—leader of the Old Guard in the Senate since Mark Hanna's death soon after the inauguration—he argued that the Bill was as necessary to the railroads as to the public, and the only means by which they could escape eventual government ownership. When, on May 16, 1906, the Hepburn Bill finally passed the Senate it was a major victory—what Professor William Z. Ripley was to call "an historic event—the most important perhaps in Theodore Roosevelt's public career. . . ."

The question of identifying the most important event in T.R.'s public career is one that has aroused considerable difference of opinion. It was not the Hepburn Bill but something entirely different, for example, that Robert M. La Follette singled out in his autobiography:

When the historian . . . shall speak of Theodore Roosevelt, he is likely to say that he did many notable things, but that his greatest work was inspiring and actually beginning a world movement for staying territorial waste and saving for the human race the things on which alone a peaceful, progressive, and happy life can be founded. . . .

Roosevelt's active interest in conservation was interwoven with his long-standing friendship with Gifford Pinchot, a lean hawk-faced Pennsylvanian whom he sponsored for the

196]   T.R.—THE STORY OF THEODORE ROOSEVELT

Boone and Crocket Club during the 1890's and who came up to Albany to spend a night at the Governor's mansion during the winter of 1899. He arrived, Pinchot later wrote, at a moment when the mansion "was under ferocious attack from a band of invisible Indians and the Governor of the Empire State was helping a houseful of children to escape by lowering them out of the second story window on a rope." After the battle with the Indians was over, Roosevelt and Pinchot put on the gloves for a friendly sparring match in which Pinchot knocked Roosevelt "off his very solid pins." They then sat down to discuss Forestry—always the subject nearest to Pinchot's heart.

The close friendship that developed from that meeting enabled Pinchot and his ally Frederick H. Newell of the Inland Waterways Commission to call on Roosevelt even before he had moved into the White House in 1901. They found the new President wholly receptive to their long-nurtured, well-developed and ably stated ideas about conservation. "We left," wrote Pinchot later, "two very happy men." Roosevelt's first message to Congress the following December contained the gist of the doctrine he was to preach and practice for the next seven years, until it became part not only of U.S. but of world policy toward natural resources: "The forest and water problems are perhaps the most vital internal problems of the U.S. . . . The fundamental idea of forestry is the perpetuation of forests by use. . . . It is as right for the National Government to make the streams and rivers of the arid region useful by engineering works for water storage as to make useful the rivers and harbors of the humid region by engineering works of another kind."

The first important legislation of T.R.'s first term was the Newlands Bill which he signed on June 17, 1902. This started the Reclamation Bureau and authorized some thirty Federal irrigation projects including Arizona's Roosevelt Dam which were under construction or finished by the time he left office in 1909. But this was merely a beginning. At the start of his second term, Roosevelt transferred the Forest Reserves from the Department of the Interior's Land Office to the Department of Agriculture's Forest Service where it came under the direct supervision of Pinchot, as Chief Forester. Under the Agriculture Appropriations Act of 1905, this meant that Pinchot and T.R. were in position to contend with the great lumber companies of the Far West for control of the nation's priceless timber resources. Along with the lumbermen, T.R. fought the cattlemen who were overgrazing public lands, the electric-power companies who were buying up choice dam sites that properly belonged to the public, and the mining and oil companies that heretofore had been able to acquire government lands at far less than their true potential value.

The climax of the conservation fight came in 1907 when Oregon's Senator C. W. Fulton secured passage of an amendment shrewdly tacked on to the Agricultural Appropriations Bill specifying that no new forest reserves should be created within Oregon, Washington, Idaho, Montana, Colorado, or Wyoming. The Appropriations Bill provided funds for all the Agriculture Department's activities for the next year. The President would surely feel obliged to sign it, thus cancelling all progress for the Forest Service for the foreseeable future.

The reaction of Roosevelt and Pinchot was speedy and characteristic. The President had ten days' leeway in which to sign the bill. During these ten days, he still had the right to create, by simple proclamation, as many Forest Reserves as he wished; and Pinchot and his subordinates knew precisely where they were needed. All that remained to be done was to draft the proclamations and have the President sign them. Pinchot's autobiography records the process: "Our field force had already gathered practically all the facts. Speedily it supplied the rest. Our office force worked straight through, some of them for thirty-six and even forty-eight hours on end to complete the job."

Before Roosevelt signed the Appropriations Bill forbidding him to create new Forest Reserves, he had created twenty-one of them in the six Northwestern states. His *Autobiography* records the consequence:

> ... When the friends of the special interests in the Senate got their amendment through and woke up, they discovered that sixteen million acres of timber-land had been saved for the people by putting them in the national forests before the landgrabbers could get at them. The opponents of the forest service turned handsprings in their wrath; and dire were their threats against the Executive; but the threats could not be carried out, and were really only a tribute to the efficiency of our action.

Probably the most controversial of all T.R.'s actions during his second term was his role in the panic of 1907—of which indeed even the cause is still in dispute. To most business-men of the time, and to many historians after them, this was in part at least T.R.'s hostility toward business in general and toward the railroads in particular. His 1906 message to Con-gress was, if anything, more severe than that of the year before; and when Union Pacific stock dropped twenty-five points in the market break of the following March, E. H. Harriman said to reporters: "I would hate to tell you to whom I think you ought to go for an explanation of all this."

T.R. himself had very different ideas about the matter. The very day after the market break, he instructed the Interstate Commerce Commission to undertake a thorough investiga-tion of the railroad industry, saying: "I desire from you rec-ommendations definite and precise in character to secure a far more thoroughgoing supervision and control than we now have over the great agencies of interstate transportation." That summer, Judge Kenesaw Mountain Landis found the Standard Oil Company guilty of fourteen hundred violations of the Elkins Act and—in a decision later set aside on repeal—imposed a fine of twenty-nine million dollars. Talk of a financial panic grew louder but Roosevelt, far from drawing back from his objective, took this as an incentive to advance. Dedicating a lighthouse at Provincetown in August, he suggested that "malefactors of great wealth" were actually trying to foment panic, hoping thus to persuade him to reverse his policy toward business "so that they may enjoy unmolested the fruits of their own evil doing." He went on to propose more vigorous criminal prosecution of lawbreakers in business.

Whatever may have been the underlying causes of the panic—at least some of which lay far deeper than Roosevelt's speeches and Wall Street's reaction to them—the immediate occasion was an attempt, by the same Auguste Heinze who had attracted his notice at the banquet in Butte, to corner the copper market. The corner failed, causing a run on the Knickerbocker Trust Company in New York which forced that institution to close its doors on October 23. J. P. Morgan, just returned from the General Convention of the Protestant Episcopal Church in Richmond, Virginia, met with James Stillman, George F. Baker and other financiers and conferred until late that night at the Manhattan Hotel. George B. Cortelyou, T.R.'s new Secretary of the Treasury, went to New York to investigate the situation and Roosevelt, having returned from a bear hunt in Louisiana the same afternoon, said to reporters: "I have had a delightful time. I am extremely gratified that I got a bear."

By afternoon of the next day, call money was being lent

at 100 per cent and stocks were falling faster than they would do again until another October twenty-two years later. Then, suddenly, the situation eased. Cortelyou had agreed to add twenty-five million dollars to the government funds in the national banks. News of this assistance, released through Morgan and Company to the President of the Stock Exchange, had temporarily restored confidence. A few days later, the crisis became grave once more. This time the weak point appeared to be the securities of the Tennessee Coal and Iron Company of which one important brokerage firm alone held some $5,000,000 which banks refused to accept as collateral. On Saturday and Sunday evening J. P. Morgan sat smoking long black cigars and playing solitaire in a room next to the famous library of his house on Murray Hill. In the library, other financiers and industrial leaders conferred on various plans of action until at last they found one that Morgan thought would do the trick. That Sunday evening, Judge Elbert H. Gary and Henry Clay Frick of United States Steel boarded a special train to Washington, consisting of an engine and one Pullman. The next morning, they reached the White House while the President was still at breakfast.

Their proposition, in a nutshell, was that United States Steel buy Tennessee Iron and Coal for forty-five million dollars, thus substituting its sound securities for the shaky ones of the smaller company. The question they wanted T.R. to answer was whether, if U.S. Steel did this, the corporation would be vulnerable to prosecution under the Sherman Anti-Trust Law. They needed an answer before the Stock Exchange opened in New York; and if they could go ahead with the purchase it would mean saving not only the firm in question but numerous others linked with it in the financial community. Roosevelt called Root to the White House and that astute counselor, far better versed in the intricacies of finance than the President, signified approval. Five minutes before the exchange opened in New York, Morgan's partner, George Perkins, waiting on a special line to the White House, got the call he was waiting for. The President had said that it was all right to make the purchase.

Detailed accounts of that White House meeting were later published by three of the four parties to it. Gary's and Root's confirmed that of the President's which, in a letter to his Attorney General, apparently written for the record, was as follows:

"Judge Gary and Mr. Frick informed me that as a mere business transaction they do not care to purchase the stock . . . because but little benefit will come to the Steel Corporation. . . . They further informed me that . . . the acquisition of the property in question will not raise [their proportion of the steel industry as a whole] above sixty percent . . . I answered that, while of course I could not advise them to take the action proposed, I felt it no public duty of mine to interpose any objections."

That the purchase by U.S. Steel of the Tennessee Iron and Coal Company did in fact end the panic has never been seriously questioned. Critics of the President then and later have asserted that he was victimized by Gary and Frick and that they had used the crisis to secure Presidential permission to pick up an important subsidiary at a fraction of its real value. Probably no evidence will ever be forthcoming to prove precisely what motives were uppermost in the minds of Roosevelt's visitors that long-ago morning. Only cynics so naive as to believe that human vanity can have no basis except a mercenary one will deride Judge Gary's later reply to the charge: ". . . Everyone connected with the United

States Steel Corporation cares more for his conduct and reputation and his character than . . . for making or losing a few
dollars."

To dwell on a few of the major episodes of any period of
history, however briefly, inevitably tends to imply that these
were the only important things that happened in it. In the
case of Roosevelt's second term in the Presidency, such distortion may be especially damaging to the truth. It was exactly
the quantity and the variety of things that suddenly appeared
to be going on all at once and everywhere that, more than
anything else, gave the era its special character. T.R. was
often the reason that the things happened or, by his lively
participation, the reason that they seemed, or were, noteworthy and important.

There was, for instance, the matter of the "muckrakers."
Writers at the turn of the century, like most of their kind
before and since, tended to take the sorry view that all was
not as it should be. Newspapers, magazines, and publishing
houses found that readers were in a mood to respond to this
point of view. A flourishing swarm of able polemicists were
soon competing with each other in discovering scandals and
shortcomings, everywhere from the halls of Congress which
provided David Graham Phillips with material for a predecessor of *Advise and Consent* called *The Treason of the
Senate,* to the hog pens of Chicago, which provided Upton
Sinclair with one of the few milieus not later explored by his
ubiquitous Lanny Budd, in a book called *The Jungle.* Even
more energetic in this field than the novelists were eminent
journalists like Lincoln Steffens, Ida Tarbell, Ray Stannard
Baker and a shoal of others, most of whom T.R. had encountered at first hand and all of whom he somehow found
time to read, along with such less perishable stuff as *The Song*

of Roland in archaic French—of which his tennis cabinet crony, Ambassador Jules Jusserand, gave him a copy that later enabled T.R. to astound Critic Hamlin Garland by his knowledge of the subject.

The "muckrakers" got their name from T.R. when, in a speech at the Gridiron Club, he suggested that maybe such polemicists were carrying the thing a bit too far. The analogy he drew was with the character in Bunyan's *Pilgrim's Progress* who had a propensity for toil of the same unsanitary category. More to the point than this christening was the way in which T.R. castigated, or co-operated with, the muckrakers, as circumstances indicated. *The Jungle,* for example, was of considerable help in enabling him to get Congress to pass a Pure Food Law which, heartily resented by the meatpackers when first proposed, later received their reluctant endorsement. Meanwhile, he engaged in a lengthy correspondence with Sinclair of which a good portion consisted of literary criticism and advice. Stressing the importance of the social message in fiction, this advice was of a kind to which many later-day critics—much less averse to "messages" when displayed in proletarian works—have tended to take grave exception.

In response to Sinclair's first letter, T.R. spoke well of his book, invited him to visit the White House and then went on to disparage a clergyman whose endorsement of *The Jungle* Sinclair had quoted. "I think the preacher furnishes his measure when he compares you to Tolstoy, Zola and Gorki, intending thereby to praise you," wrote the Chief Executive. "The abortiveness of the late revolution in Russia sprang precisely from the fact that too much of the leadership was of the Gorki type and therefore the kind of leadership which can never lead anybody anywhere save into a Serbonian bog. Of course the net result of Zola's writings has been evil.

Where one man has gained from them a shuddering horror at existing wrong . . . a hundred have simply had the lascivious, the beast side of their natures strengthened and intensified by them. . . . As for Tolstoy, his novels are good, but his so-called religious and reformatory writings constitute one of the age-forces which tell seriously for bad. . . ."

In another letter, T.R. imparted counsel when Sinclair grew upset over attacks on him by the Chicago *Tribune*: "P.S. no 2. Your second telegram has just come; really, Mr. Sinclair, you *must* keep your head. It is absurd to become so nervous over such an article. Hundreds such appear about me all the time, with quite as little foundation."

In responding to his understandable urge to keep an eye on the U.S. literary scene in general, T.R. felt no need to confine himself to works of social significance. Works of a scientific and educational nature also attracted his attention, and most especially those that dealt with his special field of biology. During the early 1900's, when animals perhaps tended to impinge more on the U.S. consciousness than they do nowadays, nature writing of all sorts abounded in the national press, from the learned studies of naturalists like John Burroughs or John Muir, to the eloquent fiction of Rudyard Kipling or Ernest Seton Thompson. While prepared to endorse such eminent practitioners, T.R. was much less pleased with many of their imitators who, in works purporting to be non-fiction, made the error of crediting animals with ability to think, act, or feel like human beings.

First object of T.R.'s wrath in this field was a clergyman named William Joseph Long whose popular works dealt with such adroit creatures as a woodcock with a broken leg who made a do-it-yourself plaster cast out of mud and grass. In 1907, Roosevelt's patience burst its bounds and he wrote an article for *Everybody's* magazine in which he attacked "nature-fakers" generally and Mr. Long in particular. No doubt amazed to find himself so singled out for Presidential censure, that unfortunate might have been interested by T.R.'s explanation in a letter to Burroughs: ". . . I ought not to do this but I was having an awful time toward the end of the session and I felt I simply had to permit myself some diversion."

Roosevelt's self-imposed concern with the world of letters went far beyond even the nature-fakers and extended to such details as the letters themselves. In 1906, he got wind of an organization called the Spelling Reform Association, headed by his good friend Brander Matthews which proposed some three hundred spelling changes like "fulfill" to "fulfil," "dropped" to "dropt," and "through" to "thru." T.R., whose own orthography had always been highly individualistic—especially in troublesome locutions such as "Cleaveland" or "do'n't"—plunged into the struggle with his usual élan. He instructed the Government Printing Office to use the new spellings in all future publication and sat back to await the storm which was not long coming. The New York *Times* stated that it would regard the novelties in question as misprints and "correct them into English." Henry Watterson in his Louisville *Courier* suggested that Roosevelt's own name should be spelt as "Rucefelt," with "the first silabel riming with goose."

This was one of the few issues on which T.R. eventually sustained a resounding, and perhaps merited, defeat. The House of Representatives reversed his order to the Printing Office and ordered it to use standard spelling in all public documents, including Presidential ones. Roosevelt surrendered promptly and explained why to Matthews: "I could not by fighting have kept the new spelling in and it was evidently worse than useless to go into an undignified contest when I was beaten." T.R., however, continued to use most of the three hundred novelties in his private correspondence.

No less noteworthy than the way in which T.R. lent the august prestige of his office to decisions about the best way to spell "thru" or the sins of the nature-fakers was his intense personal participation in matters of greater national import. In keeping with his later confession that "I took Panama," was the degree to which he kept in close touch with the progress of work on the Isthmus. When Chairman Theodore Shonts of the Canal Commission demanded dismissal of his sanitation officer, Major William C. Gorgas, T.R. looked into the matter carefully and backed Gorgas in the anti-Yellow Fever campaign—without which the whole venture would almost surely have failed. When labor difficulties threatened, he wrote Taft, by this time his Secretary of War: "That Canal is to be dug, to be dug by Chinese labor or any other labor that we can get hold of, and the labor union men are to do their work up to the handle on the Isthmus and be subordinate if they are to be well treated; nevertheless Shonts and Stevens must keep in mind the fact that they are not now working for Hill on the Great Northern but for the United States Government. . . ."

Long-standing precedent forbade the Chief Executive to leave the continental limits of the United States. T.R. was the first to break it—to go to Panama with Mrs. Roosevelt on the battleship *Louisiana* in November of 1906, when he spent three days inspecting the job in a fashion best described by himself in a letter to Kermit:

"Our visit to Panama was most successful as well as most interesting. We were there three days and we worked from morning till night. The second day I was up at a quarter to six and got to bed at a quarter to twelve, and I do not believe that in the intervening time, save when I was dressing, there were ten consecutive minutes when I was not busily at work in some shape or form. For two days there were uninterrupted tropic rains without a glimpse of the sun . . . so that we saw the climate at its worst. It was just what I desired to do. . . ."

Submarines were novelties in 1905 and, as Commander-in-Chief, T.R. naturally wanted to inspect one. When the Navy sent *The Plunger* into Oyster Bay one late August afternoon, the President wasted no time wiggling through the eighteen-inch hatch of the conning tower, followed by her blithe commander, Charles "Daredevil" Nelson. *The Plunger* spent the next three hours doing starts, turns, and "porpoise dives" in Long Island Sound, much of the time with T.R. at the controls. "I've had many a splendid day's fun in my life," he remarked on disembarking, "but I can't remember ever having crowded so much of it into such a few hours." In a letter to Speck von Sternburg he elaborated further: ". . . I went down in it chiefly because I did not want to have the officers and enlisted men think I wanted them to try things I was reluctant to try myself. I believe a good deal can be done with these submarines although there is always the danger of people getting carried away with the idea. . . ."

During the last months of his second term Roosevelt became disturbed over the poor physical condition in which some senior Army and Navy officers found themselves and issued an executive order requiring a fitness test that involved riding ninety miles in three days. As Commander-in-Chief, he naturally felt eligible for this test himself, with consequences described in a letter to Kermit:

"There has been a good deal of talk in Congress and in the papers and among the grumblers in the Army and Navy about my physical exercise order, which as a matter of fact was very moderate. So I concluded, on the suggestion of Dr. Rixey, to ride ninety miles in one day myself, which would put a stop to any grumbling because I required other people to ride ninety miles in three days. Accordingly, yesterday Dr. Rixey, Dr. Grayson, Archie Butt, and I rode out to Warrenton and back from and to the White House. It was just ninety-eight miles, altho the people at Warrenton claim it was 104. We left the White House a few minutes after half past three in the morning and got back there a few minutes after half past eight in the evening, lunching at Warrenton, where I had to shake hands with prominent citizens, say a word to the school children, &c. We had sent out relays of horses, and each rode four horses, riding each horse twice as the journey back was over the same ground. I began and ended the day on old Roswell, who is really a perfect trump. The last fifteen miles in were done in pitch darkness and with a blizzard of sleet blowing in our faces. But we got thru safely, and altho we are a little stiff and tired nobody is laid up."

According to Sir Edward Grey, Britain's long time Foreign Minister, T.R. was a man to whom adventures happened naturally. Another way of putting it might be to say that he was a man who could not help finding adventure in everything that happened. Roosevelt's capacity for adventures was revealed not only in the large number of them that occurred while he was in the White House but also in the large amount that he found to say about them, much of it exciting, funny, penetrating, or all three at once. The stream, or flood, of letters that taxed the endurance of the several secretaries to whom he liked to dictate when having his hair cut, riding in carriages, or even changing his clothes may have provided some grounds for the jibe that his motto was, or should have been, "No sooner done than said." It also happily provides for readers nowadays an enlightening picture of the strenuous life that often seemed to make the White House vibrate like a tuning fork during the seven and a half years that the Roosevelts occupied it.

The major social event of the Roosevelt's first winter in the White House had been Alice's coming-out party. The major social event of the winter of 1906 was her White House wedding to the well-to-do and well-connected young Ohio congressman, Nicholas Longworth. Warship-board romance between the two had developed the previous fall, when both were in the party of forty-odd senators, representatives, and others who accompanied Secretary of War Taft on an official tour of the Far East including Tokyo, Peking, Seoul and Manila. Between her debut and her wedding, the conduct of the President's oldest daughter had not always been of a sort to set her father's mind at rest. Escapades like setting an automobile speed record between Newport and Boston and letting her name be used with that of the young actress, Ethel Barrymore, to advertise a charity bazaar indicated a mettlesome disposition but also led to a plethora of headlines. When "Princess Alice" popped in and out of her father's office three times during a call at the White House by Owen Wister, the latter felt emboldened to ask: "Theodore, isn't there anything you can do to control Alice?"

"I can do one of two things," replied T.R. "I can be President of the United States or I can control Alice. I cannot possibly do both."

While all of Alice's escapades tended to be highly publicized, those of her younger brothers and sisters, often also of a sort to arouse parental concern, were by no means ignored in the nation's press. Indeed, the attention given to Ted, Jr., who, while Alice was touring the Orient, had become a freshman at Harvard, was so assiduous that the President felt obliged to write President Eliot to see if there was any way that he could be protected from reporters: ". . . This crass, hideous vulgarity is not merely extremely distasteful, but may have a damaging effect . . . in the very improbable event of your having any advice to give I should be glad to get it." To Ted, Jr., he took a more chatty, man-to-man tone: "It is just one of those occasions where the big bear cannot help the small bear at all though he sympathizes awfully with him. . . . I have been playing tennis with Mr. Pinchot, who beat me three sets to one. . . . Do'n't let those newspaper creatures and kindred idiots drive you one hairs-breadth from the line you had marked out, in football or anything else; & avoid any fuss, if possible."

In football, the line Ted, Jr., had marked out, since he was too small to hope to play on the varsity later, was to win a place on the freshman eleven. As the lightest man in the line on the Harvard team that lost to Yale, he suffered a broken nose in the season's climactic game and distinguished himself further by dismissing charges that Yale had singled him out for special punishment. "They played a clean straight game and played no favorites," he wrote his father, much to the latter's satisfaction. T.R. was less enthusiastic three months later, when Ted, Jr., found himself on probation for poor marks and stood in "serious danger of separation from college." This crisis led to a stern letter which, however, ended on an encouraging note: "Anyone might come a cropper like this: now get up and retrieve it."

Meanwhile, the antics of Quentin and Archie served to enhance life at the White House for visitors and staff as well as for its principal occupants. Ethel who eventually grew up enough to have her debut there in the last winter of T.R.'s second term, was by this time, according to her father, a "perfect little mother" but her two small brothers nonetheless got frequently out of hand. Typical of Quentin's peccadilloes, as recounted by Earl Looker in his book *The White House Gang*, was that of using a historic portrait of Andrew Jackson as a target in a spitball contest with several other unruly playmates, including one of the small Tafts.

The President not only participated in most of the livelier activities of his offspring but also kept those who were away from home apprised of what the latter were up to in letters, often illustrated by freehand drawings. When, near the end of his father's second term, Archie came down with diphtheria, the entire nation was almost as worried as his parents. "This dreadful time," wrote Edith Roosevelt to her sister Emily, after whom Alice had named her pet green garden snake, Emily Spinach, "has been a terrible strain on Theodore."

One thing that tended to lessen the strain upon T.R. of his immensely variegated and intricately interwoven public and private lives was the calm, resourceful, and understanding devotion of his life. According to Mrs. Stuyvesant Fish, a fashionable New York hostess of the period, "Mrs. Roosevelt dresses on three hundred dollars a year—and looks it." While almost as inaccurate as it was insolent, this comment missed the point, for it was not necessary for Edith Roosevelt to be a fashion plate to be, by many reliable accounts, the most expert hostess in White House history before or since. Intellectually as well as socially well equipped to relish the range and incongruity of the guests she was called upon to entertain, she handled them with grace, tact, and elegance.

Though Edith Roosevelt exerted constant influence on her husband's thought—among other things, she sorted his mail and read the papers for him—she was careful never to call attention to her role in his activities. Some indication of the way she influenced and at the same time assisted and amused him is implied in an incident involving the astute Ambassador

Jusserand. At Sagamore Hill, one of T.R.'s favorite forms of exercise—later emulated, after his abdication, by his erstwhile friend, the German Kaiser—was chopping wood. When one day in doing so, he inadvertently chopped down a tree that fell across the telephone wires, the news reached Mrs. Roosevelt at the family dinner table. When she smiled in what T.R. considered an altogether too understanding fashion, he suggested that the mishap might have been her fault since, in her role as Chief Forester of Sagamore Hill, she had not marked the trees he was to cut. When T.R. added that "I will not hold you up to scorn before your children if you will let the subject drop, once and for all," Jusserand ventured to point out that Edith Roosevelt had not yet mentioned it, whereupon T.R. expostulated:

"Ah! But you don't know my wife. She has a language all her own. The telephone will never ring now that my wife will not begin to chuckle to herself, and if the cursed thing ever gets out of order . . . she will tell the servant to see if the wires are still up or if the trees are down. . . . She has a humor which is more tyrannical than half the tempestuous women of Shakespeare."

Conspicuously missing in the eight volumes of T.R.'s published letters—representing a mere ten per cent of his total correspondence—are any letters at all to Edith Carow Roosevelt. In accord with her exacting sense of the appropriate, she made completely sure that none would ever be published by burning them all after his death. Thus the closest approximation of what his marriage in general and his wife's tyrannical humor in particular meant to T.R. must be inferred from what he wrote to others. Shortly before Ted, Jr., was to be married, his father wrote him from Africa: "Mother, always tender, gentle and considerate, and always loving, yet when necessary pointed out where I was thoughtless and therefore inconsiderate and selfish, instead of submitting to it. Had she not done this it would in the end have made her life very much harder, and mine very much less happy."

Writing to Lawrence F. Abbott of *The Outlook,* at about the same time, Roosevelt summed up his thoughts about love and marriage generally: "I think that the love of the really happy husband and wife—*not* purged of passion, but with passion heated to a white heat of intensity and purity and tenderness and consideration, and with many another feeling added thereto—is the loftiest and most ennobling influence that comes into the life of any man or woman, even loftier and more ennobling than wise and tender love for children. . . ."

In concept and in execution, nothing could have been more completely in the Roosevelt style than the last great act of his Presidency—the sending of the Great White Fleet around the world. This project originated from discussions with Japan about the vexing problem of large-scale immigration into Southern California of coolie laborers who caused racial difficulties by upsetting local wage scales. With the aid of Taft, a typically Rooseveltian solution to this problem was presently found in the form of the renowned "gentlemen's agreement": in exchange for a U.S. promise to welcome visiting Japanese businessmen, scholars, and tourists, Japanese authorities would keep potentially undesirable immigrants at home. Meanwhile, however, as Roosevelt later informed his English historian friend, Trevelyan, "I had become uncomfortably conscious of a very very slight undertone of veiled truculence in their communications . . . I finally made up my mind that they thought I was afraid of them . . . it was time for a show down."

A round-the-world voyage by the U.S. fleet would, among

other things, show that while the U.S. entertained no feelings whatever of hostility to Japan, this was not because she did not dare to entertain them; and also, incidentally, as T.R. later mentioned to German Admiral von Tirpitz, it would show that "there were fleets of the white races which were totally different from the fleet of poor Rodjestvensky." Secondly, it would serve to stimulate U.S. interest in the Navy and make indelibly clear for the future T.R.'s insistence that, if the U.S. really meant to take its place among the great powers, it needed first of all to be greatly powerful. Thirdly, on the practical level, the voyage would dramatize the importance of keeping hard at work to finish the Panama Canal, give the fleet a chance to perfect coaling procedures that might be needed in a war, and provide chances for practice in gunnery and like exercises. Finally, it would tell the rest of the world once more, politely but eloquently, that the U.S. was now a nation second to none and more than able to take care of itself in both great oceans of the globe. But all these individual considerations, while comprehensible enough, were not really what gave the venture Rooseveltian style.

The style had more to do with the way that it said them all together—and said them dramatically, at exactly the right time, in terms of dramatic action. It had to do with the way in which, having made up his mind that he had the power to send the fleet and should send it, that T.R. let nothing stand in his way; so that when the Chairman of the Senate's Naval Affairs Committee, Maine's Hale, objected to spending the money, T.R. replied that there was already enough money to send the fleet to the Pacific and if the rest were not forthcoming, it could stay there. Lastly and most important of all, it had to do with the way in which the deed itself—unprecedented, difficult, and fraught with possibilities for muddle or misinterpretation—was, after being prepared to perfection, carried off without a hitch, on schedule and in high good humor.

On December 16, 1907, the President, having given the order, "Proceed to duty assigned," from the deck of his yacht *Mayflower,* watched the column of sixteen battleships, manned by 12,000 officers and sailors, steam out of Hampton Roads. The voyage around South America, with gala stops at major ports, confirmed the impression of friendliness made by Secretary Root's goodwill tour the year before. On the West Coast, the torpedo-boat squadron—which had accompanied the bigger ships that far at the personal request of its officers to T.R.—was left behind. After stops in New Zealand, Australia, and the Philippines, the Fleet reached Tokyo on October 18, 1908, shortly before the U.S. presidential elections. Roosevelt had taken pains to write Admiral C. S. Sperry, who had replaced Admiral Robley D. Evans as Commander-in-Chief at San Francisco, to make sure that shore leave parties be chosen carefully with an eye to avoiding any possibility of rowdiness on shore. The three-day stay went off in festival style, with a special issue of the *Jiji Shimpon* to commemorate the event.

On the way home around the world, the battleships passed through the globe's only completed intercontinental passageway at Suez. The great earthquake at Messina had occurred just in time to enable them to set a precedent for similar naval action in Japan in 1923, by bringing help to the survivors. Then, accompanied by a flotilla of cruisers, came the voyage home and the welcome by the President at Hampton Roads, where he saw the white hulls flash over the horizon, on time to the minute, on the morning of Washington's Birthday, 1909.

T.R.'s greeting to Admiral Sperry and his men summed up the high points of the feat: "You have falsified every prediction of the prophets of failure. In all your long cruise not an accident worthy of mention has happened to a single battle-ship, nor yet to the cruisers or torpedo-boats. . . . As a war machine, the fleet comes back in better shape than it went out. In addition you, the officers and men of this formidable fighting force, have shown yourselves the best of all possible ambassadors and heralds of peace. . . . We welcome you home to the country whose good repute among nations has been raised by what you have done."

According to T.R. himself, ". . . The most important service that I rendered to peace was the voyage of the battle fleet around the world." Some later historians have argued, not always convincingly, that later events proved him wrong in this. In any event, the fleet's return in glory made an appropriate climax to the years in the White House that ended ten days later. The inauguration of William Howard Taft, whom T.R. had carefully picked and groomed as his successor, went off in fine style on March fourth. That morning T.R.'s old and close friend, Henry Adams, dropped in alone to say good-by. "I shall miss you very very much," he said to T.R. as they shook hands. No one could better have expressed the feelings of the nation.

XI

W HEN people have spoken to me as to what America should do with its ex-Presidents, I have always answered that there was one ex-President as to whom they need not concern themselves in the least, because I would do for myself. It would be to me personally an unpleasant thing to be pensioned and given some honorary position. I emphatically do not desire to clutch at the fringe of departing greatness. Indeed, to me there is something rather attractive, something in the way of living up to a proper democratic ideal, in having a President go out of office just as I shall go, and become absolutely and without reservation a private man, and do any honorable work which he finds to do. My first work will be to go to Africa for the National Museum. I am fifty, I have led a very sedentary life for ten years, and I feel that this is my last chance for something in the nature of a 'great adventure'. . . ."

For most men, seven and a half years in the U.S. Presidency, especially years like those that T.R. had spent in it, would inevitably represent the high-water mark of a career. Whatever came afterward would necessarily be anticlimax. T.R. was immune to anticlimax. In his case, the years that followed the Presidency were in many ways the most exciting and the most significant of his career. One reason for this is set forth in this excerpt from a letter to his British friend, John St. Loe Strachey, who had written a learned article about "America and Her Ex-Presidents" for the London *Spectator* of November 14, 1908, and to whom Roosevelt wished to impart some first-hand information on the subject. The information differed from that which he had already given his son Ted about the same matter chiefly in that, when writing to the latter, he had added: "I have had the best time of any man of my age in all the world . . . I have enjoyed myself in the White House more than I have ever known any other President to enjoy himself, and . . . I am going to enjoy myself thoroly when I leave. . . ."

Among the "thoroly" enjoyable aspects of departure from the White House were his relations with his successor, William Howard Taft. These relations had had their origin, when T.R., then a Civil Service Commissioner, was writing to Taft, then Solicitor General of the United States: "Can you dine with me in the *most* frugal manner, Friday night at 8 o'clock, at 721 Rhode Island Avenue? No dress suit—I haven't got any. . . ." During T.R.'s Presidency, Taft had served with distinction first as Governor General of the Philippines and later, after Elihu Root's resignation, as Secretary of War. Meanwhile, T.R.'s approval of, and affection for, Taft had so increased that by 1908, he became convinced —since Root's background as a corporation lawyer ruled him out—that Taft was his logical successor in the White House.

Having chosen Taft as his successor, Roosevelt felt it his

obligation first to get him nominated and then to get him elected. Of the two jobs the former was probably the more difficult since, given half a chance, the delegates at Chicago in 1908 would have nominated Roosevelt himself. However, by making it unmistakably clear to all his supporters that he meant to stick to his decision not to run again, and with the assistance of Lodge as the Convention's chairman, it was accomplished—despite a forty-nine minute cheer by the delegates that greeted the first mention of T.R.'s name. During the campaign against William Jennings Bryan, the Democratic party's perennial loser, Taft ran on Roosevelt's record, although Mrs. Taft, who was not a Roosevelt devotee, considered this a rather superfluous display of gratitude. Roosevelt's high opinion of the candidate was expressed as frankly to Taft himself as it was to good friends across the water like George Otto Trevelyan, to whom he wrote:

"He has no more fear in dealing with the interests of great corporate wealth than he has in dealing with the leaders of the most powerful labor unions; and if either go wrong he has not the slightest hesitation in antagonizing them. To strength and courage, clear insight, and practical common sense, he adds a very noble and disinterested character." Taft's only shortcoming, T.R. felt, was a certain engaging lack of self-confidence which he, even more than Mrs. Taft, was concerned to overcome. "You blessed old trump, I have always said you would be the greatest president, bar only Washington and Lincoln, and I feel mighty inclined to strike out the exceptions," he wrote to his elephantine protégé. During the campaign he provided sound technical advice: "Let the audience see you smile *always,* because I feel that your nature shines out so transparently when you do smile— you big, generous, high-minded fellow."

T.R.'s outspoken efforts to persuade Taft to think as well

of himself as he thought of Taft continued during the interval between election and the inauguration on March 4. When Taft first intimated that he would keep Roosevelt's cabinet intact, and then decided to dismiss all members of it except Postmaster General George Meyer, and Secretary of Agriculture James Wilson, T.R.'s reaction was characteristically generous: "Taft is going about this thing just as I would do." Mrs. Taft's unhappy decision to replace the White House staff of white ushers by colored flunkeys in livery was deeply wounding to Mrs. Roosevelt, who felt that the ushers deserved to be rewarded for their years of loyal service, but T.R. overlooked it, so far as possible. On their last night in the White House, the Roosevelts, with characteristic courtesy, invited the Tafts to dine and stay overnight. The next morning, the two old friends rode to the Capitol together but after the oath-taking, held indoors because of the bad weather, T.R. broke precedent by going directly to the railroad station, to leave on an ordinary Pullman, instead of riding back along Pennsylvania Avenue with his successor. Mrs. Taft—to her considerable satisfaction, as she later recalled—replaced him at the new President's right hand on the drive to the White House.

Any suspicion that developments like these betokened the beginning of a rift between T.R. and his successor might have been readily dispelled by a glance at their correspondence with each other. On the last day of 1908, T.R. wound up one item in it with the words: "Ha ha! *you* are making up your Cabinet. *I* in a light-hearted way have spent the morning testing the rifles for my African trip. Life has compensations!" When T.R. boarded the *Hamburg* on March 23, the new President sent Captain Archie Butt—T.R.'s stylish military aide, whom Mrs. Taft had deemed worthy of retaining in the new regime—to say farewell and bestow parting gifts. The gifts were an autographed picture and a collapsible gold ruler with a pencil in one end, inscribed: "Theodore Roosevelt from William Howard Taft, Good-bye—Good luck—and a Safe Return." With them went a touching letter whose opening phrases were especially revealing:

My dear Theodore:
    If I followed my impulse, I should still say "My dear Mr. President." I cannot overcome the habit. When I am addressed as "Mr. President," I turn to see whether you are not at my elbow. When I read in the newspaper of a conference between the speaker and the President, or between Senator Aldrich and the President, I wonder what the subject of the conference was. . . . I do nothing in the Executive Office without considering what you would do under the same circumstances. . . . I am under obligation to you to see to it that your judgment in selecting me as your successor and in bringing about the succession shall be vindicated. . . .

Roosevelt's African expedition compared to his previous shooting trips in Maine and the U.S. West more or less as his political experiences in the White House compared with those he had encountered as President of the Montana Stockmen's Association. Scheduled to last for almost a year, it involved traveling some 1500 miles from Mombasa on the East Coast, to Fashoda, on the White Nile, through all kinds of country from the highlands of Kenya to the feverish swamps of the Congo. The objective was to secure not only big game, though this had first priority for T.R. and Kermit, but also specimens of every species of creature that inhabited the whole East side of the continent. Obviously an excursion on this scale involved extensive preparation. The preliminary arrangements, which went forward simultaneously with the Taft campaign, the global circumnavigation of the Great

White Fleet and all the other pressing activities of T.R.'s last year in office, were by no means limited to the lighthearted testing of a small arsenal of big-game rifles.

Among the secondary conveniences for T.R. of having had the White House as a winter residence was that this provided an opportunity for installing certain much-needed architectural improvements at Sagamore Hill. Most noteworthy of these was a large room suitable to the entertainment of distinguished visitors. To such visitors, the new addition, known to the family as the North Room but to others as the Trophy Room, often seemed dangerously crowded even when no one at all was in it, owing to the multiplicity of heads, horns, and skins of wild animals which it soon came to contain. However, since the walls of the rest of Sagamore Hill were already adequately tenanted by previous testimonials to the owner's marksmanship, the first and most obvious necessity imposed by the African excursion was to find some suitable repository for the additional huge prizes which were sure to result from it in numbers exceeding the capacity of any private residence even if it had been empty instead of overstocked to begin with. The President solved this difficulty with his customary foresight and sense of the appropriate by choosing, as the beneficiary of his renewed efforts in the field, the Smithsonian Institution at Washington, the largest and most receptive museum in the nation. To help collect, preserve, and later write about the quarry, the Smithsonian assigned three top-notch specialists in such matters headed by the distinguished Army naturalist, Dr. Edgar Alexander Mearns.

Preserving the hides of such sizable beasts as elephants, hippopotamuses and rhinoceroses for later exhibition, either flat or stuffed, required vast stores of paraphernalia, including some four tons of salt. Hand-carrying this stupendous burden, in addition to the trophies themselves and the ordinary but extensive impedimenta of the huntsmen, including their numerous and heavy weapons, across the vast distances of the Dark Continent meant enlisting an army of some 260 bearers, of whom 200 were needed for the scientific paraphernalia alone. Underwriting the baggage charges, along with those of the scientists and the supplies, was obviously an eleemosynary venture of the first magnitude, amounting eventually to some $75,000. Fortunately, however, with the aid of Presidential prestige, the Smithsonian was able to round up a good-sized pride of philanthropists headed by Andrew Carnegie, the greatest monetary benefactor of the age, to shoulder the major part of the financial burden.

The share of the burden that was not assumed by Carnegie and his colleagues was the comparatively minor item represented by the personal expenses of T.R. and Kermit, who was in effect playing hookey from his sophomore year at Harvard to accompany his father at the latter's instigation. These Roosevelt proposed to defray himself by writing, for *Scribner's* magazine and later book publication, a running story of his adventures as they occurred for which he was guaranteed an honorarium of $50,000. Set down in longhand by lamp or candlelight after the days on safari, and dispatched to New York through the wilderness by native runners, Roosevelt's on-the-spot account of the expedition eventually appeared in book form as *African Game Trails*. The volume which netted some $40,000 over the guarantee contains some of the best writing he ever did and remains to this day a model of sporting reportage which, for action and accuracy of observation, few subsequent practitioners in the field have been able to equal let alone surpass.

Shortly after T.R.'s departure, Harvard's recently retired President Charles W. Eliot published his celebrated "Five Foot Shelf" purporting to contain the quintessence of the

world's best writing. T.R. who received a copy of the Eliot list
from Edith Roosevelt commented on it somewhat brusquely
from Kenya in a letter to the Lodges: "It is all right as
a list of books which a cultivated man would like to read;
but as *the* list it strikes me as slightly absurd." He pointed out
that a selection which included Woolman's *Journal,* Penn's
Fruits of Solitude and the *Aeneid* while omitting all of
Herodotus, Tacitus, Thucydides, Aeschylus, Sophocles,
Moliére, and Homer among many others, scarcely compelled
unanimous concurrence.

The subject was one which had a special interest for T.R.
For his own safari-reading he had just compiled an entirely
independent collection which, while it overlapped Eliot's
in some instances, went him one better in the matter of bind-
ing. Instead of a "Five Foot Shelf," Roosevelt's collection—
presented to him as a parting memento by his sister Corinne
—was a "Pigskin Library," built to withstand the ravages of
travel under primitive conditions. Among the authors of the
sixty volumes it included were Browning, Bunyan, Carlyle,
Cooper, Dante, Dickens, Euripides, Holmes, Homer, Keats,
Longfellow, Poe, Swift, Tennyson, Mark Twain, and Shakespeare. Up to then never a devotee of the Bard, T.R. found
time between marching, shooting, and discharging his own
literary obligations, to attain a further familiarity with his
works which resulted in belated appreciation. An Appendix
to *African Game Trails* contains his comment on his books:

They were for use not ornament. I almost always had some
volume with me, either in my saddle-pocket or in the cartridge-
bag which one of my gun bearers carried to hold odds and
ends. Often my reading would be done while resting under a
tree at noon, perhaps beside the carcass of a beast I had killed,
or else while waiting for camp to be pitched; and in either
case it might be impossible to get water for washing. In con-

sequence the books were stained with blood, sweat, gun oil, dust and ashes; ordinary bindings either vanished or became loathsome, whereas pigskin merely grew to look as a well-used saddle looks.

On the blustery morning of March 23, Edith Roosevelt stayed at home but a festive crowd gathered on the pier at Hoboken, N.J., to see the ex-President off. T.R. asked all Rough Riders present to hold up their arms, so that he could identify them. Then he fought his way to shake hands and say good-by to each one individually. On board the *Hamburg*, Kermit made the aquaintance of a young widow named Ruth Draper, later to be internationally famous as a monologist. When the ship stopped at the Azores and Gibraltar, the naturalists went ashore to warm up for their later efforts by bringing back the first of the expedition's specimens. At Naples, the ex-President and his party, joined now by the renowned English hunter, explorer and ivory-trader, Frederick C. Selous, transferred to another German ship, the *Admiral*, for the voyage, via Suez, to Mombasa. "My three naturalists are trumps"; T.R. wrote to Corinne, "bird skins are drying in my room at the moment, just as if we were once more on the Nile." From Mombasa, the party proceeded by rail to a station in the Kapiti plains where, under instructions from Selous, the professional hunters R. J. Cunninghame and Leslie Tarlton had been organizing the safari. T.R. made this stage of the journey perched in a chair on the cow-catcher of the engine, thereby gathering material for his first *Scribner's* article, "A Railroad through the Pleistocene."

Less than two months after leaving Hoboken, the expedition was in full swing and, in his first letter from Africa to Cabot Lodge on May 15, T.R. recorded its progress: "Our hunting trip has lasted three weeks, and so far, has been very successful. We are in the settled country, and there has been no hardship whatsoever. I have killed four big lions, and two small ones, a bull rhino (which charged viciously, and might have done mischief had it not been for a lucky rather than a skillful shot which dropped him at fourteen paces), two giraffes, a zebra and various kinds of antelopes. Kermit has had very good luck too. . . ." Similar bulletins dispatched later to Elihu Root, Ted, Jr., Arthur Lee, Cecil Spring Rice, Andrew Carnegie, and a few other favored correspondents demonstrated the futility of the toast then fashionable in conservative circles in New York: "Health to the Lions!"

The Roosevelt expedition lasted eleven months, at the end of which T.R. had shot a total of two hundred and ninety-six animals of various sorts including six buffaloes, seven hippos, eight elephants, nine lions, thirteen rhinoceroses, fifteen zebras and twenty-eight gazelles. Kermit had done nearly as well, with a bag of two hundred and sixteen. As for the scientific side of the expedition, the three naturalists had assembled in East Africa alone a total of some 11,397 mammals, birds, fishes, reptiles, and batrachians, not to mention miscellaneous invertebrates, collected mainly by the most studious of the three trumps, Dr. Mearns. Theretofore East Africa's amazing variety of beasts had been represented in European and United States museums mainly by sporadic gifts from explorers, colonial officials, and big-game hunters. Roosevelt's expedition was the first large-scale systematic attempt to study the area. From it the Smithsonian derived what is still the world's most complete collection of East African flora and fauna.

The safari wound up with a final climactic hunt in the Congo, for the rare white rhinoceros of the Lado Enclave. T.R. and Kermit bagged no fewer than nine, providing the basis for a definitive monograph on the species. At the end of February, the expedition began the return journey down the White Nile, taking occasional shots at kob, lechwe and shoe-billed storks along the way.

We reached Khartoum on the afternoon of March 14, 1910 [wrote T.R. at the end of *African Game Trails*], and Kermit and I parted from our comrades of the trip with real regret; during the year we spent together there had not been a jar, and my respect and liking for them had grown steadily. Moreover, it was a sad parting from our faithful black followers, whom we knew we should never see again.

He was filled with joy a few days later by a reunion with Edith who had come up the Nile with Ethel to meet the party. "Catch me ever leaving her for a year again, if I can help it," he had written to Cecil Spring Rice while on safari the previous October. Now, after a festive stay with the legendary Slatin Pasha, an Austrian Baron, British Knight and former crony of the late renowned General Charles George "Chinese" Gordon, who had settled down in Khartoum as adviser to the then absent British Sirdar, the Roosevelt party set off for Cairo to start their homeward journey through Europe. For excitement in the field of ceremonious gaiety and glamor, this matched or excelled everything that the African safari had provided in the field of outdoor hardship and hazard.

Shortly before T.R.'s arrival at Khartoum, Egypt had been gravely alarmed by the assassination of the Christian Prime Minister, Boutros Pasha. T.R.'s first step into the troubled waters of European and colonial politics took the form of a rousing talk to the American mission in which he stupefied the Sudan's anti-British Moslem element by deploring this crime and stating that it was "incumbent on every decent citizen of the Sudan to uphold the present order of things." Lest there be any mistake as to his views on the matter, he denounced the assassination again when he reached Cairo.

By this time, however, a new and more pressing problem confronted him in connection with Pope Pius X at Rome, which was the next major stop on his itinerary.

The difficulty in Rome concerned T.R.'s request for an audience to which the Papal Secretary of State, the Spanish Cardinal Merry del Val, had replied by cable that it could be readily arranged on one condition. Present in Rome just then was a certain group of Methodist missionaries whose tactless proselytizing activities in the Holy City had reached a nadir of impropriety when one of their number, a learned authority by the name of Ezra Tipple, saw fit to refer to the Holy Father as "the whore of Babylon." The condition was that Roosevelt agree to have nothing to do with these offensive visitors. T.R. cabled back that while Pope Pius had unquestioned right "to receive or not to receive whomever he chooses for any reason that seems good to him. . . . I must decline to make any stipulations . . . which . . . limit my freedom of conduct." When T.R.'s ship reached Naples, Merry del Val countered with a new suggestion. This was that Roosevelt secretly agree not see the Methodists while announcing publicly that no such agreement had been made. This proposal, which T.R. later characterized as one which "a Tammany boodle alderman would have been ashamed to make," he also rejected, setting forth the upshot of the matter in a letter to Lodge on April 6:

"At Rome I had an elegant row, the details of which you have doubtless seen in the papers. The Pope imposed conditions upon my reception, requiring a pledge—secret or open —that I would not visit and speak to the Methodist Mission. Of course I declined absolutely to assent to any condition whatever, and the reception did not take place. Then with a folly as incredible as that of the Vatican itself, the Methodist Missionaries, whose game was perfectly simple because the

Pope had played it for them, and who had nothing to do but sit quiet, promptly issued an address of exultation which can only be called scurrilous, and with equal promptness I cancelled the arrangements I had made for seeing them. . . . I made it understood that I feared the most powerful Protestant Church just as little as I feared the Roman Catholics. If I were in politics, or intended to run for public office, I should regard the incident as gravely compromising my usefulness as a candidate, but inasmuch as I have no idea that I shall ever again be a candidate for anything, I can take unalloyed satisfaction in having rendered what I regard as a small service to the cause of right thinking in America. . . ."

More successful than Roosevelt's relations with the Pope were those which he struck up with King Victor Emmanuel III and Queen Helene of Italy, whom he found to be "delightful people," although some aspects of their court etiquette proved mildly confusing. Especially bothersome to T.R., when he attended a royal banquet, was the business of disposing of his hat which, on arriving at the palace, he handed to a servant who promptly gave it back to him. "When I was brought up to the Queen to take her in to dinner, I again thought it was time for me to get rid of my hat. But not a bit of it! I found that I was expected to walk in with the Queen on my arm, and my hat in the other hand—a piece of etiquette which reminded me of nothing with which I was previously acquainted except a Jewish wedding on the East Side of New York. . . . Both at the Italian Court and at the East Side wedding, however, some attendant took the hat as soon as I sat down at the table."

Equally astonishing was the procedure encountered by T.R. a few days later at Vienna where he paid a visit to the Emperor Francis Joseph. ". . . The Emperor and all the Austrian guests had one horrid habit. . . . The finger bowls were brought on, each with a small tumbler of water in the middle; and the Emperor and all the others proceeded to rinse their mouths and then empty them into their finger bowls. . . . However, all of the guests were delightful. . . ."

From Vienna, the Roosevelts went on to Paris where T.R. addressed the Sorbonne, then to Brussels where he met King Albert " a huge fair young man, evidently a thoroughly good fellow," and then Het Loo in Holland where he formed a poor opinion of Queen Wilhelmina—"obviously both conceited and bad-tempered . . . immensely impressed with the dignity of her position." At Copenhagen, the Roosevelts stayed at the palace with the Crown Prince and Crown Princess in the absence of the former's father. When their luggage was delayed and they were obliged to attend a royal court dinner in day clothes, the aplomb with which Edith Roosevelt met this emergency impressed the court chamberlain as ". . . vraiment royale!"

Norway, Roosevelt found "As funny a kingdom as was ever imagined outside opera bouffe—although it isn't opera bouffe at all for the Norwegians are a fine, serious, powerful lot of men and women. . . . They have no nobles, hardly even gentry; they are peasants and small townspeople—farmers, sailors, fisherfolk, mechanics, small traders. On this community a royal family is suddenly plumped down. It is much as if Vermont should offhand try the experiment of having a king. Yet it certainly seemed as if the experiment were entirely successful. . . . On the first afternoon, shortly after arriving, I was in the sitting room when in came the King and Queen with Olaf. . . . I gave Olaf various bloodcurdling bits of information about lions and elephants. . . . He was not a bit spoiled; his delight was a romp with his father and he speedily pressed Kermit and Ethel, whom he adored, into the games. In the end I too succumbed and romped with him as I used to romp with my own children when they were small. . . ." In Norway, too, T.R. addressed "the Nobel Committee, at the University, at a huge 'Banquet' of the canonical—and unspeakably awful type." It was there that he first proposed the "League for Peace" which served as the first rough outline of what Woodrow Wilson later shaped up into the ill-fated League of Nations.

From Norway, the Roosevelts proceeded to Sweden where again, in the absence of the King, the Crown Prince and Princess were their hosts. Roosevelt found Sweden "delightful," Stockholm "a delightful city" and the Swedes "fine people." Nonetheless, to a confirmed believer in large families, some drawbacks were apparent: "I was saddened to see how Socialism had grown among the people, and in a very ugly form; for one of the Socialist tracts was an elaborate appeal to stop having children; the Socialists being so bitter in their class hatred as to welcome race destruction as a means of slaking it. Personally, as Sweden practically has not only free but almost democratic institutions, I could not understand the extreme bitterness of the Socialist attitude. . . ."

The continental phase of T.R.'s European tour was climaxed and concluded by his historic visit to Germany where he and the Kaiser, then easily the world's two outstanding international celebrities, spent a day together reviewing the world's greatest army.

"Roosevelt, my friend," said the Kaiser, "I wish to welcome you in the presence of my guards; I ask you to remember that you are the only private citizen who has ever joined the Emperor in reviewing the troops of Germany."

According to T.R.'s own later account of the occasion, the Kaiser "talked steadily" during the maneuvers, which lasted for five hours. This would have been an unusual achievement for anyone engaged in a tête-à-tête with T.R.; and numerous photographs taken by a court photographer of the two splendidly mounted dignitaries suggest that, in fact, His Majesty may have conveyed this impression to his visitor merely by occasionally interrupting. A set of these photographs, with lighthearted captions written on the reverse side, were sent to Roosevelt by the Kaiser to commemorate the occasion. Under one of them, which shows the Emperor rather pensively listening to his guest, the donor had scrawled, "The Colonel of the Rough Riders instructing the German Emperor in field tactics."

When an emissary, presumably from the Foreign Office, called to request T.R. to send the pictures back, the recipient good-humoredly refused, saying "Oh, no! His Majesty, the Kaiser, gave the photographs to me and I propose to retain them." He took them with him to Sagamore Hill where, mounted between sheets of glass to make both pictures and inscriptions visible, they were scrupulously preserved in a wooden box in the Trophy Room.

Roosevelt's comments on the courts and on the countries of Europe—in most of which he received heroic welcomes from local populace as well as sovereigns—were summed up in a long confidential letter which he wrote some sixteen months after his return and tactfully addressed in part to historian George Otto Trevelyan and in part to his friend David Gray, a Buffalo, N.Y., journalist and author. Comparable for humor, insight, and candor, to his 1903 letter to John Hay about the U.S. Far West, this communication provides an unmatched picture of the continent and its leading characters in what proved to be a final royal flowering. Typically Rooseveltian in its timing, T.R.'s tour of Europe coincided so perfectly with the end of the Edwardian era that, when the monarch from whom it took its name died suddenly of pneumonia while T.R. was in Oslo, it required scarcely a change in his railroad bookings to appear at the London funeral as President Taft's special representative with the rank of Ambassador. Nine kings and forty-four royal princes, including most of those to whom he had just been paying ceremonial visits, turned up for the obsequies also. These comprised an event which history, for all its well-deserved repute on this score, is unlikly to repeat in the foreseeable future—and of which T.R.'s confidential account constitutes a reportorial classic.

One noteworthy passage in T.R.'s reportage concerns the dinner given by King George V on the evening before the final procession: "The night before the funeral there was a veritable wake,—I hardly know what else to call it. King George gave a dinner to the special ambassadors in Buckingham Palace, the palace in which the dead king his father was lying in state. There was some seventy of us all told. Each man as he arrived said some word of perfunctory condolence to the king our host, and then on with the revel! It was not possible to keep up an artificial pretense of grief any longer, and nobody tried; and it was precisely like any other entertainment. The king sat in the middle of one side of the table, and the Emperor opposite him, and the rest of us were arranged elsewhere without as far as I could judge much attention being paid to rank. I sat with Prince Henry of Prussia on my right hand, and on my left a tall, shambling young man in a light blue uniform, whose card proclaimed him to be the Prince of Cumberland, or Prince Somebody of Cumberland, I forget which. For lack of other subjects of conversation, I said to him that although his title was English, yet that he himself seemed to be German; and with a melancholy glance at the very vivacious Emperor, who was diagonally opposite us, he answered that he ought to be Prince of Brunswick and King of Hanover, and would be 'if it were not for him,' nodding his head to indicate the Emperor. I felt like suggesting to him to relieve his feelings by throwing a carafe at the usurper.

"As soon as I entered the room the Bulgarian Czar came up to speak to me, and to thank me for various things I had done for the Bulgarians, a people who have always interested me and in whom I have always believed. He is a very competent fellow, but with some unattractive traits, and at the moment all the other sovereigns were angry with him because he had suddenly christened himself czar instead of king, which they regarded as bumptious. Moreover he had had an intricate row about precedence with the Archduke Ferdinand on the way to the funeral. The Archduke Ferdinand does not like Bulgaria or its czar, and insisted that as the heir apparent to a real and big empire he was entitled to precedence which the czar of course flatly denied; and they had a delightful row over the matter, as complicated and involved, and as utterly childish, as the rows in Washington, when it used to be a matter of no small engineering skill to have Dewey, Cannon, Frye, and the Chief Justice, all dine at the White House and yet never meet—the Speaker of the House, the President of the Senate, and the Chief Justice each pointing to the constitution as giving *him* precedence, while my beloved Dewey triumphantly based his own claims on the number of guns fired for him when he went aboard ship. With a fine sense of military subordination, by the way, the good Admiral insisted that he would walk behind the Secretary of the Navy, but ahead of all the other Cabinet officers; and as several of the latter went ahead of the Naval Secretary, this meant that Dewey would have been sandwiched into a kind of Dodo race.

"Well, the czar and the Archduke came to London on the

same express train. The Czar's private carriage was already on it, and the archduke had his put on at Vienna. Each wished to have his carriage ahead of the other, but the archduke triumphed and had his placed nearest the engine, the czar's carriage coming next, and then the dining carriage. The archduke was much pleased at his success, and rode next the engine in purple splendor; and all went well until dinner time, when he sent word to the czar saying that he should like to walk through his carriage to the dining saloon, and the czar sent back word that he could not! Accordingly, breathing stertorously, he had to wait until a station came, get out and get into the dining saloon, and after eating his dinner wait until another station was reached, get out again and pop back into his own carriage. This struck all his brother royalties as a most serious matter, and the German Emperor had heatedly sided with the Austrians. Accordingly, while I was talking to the Czar, the Emperor suddenly walked up to us, thrust himself in ahead of the Czar, turned his back square to him and said to me: 'Roosevelt, my friend, I want to introduce you to the King of Spain'; (then with a sudden ferocious glance over his shoulder at the Czar) '*he* is worth talking to!'

"The King of Spain, by the way, *was* worth while talking to. I was much impressed by him. He at first thanked me for having behaved with such courtesy and consideration to Spain while I was President, and I told him of course that I had simply done my duty, for which I deserved no thanks, and that anyhow it was a real pleasure for me to do anything I could for Spain. He then said, looking me straight in the face, 'I am glad to meet you, Mr. Roosevelt, I have admired your public career, and I have also admired your military career, though I am sorry that your honors should have been won at the expense of my countrymen.' I bowed and said: 'Your Majesty, I have always borne testimony, and I always

shall bear testimony, to the gallantry and courage your countrymen showed in battle; although frankly I cannot speak as
highly of their leadership.' "

At the dinner, T.R. encountered M. Stephen Pichon, the
French Foreign Minister, who had been sent to London to
represent Europe's major democratic government at the ceremonies. "He is a queer looking creature at best, but on this
particular evening anger made him look like a gargoyle. His
clothes were stiff with gold lace and he wore sashes and
orders, for I was the only man present in ordinary evening
dress. He had all along held me as his natural companion
and ally, because we represented the two republics, and were
the only people present who were not royalties. Before dinner
he got me aside and asked me in French, as he did not speak
English, what color coat my coachman had worn that evening. I told him I did not know; whereupon he answered
that his coachman had a black coat. I nodded and said Yes,
I thought mine had a black coat also. He responded with
much violence that this was an outrage, a slight upon the two
great republics, as all the Royalties' coachmen wore red coats,
and that he would at once make a protest on behalf of us
both. I told him to hold on, that he must not make any
protest on my behalf, that I did not care what kind of coat
my coachman wore, and would be perfectly willing to see
him wear a green coat with yellow splashes—'un paletot vert
avec des taches jaunes,' being my effort at idiomatic render-
ing of the idea, for I speak French, I am sorry to say, as if it
were a non-Aryan tongue, without tense or gender, although
with agglutinative vividness and fluency. My incautious in-
cursion into levity in a foreign tongue met appropriate punishment, for I spent the next fifteen minutes in eradicating
from Pichon's mind the belief that I was demanding these
colors as my livery. However I think it had the effect of di-

verting him from his own woe, and nothing more happened that evening.

"But next morning when at eight o'clock, in evening dress, I turned up at the palace to go to Windsor, I found Pichon waiting for me more angry than ever. He was to go in the same carriage with me, and walking hastily up, and his voice shaking, he pointed out the very gorgeous-looking carriage in which we were to go and said that it was an outrage, that all the royalties had glass coaches and we did not. As I had never heard of a glass coach excepting in connection with Cinderella, I was less impressed by the omission than he was; and he continued that 'ces Chinois' were put ahead of us. To this I answered that any people dressed as gorgeously as 'ces Chinois' ought to go ahead of us; but he responded that it was not a laughing matter. Then he added that 'ce Perse' had been put in with us, pointing out a Persian prince of the blood royal, a deprecatory, inoffensive-looking Levantine of Parisian education who was obviously ill at ease, but whom Pichon insisted upon regarding as somebody who wanted to be offensive. At this moment our coach drove up, and Pichon bounced into it. I supposed he had gotten in to take the right-hand rear seat; as to which I was totally indifferent, for my experience at the White House had given me a horror of squabbles over precedence, and the one thing upon which I had insisted with our Ambassadors was that I should sit or walk or stand wherever any of my hosts wished me to. But Pichon was scrupulous in giving me precedence, although I have no idea whether I was entitled to it or not. He sat on the left rear seat himself, stretched his arm across the right seat and motioned me to get in so that 'ce Perse' should not himself take the place of honor! Accordingly, I got in, and the unfortunate Persian followed, looking about as unaggressive as a rabbit in a cage with two boa constrictors. As soon as we had started, Pichon's feelings overcame him again, and he pointed out the fact that we were following 'toutes ces petites royautes,' even 'le roi du Portugal.' I then spoke to him seriously, and said that in my judgment France and the United States were so important that it was of no earthly consequence whether their representatives went before or behind the representatives of utterly insignificant little states like Portugal, and that I thought it a great mistake to make a fuss about it, because it showed a lack of self-confidence."

T.R.'s letter concludes with a description of two of the meetings in London which he enjoyed the most: "On another occasion Mrs. Roosevelt and I took lunch with King George and Queen Mary. It was the day after the king's birthday, and his presents were all on a table in the corner, and by it another table with a cake. They were thoroughly pleasant, homelike people—and I was much amused, by the way, to find that his sympathy went out to me because he knew that I had a horror of the type of American who wishes to hang around a foreign court, particularly the English court, and get social recognition. This is the type of American who, when wealthy enough—and the type is even more objectionable when wealthy than when poor—uses his money to marry his daughter to a foreigner of title, and it is a type which, unlike his father, he thoroughly abhors, I am glad to say. Toward the end of lunch the children came in. He was telling me about them in advance. 'They are all obedient except John (the youngest). I don't understand it. He is not obedient at all. Now you watch him when he comes in. He will go straight for that cake. You watch him.' In came the children, made their manners prettily, and then sure enough John, a nice, solid-looking little boy, made a beeline for the cake. The king turned to me with an air of pride in the way the event had justified the prophecy. 'There, didn't I tell you so? Now you listen to the way he answers me. He isn't like any of the other children. You just listen.' Then to John, 'John!' John, 'What?' The king, 'Don't say "What" when I speak to you. Come here.' Turning to me, 'Didn't I tell you so? He is not obedient, and all the other children are so obedient.' John started solemnly towards us, and on the way he met a rather hairless little dog called 'Happy,' which he stooped over and began to pat, at the same time saying something to his father. The latter turned to me with another smile of triumph. 'Did you hear that? " 'appy is 'airy!" Not an h to him! I don't know where he gets it from; it must be his nurse!' I thoroughly liked the king. He had been much bothered over the accusations brought against him that he was already secretly married and that he drank to excess, and wanted to know what I would advise his doing. I told him that unless the accusation appeared in public, I would take no notice of it; that of course if any public accusation was made it should be promptly and effectively met, but that it was always a mistake to refute private slander by a public statement.

"I managed to visit two or three of my old friends, spending either a week end or a night at their houses,—Trevelyan, Edward North Buxton and Selous.

"I thoroughly enjoyed my stay in England. The men I met were delightful, and I felt at home with them. As a whole, they had my ideals and ways of looking at life. But the twenty-four hours I really most enjoyed not only in England but in all Europe, were those I spent with Edward Grey, the last twenty-four hours I was in England. He is very fond of birds, and I had been anxious to hear and see the English birds which I knew so well in the books. He took me down to the Valley of the Itchen, which we tramped along, and then motored to an inn near the New Forest where we took tea (having already eaten our lunch on a bank); and then tramped through the New Forest, reaching the inn on the other side of it about nine in the evening, tired and happy and ready for a warm bath, a hot supper, and bed. Grey is not a brilliant man like Balfour, or a born leader like Lloyd George, but he is the kind of high-minded public servant, as straight in all private as in all public relations, whom it is essential for a country to have, and I do not remember ever meeting anyone else except Leonard Wood to whom I took so strong a fancy on such short acquaintance."

The main reason for T.R.'s visit to England, which in turn had been the main reason for his continental tour on the way there, was in invitation to deliver the annual Romanes lecture at Oxford. T.R. had composed the lecture, in which he developed complex comparisons between various extinct animals from bygone geologic eras with certain more or less modern kingdoms and principalities, before leaving the White House. Then, in order to check his scientific references, he had sent the manuscript to his friend and fellow-naturalist, Henry Fairfield Osborn of the American Museum of Natural History, who later recalled the consequences: "I drew heavy pencil lines across . . . pages with the word 'omit' in the margin and wrote: 'I have left out certain passages that are likely to bring on war between the United States and the governments referred to.' "

As delivered at Oxford, the lecture received qualified approval from its listeners including the Archbishop of York to whom T.R. remarked that it would have been "a great deal stronger had not one of my scientific friends in America blue penciled the best part of it." Some years later, in relating this comment to Osborn, the Archbishop also defined the audience reaction further: ". . . In the way of grading which we have at Oxford, we agreed to mark the lecture 'Beta Minus' but the lecturer 'Alpha Plus'. . . ."

Most noteworthy of all the speeches made by T.R. in England—which also included one at Cambridge, where the undergraduates provided a Teddy bear with outstretched paw to welcome him on his arrival—was the address delivered at the London Guildhall where he was made a Freeman of the City of London before a distinguished audience. In subsequent years, it became the fashion, scrupulously followed by a later Roosevelt, for U.S. politicians to urge the British to disown the burdens of Empire. T.R., referring to his recent experiences in Egypt, and relating them to the policies pursued by himself in the Philippines despite interference from domestic mugwumps, took the opposite slant:

"In Egypt you are not only the guardians of your own interests; you are also the guardians of the interests of civilization; and the present condition of affairs in Egypt is a grave menace to both your Empire and the entire civilized world. . . . Now, either you have the right to be in Egypt or you have not; either it is or it is not your duty to establish and to keep order. If you feel that you have not the right to be in Egypt . . . then, by all means get out of Egypt. If, as I hope, you feel that your duty to civilized mankind and your fealty to your own great traditions alike bid you to stay, then make the fact and the name agree and show that you are ready to meet in very deed the responsibility which is yours."

For an outsider not merely to lecture the British about how to run their Empire but even to urge them not to loaf on the job was a novelty of a sort guaranteed to create commotion. Theretofore, T.R. had so delighted Britain that the closest approach to adverse comment had been a *Punch*

242]   T.R.—THE STORY OF THEODORE ROOSEVELT

cartoon showing the famous stone lions on Trafalgar Square guarded by policemen and further protected by signs reading "NOT TO BE SHOT." Now, however, a storm of criticism arose in the press led by the *Standard* which called his address "a social crime not far from sacrilege." The storm was presently quieted by Foreign Minister Grey who explained that he and other responsible members of the government had, like Osborn in the case of the Romanes lecture, been privileged to read the speech beforehand. Grey commented later: "It would have been a poor and paltry thing . . . to ask him to let the tribute stand, but to leave out the advice. . . . I had no hesitation in deciding that . . . I would ask for no alteration."

A few days after the Romanes lecture, and after spending his last afternoon on the memorable Itchen River bird-walk with Sir Edward Grey, T.R. boarded the *Kaiserin Auguste Viktoria,* for the voyage home. During the crossing, he was accompanied not only by Edie, Kermit, and Ethel but now also by Alice Longworth and by his old friend Seth Bullock, United States Marshal of Oklahoma, who had accepted T.R.'s invitation to join him in London to see the sights. Along with their pleasant company and the agreeable recollections of the year just past, he had ample food for thought in the prospects of what awaited him on his return to his native shores.

Indications that his successor was by no means fully living up to T.R.'s glowing predictions had been discernible almost as soon as he left Hoboken. First was the news that Henry White—of whom T.R. had supposed that Taft shared his high opinion—had been summarily relieved of his post as Ambassador to France and demoted to a job in the Embassy in London, where T.R. had seen him and heard the whole story. The facts that the new President's dismissal of White had been caused by some long-remembered slight involving Mrs. Taft, and that he had been replaced by T.R.'s good friend, Morgan partner Robert Bacon, the handsomest man in the Harvard class of 1880, by no means served to repair what T.R. could not help regarding as a rudeness to himself as well as an injustice to White and an injury to the Foreign Service.

Even more troubling than the removal of White had been the news brought to him in the heart of Africa by special runner, that Gifford Pinchot, possibly his closest friend next to Lodge, had been ousted from his post as Chief Forester as the result of a row with the Secretary of the Interior, Richard A. Ballinger. Later, when the Roosevelts were spending a week at Emily Carow's Italian villa at Porto Maurizio, Pinchot himself, having crossed the ocean for the purpose, had told T.R. the whole story of his ousting. This apparently represented not merely a personal slight and an administrative blunder, like the dismissal of White, but a blow to T.R.'s entire conservation policy.

Finally, there were indications, most notably Taft's handling of the new Tariff which had been the major business of his first Congress, that the trend of the new administration as a whole, far from upholding and advancing T.R.'s progressive Republicanism, was to revert to the old-guard, standpat conservatism against which he had spent a lifetime fighting and which in his opinion would ultimately lead to disaster for the party. In his absence, Taft had turned for encouragement and guidance, not to T.R.'s close friends but to his longtime adversaries, like Speaker Joseph Cannon in the House and Rhode Island's affluent Nelson W. Aldrich, whose daughter had married John D. Rockefeller, Jr., in the Senate. From Pinchot and Root—who was now a New York Senator and whom he had seen in London—T.R.

learned also that Taft's closest personal advisers were his
nervous and socially-ambitious wife and his pompous older
half-brother, Charles.

What all this meant was simply that when he got home,
T.R. would be faced with a harrowing choice of loyalties:
whether to give support to friends who had fought for him
and his policies during his two terms in the White House,
and who were now being pushed aside, or to the President
whom he had chosen and installed and who now took this
strange way of discharging the obligations so generously acknowledged in his farewell letter. Moreover, the choice was
one that would have to be made soon after he returned, in
the form of a decision as to what role, if any, he should take
in the forthcoming Congressional elections.

The welcome provided for T.R. on his arrival in New
York set the pattern for all the justly celebrated ticker-tape
parades that followed in subsequent decades—of which none
have equalled the original in sheer intensity of exuberance.
A twenty-one gun salute—normally reserved for functioning
Presidents—by the guns of Fort Wadsworth greeted his ship
as it came through the Narrows. The battleship *South Carolina* and a flotilla of destroyers, yachts, ferryboats, tugs, and
miscellaneous smaller craft accompanied the liner into the
harbor. Among them was the revenue cutter, *Manhattan*,
carrying a cargo of notables including Archie, Quentin, Ted,
and the latter's fiancée, Eleanor Alexander, whose wedding
was scheduled for two days later. Also on board, and again
unnoticed, were young Franklin Roosevelt, by this time an
Assemblyman at Albany, and his diffident young wife.

The cutter came alongside the liner and T.R. descended
a gangplank to the former in which he came ashore to be
welcomed by a "Court of Honor" at the Battery and a covey
of cabinet members, cowboys, and miscellaneous celebrities

among whom the only one apparently missing was William Howard Taft. Realizing that he would only be in the way, the President was again represented by Captain Archie Butt, for whom the developing split between the two men would pose a problem in loyalties perhaps even more acute than that confronting T.R. himself. There followed a speech of welcome by Mayor William J. Gaynor and then a procession up Broadway and Fifth Avenue, with a troop of Rough Riders as Guard of Honor, cheering thousands lined along the curbs and T.R. bowing from an open carriage as far as Fifty-ninth Street.

From the nation's press—which no one in U.S. public life before or since has dominated as completely as T.R.—his arrival in New York aroused a response that would have been appropriate to the Second Coming. Almost as a matter of course, the humorous magazine *Life,* which had already devoted one special issue to T.R.'s departure, devoted another to his return. Most noteworthy item in the latter was a single unsigned quatrain:

Little Boy Blue

Teddy, come home and blow your horn,
The sheep's in the meadow, the cow's in the corn.
The boy you left to 'tend the sheep
Is under the haystack fast asleep.

XII

—————

In April of 1907, a reporter
asked the aged mother of William Howard Taft to name her
candidate for the Presidency of the United States.

"Elihu Root," replied the old lady.

Notable for its honesty, this answer was even more remarkable for its sagacity. It sprang from reasons which she had
four months earlier spelled out in a letter to her son, when
he had written her about his dissatisfactions with public life:

"So near the throne, you realize that 'uneasy lies the head
that wears a crown.' Roosevelt is a good fighter and enjoys it,
but the malice of politics would make you miserable. They
do not want you as their leader, but cannot find anyone
more available."

Like her son, the senior Mrs. Taft believed that his talents
were judicial rather than executive and that the goal of his
ambition should be the Supreme Court. In this, her views
differed sharply from those of her daughter-in-law, who in
1906, when Roosevelt had offered his Secretary of War a

place on that bench for the third time, hurried to the White House to explain that he had other things in mind. "The subject of my husband's appointment to the Supreme Court cropped up with what seemed to me annoying frequency," she later observed in her autobiographical *Recollections.* Helen Taft—whose husband when away from home wrote her a daily report of his doings—suspected that T.R.'s readiness to make Taft a Supreme Court Justice was motivated less by consideration of the latter's wishes than by his own eagerness to occupy the White House more or less permanently. She regarded T.R.—to whom she liked to refer as "Teddy," a nickname which she was fully aware that he disliked—less as a benefactor than as a rival to her husband, and an obnoxiously persistent one.

Two years earlier, when T.R. had offered Taft the position of Secretary of War, her reactions had been somewhat different. Then High Commissioner to the Philippines, Taft had accepted the promotion with reservations which he expressed in his reply: "You know, too, the obligations that are usually felt by cabinet officers in the matter of entertainment, and you know that kind of dog's life, not that a cabinet officer, but that his wife, has to live in trying to keep up appearances on an insufficient salary." T.R. wrote back that, during his days as Civil Service Commissioner, Mrs. Roosevelt ". . . never minded our not having champagne at our dinners, for instance. At first I did, but I got over it; and moreover I found out that we could do most of our entertaining at Sunday evening high tea." This helpful suggestion did not have altogether the desired effect upon the Taft ménage, then domiciled at Manila's spacious Malacañan Palace. In a subsequent letter to a friend, Taft recorded his wife's reactions: "The President said he hoped I would live quietly and modestly. . . . You should see Nellie's lip curl at the suggestion of Sunday high teas and dinner parties without champagne."

Harmony in the Taft family was preserved by Charles P. Taft, the future President's older half-brother, a prosperous lawyer and publisher, who shared his sister-in-law's firm views as to the future President's role in public life. He felt able to add to the Secretary's salary of $8,000 a year $6,000 more out of his own pocket. This arrangement made the cabinet post one that Mrs. Taft found entirely appropriate. It was, she stated in her *Recollections,* "in line with the kind of work I wanted my husband to do, the kind of career I wanted for him and expected him to have."

The reactions of his family to the career problems of William Howard Taft sheds considerable light upon the character of the latter. Oldest of five children born of Alonzo Taft's second marriage, he was one of those openhearted, friendly souls who, by their sanguine approach to life, arouse immediate and indulgent affection. Taft was as hard to dislike as Santa Claus to whom, with his 320-pound physique, his ram's-horn mustachios and his jovial disposition, he bore a resemblance which was not wholly confined to appearances. From early days at Yale—where he had been the outstanding member of the class of 1878—his difficulty had never been that of finding friends and well-wishers. Rather it was that in his case the well-wishers were so numerous and so diverse that they naturally failed to see eye-to-eye with each other and thus became rivals whose mutual mistrust was often proportionate to the degree of the confidence they felt in their beneficiary.

Among Taft's rival benefactors, no one was more diligent than T.R. who had said of his successor, "I almost envy a man possessing a personality like Taft's. People are always prepossessed by it. One loves him at first sight." Moreover, as President of the United States, he was in a pre-eminent position among them and able to express his enthusiasm more effectively than the rest in terms of honors, appointments, and simple good-fellowship. The latter was perhaps the most eloquent of all his tributes to the man who became, next to Lodge, his closest friend during his sojourn in the White House. With Elihu Root, Taft and T.R. made up what they liked among themselves to call "the Three Musketeers" of the cabinet, and of the three the closest personal bond was that between T.R. and his Porthosian Secretary of War. One afternoon, when Archie Butt, then T.R.'s devoted aide, was chatting with Mrs. Roosevelt, they heard from one of the White House rooms, the infectious sounds of T.R.'s high-pitched laughter accompanied by Taft's deep, rumbling chuckle. Mrs. Roosevelt smiled and said: "It's always that way when they're together."

Edith Roosevelt's enthusiasm did not extend to Root. Taft, in a letter to his wife, explained why. "Her reason for disliking Mr. Root is a funny one. The President and Mr. Root, as you remember, used to go out on long walks and the President insisted on climbing precipices. He carried poor old Root through the same places until Root got out of patience. One day when Root was not along, the President in his wild career had a severe fall which lamed him, and when Mrs. Roosevelt told Root about it, he laughed and said he was very glad. Mrs. Roosevelt was very indignant on the subject and did not see why he should express himself in such a brutal manner."

Root's wit, often on the sharp side, had no terrors for Taft. In the Philippines, where he had suffered severely from the heat, the High Commissioner had once taken a trip to the mountain resort of Baguio and reported by cable to the Secretary of War on his arrival: "Stood trip well. Rode horseback twenty-five miles to five thousand feet elevation." Root

cabled back: "Referring to your telegram . . . how is the
horse?" That this joke presently found its way back to the
U.S. and became a classic of the 1908 Presidential campaign
was due to Taft's own enjoyment of it, as recorded in a
further item of dutiful correspondence with his superior.

"Your cable enquiry about the condition of the horse that
brought me up the mountain was too good to keep, so I published the despatch and have been made the subject of jokes
in the local newspapers ever since. The horse which I did
ride was the horse which General Chaffee used to ride, and
is a magnificent animal 17½ hands high, a single-footer,
gentle and intelligent and of great power. He stood the trip
without difficulty."

Other Taft jokes, which became numerous enough to fill
a sizable anthology, were comparably sympathetic. Associate
Justice Brewer of the Supreme Court got a fine laugh when,
in an address at Yale, he remarked of that institution's most
renowned alumnus: "Secretary Taft is the politest man alive.
I heard that recently he arose in a street car and gave his
seat to three women." Even Speaker Joe Cannon, whose art-
fully rustic humor often had a mordant edge, paid tribute
to Taft's impartiality when he said: "The trouble with Taft
is that if he were Pope he would think it necessary to appoint
a few Protestant Cardinals." Of the innumerable comments
on Taft as President, the sharpest, as it was also perhaps the
most discerning, was that of Iowa's astute Senator Jona-
than P. Dolliver: "President Taft is a large body completely
surrounded by men who know exactly what they want."

The closest thing to a rebuke to his Secretary of War ever
administered by Roosevelt was the consequence of Taft's
advocacy of lower tariffs on sugar and tobacco to benefit his
own beloved protégés, the Philippines, in campaign speeches
in 1904. When domestic sugar and tobacco growers were

moved to protest, Roosevelt issued a mild remonstrance to which Taft wrote back that ". . . Of course he would not expect me to retract my position but that if my presence in the Cabinet embarrassed him I would retire at once." Roosevelt's response was as emphatic as it was prompt: "Fiddle-deedee. I shall never send you another letter or complaint if it produces such awful results. . . . As for your retiring from the Cabinet, upon my word, Will, I think you must have nerves, or something."

One evening in 1906, the Tafts dined at the White House and after dinner T.R. took them to the second floor library where he threw himself into an easy chair and closed his eyes: ". . . I have clairvoyant powers and I see a man weighing three hundred and fifty pounds," he intoned in suitably oracular tones. "There is something hanging over his head. I cannot make out what it is. . . . At one time it looks like the Presidency, then again it looks like the Chief Justiceship."

"Make it the Presidency," said Mrs. Taft.

"Make it the Chief Justiceship," said her husband.

In view of the circumstances as well as of their relationship, the wonder was not that T.R. followed Mrs. Taft's suggestion and then hovered over his protégé during the campaign of 1908 to make sure that nothing went wrong. It was rather that, after T.R. had seen Taft safely installed in the White House, and after Taft had acknowledged his gratitude with almost pathetic devotion, a friendship between public men unparalleled since that of Damon and Pythias broke up in a bitter personal quarrel. But the break between Roosevelt and Taft that rocked the U.S. in 1912 was far more than the dramatic disintegration of a close friendship between two notables. It involved a head-on collision between major forces in the nation of which the reverberations were still plainly audible in U.S. politics half a century later.

The forces at issue were on the one hand the interests of property, privilege, and big business which, since the Civil War, had profitted increasingly from the coming of the industrial age, and, on the other hand, the interests of the farmers, small businessmen, and workers for whose benefit U.S. society was traditionally supposed to function. The latter were represented in Congress primarily by a group of "insurgent" Senators—notably La Follette of Wisconsin, Dolliver of Iowa, Bristow of Kansas and Beveridge of Montana—who believed that the Republican party should be more responsive to their wants and less to those of Eastern leaders of business and finance. These, meanwhile, were represented in the Capital by such men as Aldrich and Cannon, whose viewpoint, following the precedents set by the succession of post-Civil War Republican Presidents prior to T.R., remained the dominant one within the party.

Roosevelt realized that, if they were to remain the nation's majority party, the Republicans would have to represent both groups. Moreover, by his understanding of both, based on his unique range of personal experience, by the cogence with which, as a professional writer, he could make this understanding intelligible, and by the political skill, developed through three arduous decades of public life, which enabled him to apply it, he had been able to make the party do exactly that. To the old guard he had pounded home the viewpoint that Big Business, to insure its own survival, must be the servant of the community rather than its master. To insurgents he had expounded with equal vigor the doctrine that a working partnership with business was the most effective way of realizing their own apparently separate objectives. Fighting the extremists of both factions, he held the party together while he revitalized it with the spirit of progress, practical reform, and—in the resounding phrase recalled from his frontier days—the Square Deal.

Like a good many other close associates of T.R., Taft had responded wholeheartedly to the policies and programs pushed through by the President. What this proved, however, was less that Taft himself believed in them than that he was exceptionally susceptible to leadership. When Roosevelt was no longer available to provide it, Taft naturally turned first to the most accessible substitutes, his wife and his older half brother, and then, both through their influence and his own habit and inclination, to members of the ultraconservative wing of the party. That Taft, with every intention of doing just what T.R. wanted him to do, should instead have completely betrayed T.R.'s most essential purposes was perhaps less remarkable than that T.R. should ever have expected any other result, let alone the opposite one.

The most likely explanation of Roosevelt's failure to perceive the fundamental flaw in Taft's equipment for the Presidency was simply that Taft's response to his leadership was so wholehearted as to seem self-generated. What supports this explanation most impressively is that, while the future course of events remained unthinkable to T.R., it was plainly apparent to almost anyone else who had the advantage, inevitably denied to T.R., of seeing Taft when T.R. was elsewhere. The matter was perhaps best summed up by Archie Butt, who knew both men well and had a unique opportunity to observe both separately. Before Taft had even named his cabinet, he wrote that T.R. "feels very deeply the fact that Mr. Taft seems determined to sever all the ties which have bound them together in the past. Roosevelt was the only one who did not foresee this, and I think he will be bitterly disappointed when he sees many of his policies reversed. He was so cocksure that Mr. Taft would continue all his policies, and I fear that a general reversal will be the line he will follow." The perceptiveness of this comment soon became all too painfully apparent.

Before leaving London, Roosevelt had received from Taft a letter which the latter's able biographer, Henry Pringle, had described with only numerical exaggeration, as "the most poignant letter, perhaps, among all the untold millions that Presidents of the United States—so often bothered and troubled men—have written." In it, the President rendered a diligent account of his first year and a quarter in office. Between the lines it was not difficult to decipher his woeful inability to cope with the painful predicament which, for him, the Presidency clearly constituted. In one paragraph he candidly confessed it:

"It is now a year and three months since I assumed office and I have had a hard time. I do not know that I have had harder luck than other presidents, but I do know that thus far I have succeeded far less than have others. I have been conscientiously trying to carry out your policies but my method of doing so has not worked smoothly. . . . My year and two months have been heavier for me to bear because of Mrs. Taft's condition. A nervous collapse, with apparent symptoms of paralysis that soon disappeared, but with an aphasia that for a long time was nearly complete, made it necessary for me to be as careful as possible to prevent another attack. Mrs. Taft is not an easy patient and an attempt to control her only increased the nervous strain. . . ."

Roosevelt's reply was graciously noncommittal:

"Dear Mr. President: Your very kind letter which greatly pleased me has just come. . . . I am of course much concerned about some of the things I see and am told; but what I have felt it best to do was to say absolutely nothing—and indeed to keep my mind as open as I kept my mouth shut! . . . Indeed you have had a hard time, as you say, and of course the sickness of the one you love most has added immeasurably to your burden. . . . Will you give her our warmest regards? . . . Again very heartily thanking you for writing me, I am, Most sincerely yours. . . ."

While as yet there was nothing like an open split between T.R. and his successor, it was clear that this letter, making all due allowances for changed circumstances, had a tone quite foreign to the jaunty communications addressed to "Dear Will" when the latter had been a member of the cabinet. Nonetheless, had T.R. been able to adhere to the policy of saying nothing and keeping his mind open things might eventually have worked out so that he gave a sympathetic hearing to Taft's side of the Pinchot affair, the fight against Speaker Joe Cannon and the Tariff Bill. This proved to be impractical; and from the moment of T.R.'s triumphant return to the United States, events moved steadily toward the total break that followed three years later.

First link in the chain of circumstances that led to the break was the Harvard Commencement of June 29, where Roosevelt and Charles Evans Hughes, then Governor of New York, fell into such animated conversation that they failed to notice the start of the academic procession in which they were fellow marchers. The consequence of Roosevelt's conversation with Hughes was a statement to the press that evening in support of the direct primary bill, to pass which Hughes had just called a special session of the Assembly. The bill was defeated and to secure vengeance against the state bosses who had defeated it, T.R. felt obliged to strike back. But when he offered to serve as temporary chairman of the

Republican State Convention, the state committee roundly snubbed his offer by nominating instead Taft's Vice-President, James S. Sherman. "Have you seen the papers this afternoon?" Taft asked Archie Butt, not without a trace of satisfaction, "They have defeated Theodore."

T.R. secured revenge of sorts for the committee's snub by going to the convention, getting himself elected temporary chairman and securing the nomination for governor of his friend, Henry L. Stimson—who was later defeated by his Democratic opponent, John A. Dix. Meanwhile, however, he had been drawn into the Congressional election campaign which posed further difficult problems. To support the record of the administration would be to desert many of his staunchest friends and the principles to which he and they were loyal. Not to do so would be to ignore his obligation to the party that had given him two terms in the White House as well as to disown his own major share of responsibility for putting Taft there as his successor. Roosevelt solved the dilemma after a fashion by setting forth on a speaking tour which was paid for not by the party but by *The Outlook* to which, on his return from Africa, he had become a regular contributor. "My speeches," said Roosevelt, "will represent myself entirely, nobody else."

During his sojourn abroad, Roosevelt had received a copy of Herbert Croly's book *The Promise of American Life* which he had read with interest and approval. Croly's influence and his own dissatisfaction with the administration combined to produce a fresh synthesis of his political philosophy which he described as the "new nationalism" and which he defined most eloquently in a speech at Osawatomie, Kansas. There he took as his theme Lincoln's statement that: "Labor is prior to, and independent of, capital. Capital is only the fruit of labor and could never have existed if labor had not first existed. Labor is the superior capital, and deserves that much higher consideration." Roosevelt pointed out that if he himself had uttered such sentiments he would be "even more strongly denounced as a Communist agitator than I will be anyway." He went on to add that "I mean not merely that I stand for fair play under the present rules of the game, but that I stand for having those rules changed so as to work for a more substantial equality of opportunity and of reward."

Pronouncements like this, while gratifying to the insurgents, were understandably puzzling to Taft. To his brother Charles in Europe, he wrote somewhat plaintively that Roosevelt has said that "he intends to work for my renomination and election but if this is true he has taken a peculiar course to bring it about. . . . He has made some speeches that indicate that he is going quite beyond anything that he advocated while he was in the White House, and has proposed a program which it is absolutely impossible to carry out except by a revision of the Federal constitution. . . . His attitude toward me is one that I find difficult to understand and explain. . . ."

To Archie Butt, the President had expressed himself more freely by saying of Roosevelt: "If I only knew what the President wanted. . . . I would do it but you know he has held himself so aloof that I am absolutely in the dark. I am deeply wounded. . . ." His bewilderment became such that, always somewhat inclined to torpidity, he now often fell into a doze as soon as he sat down in a chair. At the same time, he grew so irritable that once, after making an especially bad shot at golf, he threw his club after the ball to a distance of twenty-five feet.

For T.R., the climax of the Western tour was reached in St. Louis, where he encountered the renowned Aviator, Arch

Hoxsey, just after the latter had completed a record flight from Springfield, Illinois. When Hoxsey—who died when his plane crashed the following year—invited him to take a "hop," T.R. reacted characteristically: "By George," he exclaimed, "I believe I will." Hoxsey's record-breaking plane was a primitive contrivance in which the passenger perched in a tangle of struts and wires, exposed to wind and weather with a good view of the ground beneath his feet. Having circled the field twice the plane landed safely after a four-minute flight. "It was great," exclaimed T.R. "I wish I could have stayed up for an hour."

T.R.'s reactions to his own forensic activities were not much more favorable than the President's. His estimate of the effect of his Western speeches was contained in a letter to Joseph Bucklin Bishop: "The lunatic Insurgents . . . were not contented with anything short of denunciation of Taft; the reactionaries literally went insane in their opposition. . . ." To Root, he confided that "I have never had a more unpleasant summer." The results of the elections did little to compensate for its miseries. The Democrats won a resounding victory which included control of the House by 228 to 162, and twenty-six out of the forty-eight governorships. Among the latter was New Jersey, whose new chief executive was the lantern-jawed former president of Princeton, Woodrow Wilson.

During this period of increasing rift, Roosevelt and Taft met on three separate occasions. The first was just after the Harvard Commencement of 1910, when T.R. and Lodge called at the new summer White House in Beverly, Mass., where they sat on the porch with the President and Archie Butt while Roosevelt told stories about the royal wake in London. When they left, the President said: "This has taken me back to some of those dear old afternoons when I was

Will and you were Mr. President." The second, which had a less nostalgic impact, was a brief encounter in the following September which ended awkwardly for all concerned when a Taft follower announced that Roosevelt had sought the meeting so as to secure the President's aid in his venture into the New York political arena and T.R. felt obliged to deny having done so. The third was in June of 1911, at a ceremony in honor of Baltimore's Cardinal Gibbons. T.R. and Taft whispered to each other and enjoyed a laugh together, thus causing the perceptive audience of several hundred to applaud and cheer.

None of these encounters led to a lasting rapprochement for reasons which each revealed privately to friends. Said T.R. to Cabot Lodge "For a year and a quarter after he had been elected, I would not let myself think ill of anything he did. I finally had to . . . admit to myself that deep down underneath I had all along known he was wrong on points to which I had tried to deceive myself by loudly proclaiming to myself that he was right." And Taft confided to his military aide: "I don't understand Roosevelt. I don't know what he is driving at except to make my way more difficult. I could not ask his advice on all questions. I could not subordinate my administration to him and retain my self-respect, but it is hard, very hard, Archie, to see a devoted friendship going to pieces like a rope of sand."

While the breach grew wider, intimates of both men naturally became increasingly aware of it—and frequently helped to accelerate its growth by repeating to each what the other had said of him in private. Meanwhile, both Taft and T.R. were careful to say nothing derogatory about each other for public consumption. Astonishingly enough, the first open acknowledgment of their differences was delayed for thirty months, until October of 1911. However, when the break was finally acknowledged, the explosion was loud enough for all to hear and damaging enough to prevent any chance of reconciliation.

Occasion for the revelation was a characteristically well-intended effort on the part of Taft to redeem his administration in the eyes of Progressives, including T.R.'s. This took the form of a bold, if somewhat belated, foray into the field of trust-busting of which the target was the United States Steel Corporation. Unfortunately, and also characteristically, Taft had neglected to read the bill of particulars prepared by a special assistant to the Attorney General. This included the already thoroughly shopworn charge that, in the summer of 1907, Roosevelt had been duped by Messrs. Gary and Frick into letting the U.S. Steel Company acquire the Tennessee Iron and Coal Company for much less than its actual value.

T.R.'s reaction to the charge—which was announced on October 27, his birthday, and which, as he pointed out made "me either a fool or a knave"—was typically prompt and vehement. In an article in *The Outlook,* he asserted that the Administration's assertion that "I was misled . . . is not correct. The representatives of the steel company told me the truth. . . . I was not misled. . . . Any statement that I was misled is itself not in accordance with the truth." Furthermore, he insisted, "nothing . . . is gained by breaking up a huge industrial organization which has not offended otherwise than by its size"; Taft's attack on the Steel Trust was "destructive litigation." In contrast, he cited anti-trust suits made under his administration in which "we felt so sure of our facts that we could be fairly certain there was likelihood of success."

Thereafter events moved rapidly. Roosevelt supporters across the nation, sensing the changed temper of the situation, converged upon Sagamore Hill according to Mark Sullivan, who was one of them, "like iron filings mobilizing to the pull of a revitalized magnet." Within weeks, the demand that he announce his candidacy for the Republican nomination in 1912 impelled T.R. to write a long letter to publisher Frank Munsey setting forth among other things the conditions under which he would do so.

"If I should consult only my own pleasure and interest, I should most emphatically and immediately announce that I would under no circumstances run. I have had all the honor that any man can have from holding the office of President. From every personal standpoint there is nothing for me to gain either in running for the office or in holding the office once more, and there is very much to lose. If, as I deem probable, Mr. Taft is nominated, and my name continues to be mentioned, my opponents will all say that I secretly or openly strove for the nomination and was defeated. If Mr. La Follette is nominated, the same thing will be said. If the utterly unexpected happens and I am nominated, I may very probably be defeated, in which case I shall be not only assailed but derided. If I won, I should take office carrying a burden for which I am not responsible, and facing conditions such as to make it almost certain, not only that I should not be able to accomplish all that I would like to accomplish, but that I should be very severely condemned, probably by a considerable majority of the people, for failure to accomplish what it would probably be beyond the power of any human being to accomplish.

"Under such circumstances, if I consulted only my own interest, the obvious thing to do would be to announce that I would not obey any popular mandate, that I would not run if nominated. I shall not follow this course, because I am sincerely endeavoring to look at the matter only from the standpoint of the popular interest. It is not only necessary for the people to have the right instrument, the right tool, with which to work in any given emergency, but it is necessary that they themselves shall choose, and shall believe in the sufficiency of, that instrument. If at this particular crisis, with the particular problems ahead of us at this particular time, the people feel that I am the only man in sight to do the job, then I should regard myself as shirking a plain duty if I refused to do it."

By mid-January, it had become reasonably clear that public demand was sufficient to meet the conditions that Roosevelt had specified. The next question was how he could most effectively and most appropriately acknowledge it. Governors of several states had by this time independently written T.R. urging him to run. He suggested that they sign a round-robin to which in reply he could say publicly what his letter to Munsey had said privately. The round-robin was duly despatched by the Governors of West Virginia, Nebraska, New Hampshire, Wyoming, Michigan, Kansas and Missouri and published on February 11.

"We . . . declare it our belief, after a careful investigation of the facts, that a large majority of the Republican voters of the country favor your nomination, and a large majority of the people favor your election, as the next President of the United States. . . . We believe that in view of this public demand you should soon declare whether, if the nomination for the Presidency comes to you unsolicited and unsought, you will accept it. . . ."

On February 24, T.R. gave his answer: ". . . I will accept the nomination for President if it is tendered to me, and I will adhere to this decision until the convention has expressed its preference. . . ." Three days before, he had said the same thing in a breezier way that added another famous phrase to the U.S. vernacular. To a reporter in Cleveland—

who, oddly enough, thought so little of the statement that he failed to despatch it for two days—T.R. had blithely remarked: "My hat is in the ring."

The news of T.R.'s formal decision to accept the nomination if it was offered reached the White House just before dinner on the evening of February 25. Archie Butt, who was dining with the Tafts, later, as was his wont, recorded the table talk. Mrs. Taft—by now amply recovered from her aphasia—opened the conversation by saying to her husband:

"I told you so four years ago and you would not believe me."

The long-suffering but almost imperturbably good-humored President replied with his famous chuckle: "I know you did, my dear—and I think you are perfectly happy now. You would have preferred the Colonel to come out against me than to have been wrong yourself."

This informative entry was almost the last in Butt's famous letter-diaries, published many years later. The strain of the trouble between Taft and T.R., to both of whom he felt strong ties of loyalty and affection, had affected his health even more than the President's. In the winter of 1912, feeling that his aide needed a change, Taft urged him to take a vacation in Europe and Butt, by now a major, did so. He booked passage home on the *Titanic* and the ship's orchestra was playing his favorite hymn, "Nearer My God To Thee," when she sank in mid-Atlantic with the loss of 1500 lives, including his.

Once acknowledged, what had been an unhappy but gradual drawing apart of good friends speedily became the biggest and most bitter personal feud in the history of U.S. politics. Whose fault it was that the feud ever started, what effect it had upon the nation, and even whether T.R., Taft, or either of them, finally won are matters about which historians are still in disagreement. What remains indisputable is that the battle was fought on the heroic scale with no holds barred across the length and breadth of the land and that it aroused the American people to extremes of devoted allegiance and fierce hostility never equaled by any personal contest in U.S. politics before or since.

Round One in the fight was the struggle for delegates to the Republican National Convention scheduled for June 17 in Chicago. Since Taft controlled the state machines, Roosevelt's only chance was to go directly to the voters through the primaries in the states that had them, to try to persuade other states to institute primaries and, where neither method would work, to appeal directly for delegates. Meanwhile, in addition to making full use of the powers of patronage and of the state machines, Taft soon found it necessary to ignore the unwritten rule that forbade campaigning by a President in office. At the outset, the tide seemed to be running against T.R. State Conventions in New York, Indiana, Michigan, and Massachusetts—where Lodge stood by the President rather than by his closest friend—chose delegations instructed for Taft. Wisconsin and North Dakota stuck to Robert La Follette—whose position as leader of the Progressive movement had made him a possible nominee until T.R. tossed his hat into the ring. Then, in April, Roosevelt began to show his strength by primary victories in Pennsylvania, Maryland, California, and even the President's home state of Ohio. But the primaries were only a small part of the excitement.

On March 3, Taft had had a talk with Roosevelt's old friend, Henry White, which the latter summarized in a letter to T.R.: "He said that nothing would induce him to say—or to allow anyone whom he could control to say—anything against you personally; that he had never ceased to avail himself of every opportunity to express his gratitude for all you have done for him; that you made him President . . . and . . . that he could not help hoping that when all this turmoil of politics had passed, you and he would get together again and be as of old." Even before this, however, and even before Roosevelt's declaration, Taft, with even more than his customary verbal ineptitude, had used one of the phrases that did most to make the quarrel bitter. Speaking in Boston on Lincoln's birthday, he had referred disparagingly to various progressive policies and gone on to say of the progressive leaders: "Such extremists are not Progressives, they are political emotionalists or neurotics." The word "neurotic" had a special sting, doubtless unintended by the President, since a cliché especially favored by Roosevelt's least scrupulous enemies was to accuse him of heavy drinking or lack of mental balance. However, it was not until April 25 that in another visit to New England climaxed by a speech at Boston, Taft directed his attack directly against T.R. by name.

"This wrenches my soul," said the President to crowds that gathered where his train stopped on the way, "I am here to reply to an old and true friend of mine, Theodore Roosevelt, who has made many charges against me. I deny those charges, I deny all of them. I do not want to fight Theodore Roosevelt, but sometimes a man in a corner fights. I am going to fight."

Taft's Boston speech lasted for two hours and amounted to a point-by-point defense of his administration against the charges brought by "one whom in the past I have greatly admired and loved." The tone was set by Taft's introduction. "Mr. Roosevelt prides himself on being a true sportsman, and he likes to take from the rules and language of sport, maxims to be applied to life in general. The maxim which he has exalted above all others, to which he has given currency the country over, and which he . . . wishes to have it thought he exemplifies, is that every man is entitled to a square deal. I propose to examine the charges he makes against me, and to ask you whether in making them he is giving me a square deal." He then proceeded to take up T.R.'s charges in interminable detail. In sum, they were "unjust and unfounded"; and T.R. had "garbled" his words and "misrepresented" his actions.

Immediately after delivering his major speech, Taft spoke briefly to another overflow gathering to which he said bluntly: "Mr. Roosevelt does not understand the rule for fair dealing." Later still, a reporter on the Presidential special train went to see Taft in his private car and found him sitting slumped over with his head in his hands. The President looked up and said: "Roosevelt was my closest friend." Then he put his head down again and began to weep.

Taft's major speech in Boston had been delivered from a carefully prepared text which ran to ten pages when reprinted in the next day's papers. Roosevelt read it there and replied at Worcester, Massachusetts, the next evening, in a speech that also lasted for two hours but was delivered extemporaneously, in blazing anger and often with clenched fists. "President Taft," said T.R., "has not only been disloyal to our past friendship, but he has been disloyal to every canon of decency and fair play. . . . President Taft served under me for over seven years without finding fault with me. He only discovered I was dangerous when I discovered that he was useless to the American people. . . .

"If he had given the people a square deal, he could have counted on my enthusiastic support. I do not believe he has given the people a square deal. I believe that he has yielded to the bosses and to the great privileged interests." Referring to the reading by Taft of a letter from himself, T.R. read excerpts from Taft's letter of thanks written on his departure for Africa. "Mr. Taft is President," he said, "only because I kept my promise in spite of infinite pressure to break it. It is a bad trait to bite the hand that feeds you."

In Boston, Taft had been interrupted by enthusiastic shouts from an audience of ten thousand who said, "We'll hang Teddy's hat to a sour apple tree." T.R.'s reply was greeted by an equally partisan crowd which shouted "Hit him again, Teddy! Hit him between the eyes! Soak him! Put him over the ropes!" It was a new sort of political show and not, perhaps, an altogether edifying one. Commenting on Taft's speech, the New York *Times* spoke of "These damning charges, made by a President of the United States against an ex-President. . . ." as "one of the most deplorable occasions in the history of our politics." Of T.R.'s allusion to Taft's ingratitude *Life* sardonically pointed out: "What was it that Mr. Roosevelt's since-bitten hand fed to Mr. Taft? It was us, our country. . . . WE were that dog biscuit, for which Mr. Taft was so grateful. . . ."

As May progressed, the contest grew, if possible, even more acrimonious. T.R. referred to his successor as "a fathead" and a "puzzle-wit" adding that he had "brains less than those of a guinea-pig." Taft described his predecessor as "a dangerous egotist," a "demagogue," and a man who "could not tell the truth." Feeling the need to enlarge upon his previous statements of his position, the President of the U.S. in Hyattsville, Maryland, resorted to a revealing metaphor: "I am a man of peace and I don't want to fight. But when I do fight I want to hit hard. Even a rat in a corner will fight."

While the former cronies denounced each other in such terms, the struggle for delegates continued also. In this, the final comparative figures told the whole story. Of states with primaries, representing a total of 388 delegates, T.R. had won a total of 281 to 71 for Taft and 36 for La Follette. The former's grand total of 1,157,397 primary votes to Taft's 761,716 showed clearly that he and his supporters were entirely justified in considering him the overwhelming choice of the party's rank and file. Taft, however, had a substantial majority of the delegates instructed by state conventions and thus an apparent majority of the total of 1,078 votes in the convention. And, most important of all, in some 252 cases the elections of delegates—some chosen by primaries and some by conventions—were contested. On the outcome of these contests—on which the forty-eight members of the Republican National Committee would give a preliminary ruling twelve days before the National Convention—the nomination itself was likely to depend.

Round Two was the convention itself, before which the National Committee—as was to have been expected—had ruled in favor of the President on all the disputed delegates. This meant that, unless Roosevelt's forces could somehow alter the Committee's ruling from the floor, Taft would get the nomination on the first ballot. To upset the ruling, the first essential was to elect a chairman favorable to T.R.; and the candidate selected in the hope—which proved unjustified —that he would get the support of La Follette's delegates as well as T.R.'s was Governor Francis E. McGovern of Wisconsin. The Taft candidate was Elihu Root, once the third of the Three Musketeers; and when, after a furious contest, Root won by 558 votes to 501, Roosevelt's always slim chance to win the Republican nomination vanished for good.

The ruling on which the issue finally turned was a motion by Roosevelt's floor leader, Governor Hadley of Missouri, that some seventy-two Taft delegates, mostly chosen by state conventions, be disqualified and replaced by seventy-two Roosevelt delegates, mostly chosen in primaries. This in turn depended on whether or not the delegates whose seats were contested were to be disqualified as a group from voting on the question of the contested seats. Root—serving as a "difficult and embarrassing duty"—conceded that "no man can be permitted to vote upon the question of his own right to his seat" but quoted a House of Representatives rule to the effect that "the disqualifying interest must be such as effects the member directly, and not as one of a class." In short, each of the contested delegates was disqualified from voting on his own case but not from voting on the seventy-one others. This caused the defeat of the Hadley motion, by a vote of 567 to 507, and gave Taft a comfortable majority—provided by delegates from states where the voters had in fact indicated a substantial preference for T.R.

For uproar, confusion, and vituperative excitement, the Republican Convention of 1912 remains unique in the annals of U.S. political history. Since Root himself had been elected by a roll call in which the contested delegates were included, this distinguished statesman had already been denounced from the floor by one of Roosevelt's lieutenants as "a receiver of stolen goods." The Chicago Chief of Police, amply qualified as an expert on such matters, called this "a plain breach of the peace." Lest the Roosevelt forces attempt to take possession of the Chicago Auditorium by main force, an extra guard, in addition to the 500 police already assigned to the affair, were detailed to special night duty.

The vote on the disputed delegates was, to T.R.'s followers, clear proof that the Taft forces were resorting to what T.R. himself called "naked theft." They accused Root of running a steam roller over popular opinion and, to drive the point home, whenever the Chairman arose to make a speech or a ruling, tried to drown out his voice by tooting, whistling, or rubbing sheets of sandpaper together to imitate the sound of a steam engine. Before the convention started, Finley Dunne's

Mr. Dooley had predicted that the gathering would resemble "a combination iv th' Chicago fire, Saint Bartholemew's massacre, the battle iv the Boyne, th' life iv Jesse James, an' th' night iv the big wind." After five days of commotion that amply justified the description, Taft's name was finally put in nomination, by Warren Gamaliel Harding of Ohio. When the roll was called on Saturday evening, the result was 561 votes for Taft, 107 for Roosevelt, 41 for La Follette, 19 for other candidates and 344 abstaining. Given the abstaining votes and those of the disputed delegates, T.R. would have had enough to win by a comfortable margin.

T.R. had arrived in Chicago on June 14 and set up headquarters in the Congress Hotel. There he told reporters that he felt as fit "as a bull moose." The night before the convention he addressed a huge meeting in the Chicago Auditorium at which he denounced the theft of the delegates, claimed "a large majority of the legally elected members of the convention" and finished with a ringing peroration: "We fight in honorable fashion for the good of mankind, unheeding of our individual fates; with unflinching hearts and undimmed eyes, we stand at Armageddon, and we battle for the Lord."

During the course of the convention T.R. had told his followers: "If you are voted down the real and lawful majority will organize as such. . . ." Now the Roosevelt delegates who had abstained from voting, the delegates who had been refused seats and hundreds of other Roosevelt followers from the galleries and elsewhere marched out of the Coliseum and pledged their support to Roosevelt at a wildly enthusiastic meeting in Orchestra Hall. This was the birth of the "Bull Moose" or, more formally, the Progressive party, organized at a convention of its own on August 5. Thirty years after his discovery that the time rarely came for a man to quit his party, T.R. had found such a time. As to the Republican party,

"The only question now," said Chauncey DePew, "is which corpse gets the most flowers." On July 2 at Baltimore, the Democrats nominated Woodrow Wilson.

Round Three was, of course, the election campaign itself. Since Taft had sought somewhat belated refuge in the convention that an incumbent President should not jeopardize the prestige of office by direct appeal for votes, the real protagonists now were Wilson and T.R. Backed by funds provided mainly by Frank Munsey and Morgan partner George Perkins, the Bull Moose party named California's Governor Hiram Johnson as T.R.'s running-mate. To a gathering of 15,000 followers who cheered him for fifty minutes in the Coliseum where Taft had been nominated seven weeks before, T.R. spelled out the new party's platform in what he called a "Confession of Faith." It called for a program which combined the reforms for which he had fought in the White House with those he had proposed since his departure: strengthened regulation of big business, popular recall of judicial decisions, easier methods of amending the constitution, social welfare legislation, steeper inheritance and income taxes, health insurance, workmen's compensation, and even— though this was not a plank to which T.R. ascribed much significance—votes for women.

Who were the people who actually made up the new party? Editor William Allen White of the Emporia, Kansas *Gazette*, long one of T.R.'s closest friends, gave a picture of the delegates at the Coliseum: "Here were the successful middle-class country-town citizens, the farmer whose barn was painted, the well-paid railroad engineer, and the country editor. . . . Looking over the crowd, judging the delegates by their clothes, I figured that there was not a man or woman on the floor who was making less than two thousand a year, and not one, on the other hand, who was topping ten thousand. . . .

On the speaker's stand, we had notables from all over the
land: college presidents, heads of scientific foundations. Our
prize exhibit was Jane Addams. . . ."

Later sociologists have offered the fruits of further investigation and speculation. According to Richard Hofstadter,
cited by William Henry Harbaugh in his authoritative *Power
and Responsibility,* the nucleus of the new party was the long-
established, well-to-do U.S. aristocracy of brains and gentility
which, with the upper middle class, had lost status to the
nouveaux riches plutocrats created by the post-Civil War industrial boom. Certainly it was a thoroughly mixed bag the
extremists among which, as was the case with all extremists,
aroused little enthusiasm in T.R. For the wilder radicals in
his following he promptly coined the enduring term "lunatic
fringe" and addressed a classic letter to one member of it:

"Sir: When I spoke of the Progressive Party as having a
lunatic fringe, I specifically had you in mind. On the supposi-
tion that you are of entire sound mind, I should be obliged to
say that you are absolutly dishonorable and untruthful. I
prefer to accept the former alternative. Yours truly, . . ."

Roosevelt himself had no illusions that victory was likely,
or even possible, as he made clear in a letter written in the
heat of the campaign, to Arthur Lee. In this he predicted that
Wilson whom he called "an able man" who would not show
"Taft's muddle-headed inability will win and that I will do
better than Taft." In view of what he considered the probable
outcome, T.R. declined the support of men in government
jobs who might jeopardize these by giving it to him. In a
letter to one such, he revealed his feelings further: "Events
shaped themselves so that I had no alternative except to lead,
but I am under no illusion about it. It is a forlorn hope."
Nonetheless, there were occasions when it was a commander's

"highest duty to fight no matter how great the risk of defeat";
and this was one of them.

T.R.'s campaign was so vigorous that the condition of his
throat—a politician's most vital organ during the era before
radio, TV, and platform-amplifiers—made it necessary for him
to cancel speeches in Indiana and Wisconsin in mid-October.
He insisted however on going to Milwaukee to speak on the
fourteenth and it was there, as he was leaving his hotel for the
auditorium, that a would-be assassin fired the shot at point-
blank range that wounded him severely in the right breast.
T.R. staggered, coughed, stood up straight again, and shouted
at the crowd, which was preparing to lynch his assailant:
"Stand back. Don't hurt the man."

Since Roosevelt himself had succeeded to the Presidency
through the death by assassination of his predecessor, he
might well have been excused for experiencing some alarm
when a bullet entered his own chest. If he felt any, he concealed it. Waving aside policemen and doctors, who urged him
to go to a hospital, he went instead to the auditorium where
he proceeded to give his speech as scheduled. Slowed down
by the hole in his manuscript, as well as by his difficulty in
breathing, the speech took over an hour, after which he submitted to examination to ascertain his chances of survival.
The bullet had pierced his coat, shirt, and spectacle case as
well as the folded manuscript but, with its force thus partially
expended, had merely smashed a rib instead of entering his
heart or lungs. It was nonetheless too deep for removal and
T.R. cheerfully retained it—as one more bit of evidence
that whatever he preached he also took pains invariably to
practice.

Roosevelt's comments on the attempted murder in his correspondence with some of his worried friends were charac-

teristic. To Spring Rice he wrote: "I did not care a rap for being shot. It is a trade risk which every prominent public man ought to accept as a matter of course. For eleven years, I have been prepared any day to be shot; and if anyone of the officers in my regiment had abandoned the battle merely because he received a wound that did nothing worse than break a rib, I would never have trusted that officer again."

Later when Roosevelt was in the hospital recovering from the wound, Wilson, with a generosity to his rival that contrasted favorably with his later behavior toward him, offered to cancel his speeches until T.R. recovered. T.R. gallantly declined but by this time it was too late to have made much difference, though he recovered in time to deliver one more major speech at New York's Madison Square Garden. A few days later when the votes were counted, T.R.'s prediction to Lee had been precisely fulfilled. He had beaten Taft by 4,126,020 votes to 3,483,922 and together they had amassed more than half the popular votes cast. Wilson, however, had a total of 6,286,124—enough to give him a landslide of 435 electoral votes with eighty-eight for Roosevelt and eight for Taft, who carried only Vermont and Utah.

Taft's hope that he and T.R. would later on "be as of old" was not fulfilled, but there was at last a reconciliation of sorts. One night in the summer of 1918—during the last year of T.R.'s life—Taft spied him dining alone in Chicago's Blackstone Hotel. He hurried across the room to shake hands. Roosevelt asked him to sit down and the two sat together talking for some time, while the other diners stared and murmured. Intermittent correspondence followed this brief reunion. When Roosevelt died, on January 5, 1919, Taft attended the funeral two days later and, after the other mourners had left, stood for a few minutes alone looking down with sorrow at his old friend's grave.

XIII

"ROOSEVELT lies and curses in a most disgusting way; he gets drunk too, and that not infrequently, and all his intimate friends know about it. . . ."

When he printed this bold assertion in the Ishpeming, Michigan *Iron Ore* for October 12, 1912, George S. Newett, the editor of that obscure provincial weekly, could hardly have been prepared for the consequences. For many years, T.R. had been plagued by rumors to the effect that he was a heavy drinker. During the Bull Moose campaign these rumors had become increasingly virulent and T.R. had resolved to stop them as soon as some publication was unwary enough to phrase them in a way that would make this possible. When the *Iron Ore* obliged him by doing so, he promptly brought a suit for libel which, for the five days it lasted, made Marquette, where the case was tried, a major source of national headlines.

In fact, so far from being addicted in any way to strong drink, T.R. was only slightly less averse to it than he was to

tobacco, which he never used in any form. The only stimulant
for which he had ever displayed noticeable enthusiasm was
coffee which he liked so much, especially at breakfast, that a
special pot was provided for him at this meal, along with a
cup, which according to Theodore, Jr., was "in the nature of
a bathtub." T.R. was also a tea drinker and, though cigars and
wine were customarily served both at the White House and
Sagamore Hill, sometimes enjoyed inflicting this beverage
upon guests who would have much preferred something
stronger. One afternoon when Boss Tom Platt came to call
at Sagamore Hill, he was asked what he would like to drink.
"I'll take whatever you do, Mr. President," said the accom-
modating Platt. "I always take tea," said T.R., requesting
two cups.

So far as the rumors of T.R.'s drinking had any foundation
at all, this consisted of T.R.'s natural exuberance which,
especially upon the rostrum, was often such that he seemed
as exhilarated when sober as other men when in their cups.
As Henry Adams had once sardonically expressed it: "Theodore is never sober—only he is drunk with himself and not
with rum." The same form of exhilaration was doubtless
what also gave rise to the related report, likewise widely
circulated in 1912, that Roosevelt was not merely neurotic
but literally insane—a canard which long continued to enjoy
credence among first-growth Roosevelt haters, especially in
the South. In actual fact, Roosevelt was so thoroughly immune to the dangers of alcoholism that he could afford to
joke about it. Once, when asked if he had any bad habits, he
gaily replied: "Yes, prize-fighting and strong drink!" On
another occasion, a lady at whose Midwestern house he was
taking tea informed him of an invitation to address a meeting
of the local Young Women's Temperance League. Teacup in
hand, he replied: "My dear Madam, will you kindly say to

those young temperance women that Colonel Roosevelt is drinking very heavily and will see them in perdition first."

Outside of such facetious comments by T.R. himself, evidence to support the *Iron Ore's* charge proved to be entirely lacking. An imposing array of celebrated witnesses, in person or by deposition, testified that they had rarely seen Roosevelt drink and had never seen him in any way under the influence of liquor. Roosevelt himself dealt with the subject in full from the witness stand:

"I have never been drunk or in the slightest degree under the influence of liquor. . . . I do not drink either whiskey or brandy, except as I shall hereafter say, as I drink it under the direction of a doctor; I do not drink beer; I sometimes drink light wine. . . . I have never drunk a highball or a cocktail in my life. I have sometimes drunk mint juleps in the White House. There was a bed of mint there, and I may have drunk half a dozen mint juleps in a year, and certainly no more. At home, at dinner, I may partake of a glass or two glasses of white wine. At a public dinner, or a big dinner, if they have champagne I will take a glass or two glasses of champagne. . . . In the White House, I have drunk light wine, and not usually at all if we were alone; if there were guests I might drink a glass or two of light wine, and I might not drink anything; and in the White House I never touched brandy or whiskey except as I have described it in connection with the mint juleps or under the doctor's direction. . . . In Africa the expedition took with it a case of champagne, a case of whiskey and a bottle of brandy. I never touched a drop of either the champagne or the whiskey. . . . The only brandy I took was at the time of my two fever attacks. I drank in those two fever attacks, by direction of the doctor, about seven tablespoonfuls. . . . After the second fever attack I refused to take any more, and took tea. . . . Never, on any

occasion, on any day, in the entire time that I was in the
White House, had I ever touched a drop of anything prior to
lunch, never under any circumstances. . . . If Mrs. Roosevelt
and I were alone we had only tea or milk or water, whatever
it was, at lunch. If there were any guests, there would usually
be light wine on the table. . . . If we dined alone we had
no wine and no liquor of any kind on our table.

Since there was clearly no basis whatever for the offend-
ing statement, Editor Newett had the grace to withdraw it,
admit that he had been completely wrong and offer an apol-
ogy which T.R. accepted with characteristic good grace:

"In view of the statement of the defendant, I shall ask the
court to instruct the jury that I desire only nominal damages.
I did not go into this suit for money. I did not go into it with
any vindictive purpose. I went into it, and, as the court has
said, made my reputation an issue, because I wished, once for
all, during my own lifetime, to deal with these slanders, fully,
and comprehensively, so that never again will it be possible
for any man, in good faith, to repeat them. I have achieved
my purpose, and I am content."

The Newett case which was tried in May of 1913, and in
which damages were set at six cents, was one of several en-
terprises that helped T.R. pass the painful year after his defeat in 1912. Another was his literary work comprising articles for *The Outlook,* the completion of his *Autobiography,*
a book in collaboration with Edmund Heller on *The Life
Histories of African Game Animals* and an essay on *History as
Literature,* delivered as a lecture to the American Historical
Association in Boston in late December. Of the three, the
last has special interest as an expression of the Rooseveltian
viewpoint on life and letters generally and history-writing in
particular. In numerous earlier pronouncements, T.R. had
made the point that, in political life, words were useless ex-

cept as they related to action. By the same token, novels and other literary works were to be judged in some part for their presumptive influence upon the subsequent actions of their readers. Now, in *History as Literature,* he drew the further corollary that, to be truly effective, history needed to be much more than a dry recital of facts. The important thing was what got off the page into the mind of the reader and this depended upon the eloquence and insight of the historian. If he failed in this job, then novelists and poets would perforce do it for him, with or without historical accuracy—as Keats had proved in his famous line crediting "stout Cortez," rather than Balboa, with the discovery of the Pacific. The last paragraph of the essay sums up what T.R. wanted from the historians. As usual, it was a tall order:

> We shall sit at feast with the kings of Nineveh when they drink from ivory and gold. With Queen Maeve in her sunparlor we shall watch the nearing chariots of the champions. For us the war-horns of King Olaf shall wail across the flood, and the harps sound high at festivals in forgotten halls. The frowning strongholds of the barons of old shall rise before us, and the white palace-castles from whose windows Syrian princes once looked across the blue Aegean. We shall know the valor of the two-sworded Samurai. Ours shall be the hoary wisdom and the strange, crooked folly of the immemorial civilizations which tottered to a living death in India and in China. We shall see the terrible horsemen of Timour the Lame ride over the roof of the world; we shall hear the drums beat as the armies of Gustavus and Frederick and Napoleon drive forward to victory. Ours shall be the woe of burgher and peasant, and ours the stern joy when freemen triumph and justice comes to her own. The agony of the galley-slaves shall be ours, and the rejoicing when the wicked are brought low and the men of evil days have their reward. We shall see the glory of triumphant violence, and the revel of those who do

wrong in high places; and the broken-hearted despair that lies beneath the glory and the revel. We shall also see the supreme righteousness of the wars for freedom and justice, and know that the men who fell in these wars made all mankind their debtors.

Some day the historians will tell us of these things.

In February, T.R.'s *Chapters for an Autobiography* began to appear in *The Outlook* where he commented also on subjects of general interest. Most noteworthy of these was the famous Armory Show or International Exhibition of Modern Art, of March, 1913, which gave the U.S. its first disturbing glimpse of what painters had finally cooked up in riposte to the camera whose accomplishments in the preceding decades had caused them to suspect that mere representation was no longer adequate as an aesthetic *raison d'être*.

By far the most controversial single item on the walls of the Sixty-Ninth Regiment Armory was Marcel Duchamp's famous *Nude Descending a Staircase* which the ex-President, like a vast majority of other viewers, including most of New York's professional art critics, found somewhat confusing. Of it, he remarked with somewhat less than his usual precision, that for some reason "it is called 'A Naked Man Going Down Stairs' but could just as fittingly have been called 'A Well-Dressed Man Going Up a Ladder.'" More noteworthy than this mild rebuke, and a few similar reflections upon the early cubists—whom he found analogous to the "lunatic fringe" of the Progressive party and whose contributions resembled the "later work of the paleolithic artists of the French and Spanish caves,"—was T.R.'s reaction to the show in general. Unlike that of most professional critics this was basically favorable, and for exactly the right reasons:

"There was one note entirely absent . . . and that was the

note of the commonplace. There was not a touch of simper-
ing, self-satisfied conventionality anywhere in the exhibition.
Any sculptor or painter who had in him something to express
and the power of expressing it found the field open to him.
. . . There was no stunting or dwarfing, no requirement that
a man whose gift lay in new directions should measure up or
down to stereotyped and fossilized standards."

To many middle-aged men of industrious habit, the writing of two major books along with a career as a practicing
columnist on a weekly magazine and the busy social life inevitable for any ex-President, even an out-of-favor one, might
well have seemed adequate to pass the time. In T.R.'s case,
such activities merely served to emphasize the fact that he
needed something to do. He tried to fill in the gap by a trip
with Archie and Quentin to Arizona where among other
perilous pastimes he hunted cougar and participated in snake-
washing ceremonies involving rattlers and Hopi Indians. This
lasted only a month and by August he was back at Sagamore
Hill to prepare for the trip to South America that almost
ended his life and without doubt materially shortened it.

Among the projects that T.R. had seriously considered
after the campaign of 1912, one of the most inviting was a
journey to the North Pole. This geographical vantage point,
largely ignored by the vast majority of human beings for all
the preceding centuries of their existence, had come in for an
unwonted burst of attention during the months that T.R.
had spent in the Dark Continent when not one but two explorers suddenly claimed to have been there. One of these
was a persuasive travel-orator named Dr. Frederick Cook who,
as it later turned out, had deduced that, since witnesses
to such a discovery would be scarce in any case, it might

be feasible to gain the kudoes without bothering to make the trip. The other was a more conscientious and hard-bitten adventurer, Captain Robert E. Peary, who, preparatory to a dash across the ice by dogsled, had made the voyage to the Arctic in a ship called the *Roosevelt*. Apprised by mail of the controversy between the two, Roosevelt exercised his customary insight from a camp on the Nzoi River, near Mt. Elgon, and wrote back: "Perry is straight goods, and Cook has all the earmarks of a fake."

Under the existing circumstances the North Pole naturally seemed to T.R., when in the mood for travel, to provide an almost ideal destination. Not only did it present, in unrivalled combination, the virtues of being both conspicuous and dangerous, each to a supreme degree, but it also had a symbolical suitability which he had summed up wrily on his return from his own triumphant tour of Europe and Africa. "I am like Peary at the North Pole—there is no way for me to travel except South." That he chose instead an excursion that, while even more perilous, was considerably less glamorous, was due primarily to one of his White House author-friends, a Jesuit priest named Father John A. Zahm, of whom he explains at the start of his later book on their excursion: "Father Zahm and I had been cronies for some time because we were both of us fond of Dante and of history and science —I had always commended to theologians his book *Evolution and Dogma*. He was an Ohio boy. . . ."

The Ohio boy's earlier researches into his assorted specialties had in due course taken him to South America and, while T.R. was still in the White House, he had proposed that on his departure they explore the interior of that continent together. T.R.'s African trip had made this impractical but when in 1913, he accepted invitations to lecture in several Latin American capitals, he recalled the suggestion and resolved to act on it. First step in this direction was a lunch with Frank Chapman, Curator of Ornithology at the American Museum of Natural History, at which Zahm also unexpectedly turned up and where the project was outlined in more detail. The plan devised was to ascend the Paraguay River to its headwaters, cross the Brazil Highlands to the basin of the Amazon and then descend one of its tributaries so as to emerge eventually at Belem, then known as Para. In addition to T.R. and Zahm, the group would include an ornithologist and a mammalogist to be picked by the Museum which was understandably eager to secure as many specimens as possible of wildlife from what was then, and remains now, one of the world's least known and most impenetrable regions, the celebrated Mato Grosso, or great jungle, of Brazil.

Further embellishments were introduced later. One was the addition of Kermit, by now employed in South America by a contracting firm and recuperating from a job injury involving the loss of two teeth, two broken ribs, and a knee-dislocation, for which, according to the Rooseveltian pharmacopoeia, a scramble through the Mato Grosso would provide precisely the proper palliative. Another was to enlist the aid of Brazil's most famous indigenous explorer, an old Mato Grosso hand of Indian ancestry named Colonel Candido Mariano da Silva Rondon. The third was the proposal of an objective, made when T.R. reached Rio de Janeiro by Lauro Muller, the Brazilian Minister of Foreign Affairs, which appeared to T.R. to provide the further scientific significance needed to distinguish the trip unmistakably from ordinary tourist sight-seeing. This was that, instead of descending one of the known affluents of the Amazon, as originally planned, the party undertake to come down a mysterious stream named by Rondon the "Rio de Duvida," or River of Doubt. Rondon had discovered its sources deep in the interior but neither he nor anyone else knew what happened to its waters thereafter except that they flowed North in the general direction of the Amazon, of whose tributary system the stream seemed indisputably to be a part.

Roosevelt's lectures were delivered in Brazil, Uruguay, the Argentine, and Chile during the late autumn of 1913. On December 9, he boarded a river steamer to begin the ascent of the Paraguay, meeting en route Colonel Rondon and the two naturalists, who had already started their collecting. There followed some two months of reasonably arduous travel as the party proceeded across the country from the headwaters of the Paraguay toward those of the Duvida, hunting and collecting as they went. Finally, the expedition was divided into two parts of which one was to descend the River Gy-Parana which, while unexplored, was known to flow into the Madeira, a major affluent of the Amazon, while the other descended the Duvida.

The possibilities concerning the latter were that it might flow more West than North and enter the Gy-Parana, perhaps after a relatively short course; that it might flow more North than West and enter the Madeira, after a relatively long course; or finally, though this seemed unlikely, that it might flow Northeast and enter the Tapajos, another major affluent of the Amazon, that joined the latter down stream from the Madeira. The expedition that set forth on February 27, shortly after midday, consisted of T.R., Kermit, Rondon, Ornithologist George K. Cherrie, a Brazilian doctor and geologist named Eusebio de Oliveira and Rondon's subordinate, Lieutenant João Lyra, along with sixteen native paddlers, or *camaradas,* in seven dugout canoes. With them they took enough provisions to last for some fifty days, hoping to be able to supplement these stores by shooting game, catching fish, and eating local vegetation such as nuts and palm-tops.

"It was at the height of the raining season and the swollen torrent was swift and brown," T.R. noted in the opening passage of his running story of the venture, which was soon to develop into a series of disasters.

First of the catastrophes that befell the expedition was the death by drowning of one of the camaradas some two weeks after their departure, when a canoe that also contained Kermit and another paddler was swept into one of the savage rapids of which the river proved to be largely composed. Kermit and the other camarada barely escaped with their lives. The second was a personal feud between a surly and lazy camarada and one of his hard-working companions a few days later which ended in the murder of the latter, the culprit then running off into the jungle. The third catastrophe was a serious injury to T.R. when, working to extricate two canoes that had become jammed against the rocks in fast water, he bruised the leg which had been injured a decade before in the Pittsfield trolley accident and which had been periodically subject to painful infections ever since. T.R.'s own account of this mishap was characteristically laconic: "While in the water trying to help with an upset canoe I had by my own clumsiness bruised my leg against a boulder; and the resulting inflammation was somewhat bothersome." A more explicit description was later provided by the naturalist, Cherrie.

Cherrie, when recruited for the expedition by the Museum, had experienced some qualms about joining. Though well qualified as an expert on birds, as an experienced sojourner in South American jungles and even as an enthusiastic supporter of the Progressive party, he stood so much in awe of its founder as to doubt whether he would be up to sharing the intimacies of outdoor life with such an important dignitary. His nervousness on this score was not completely resolved until one day when, on returning to camp after a brief reconnoitering excursion, he found that T.R., already too ill to leave camp, had, while cleaning up his own kit, washed some of Cherrie's shirts along with his own. Meanwhile, T.R. had formed a good opinion of the ornithologist for reasons set down in his own account of the journey:

"Twice he had been behind the bars . . . on one occasion spending three months in a prison of a certain South American state, expecting each day to be taken out and shot. In another state he had, as an interlude to his ornithological pursuits, followed the career of a gun-runner, acting as such off and on for two and a half years. The particular revolutionary chief whose fortunes he was following finally came into power, and Cherrie immortalized his name by naming a new species of ant-thrush after him—a delightful touch, in its practical combination of those not normally kindred pursuits, ornithology and gun-running."

Cherrie's account of the expedition's most critical phase was recorded by a stenographer from his address to the Roosevelt Memorial Meeting of the Explorers Club on March 1, 1919, two months after its subject's death. It sheds light not only on that crisis but also—albeit a less charitable one than that focussed by T.R.—upon Foreign Minister Muller and the redoubtable Candido Rondon to whom T.R. later dedicated his book, *Brazilian Wilderness:*

"There were a good many days, a good many mornings, when I looked at Colonel Roosevelt and said to myself, he won't be with us tonight; and I would say the same thing in the evening, he can't possibly live until morning. I can't speak of the others, but I know as far as Kermit and myself were concerned, the fact that the Colonel was with us gave us energy to do things we couldn't possibly have done otherwise.

"We had lost three or four canoes, and were in dire straits indeed. We had come down to the foot of the rapids, and the canoemen were to run the rapids with the empty canoes. We had carried the contents to the foot of the rapids, and the men had succeeded in getting down most of the canoes successfully. I had wandered away from the rest of the party, and was at the foot of the rapids, watching the canoemen coming down. They had a balsa, two boats lashed together side by side, an unwieldy craft that was caught in the angry whirl of waters and capsized. By some strange chance the two canoes instead of being whirled away and crushed were thrust down and held by the force of the current against some rocks. The two canoemen had managed to keep hold of the canoes and stood waist-deep exerting all their strength to try and hold them, although as a matter of fact it was hardly necessary, for the force of the current held the boats. I rushed in but couldn't do anything alone, so getting out I ran as fast as I could to the foot of the rapids, and gave the alarm 'Two boats have capsized and held against the rocks by the current. If they wash loose they will be crushed among the boulders!' The Colonel and other members of the party responded instantly, but the Colonel was the first one in the water. We all followed as quickly as we could, and working in the water up to our armpits, finally, with our united efforts, we were able to raise the two boats and save them.

"At that time the Colonel received a severe bruise on one of his legs, a wound that troubled him from that time forward. Indeed, it was the first night after that accident that he was seriously ill, his temperature going up to something like one hundred and five degrees. From that time on he was a very sick man.

"We lost one boat after another, and lost so much of our food that we were on very much less than half rations. Kermit and I had to watch the Colonel to prevent his giving to the camaradas his share of food. He began to fail, almost immediately after he was sick with the fever. He seemed to feel that he was a burden, that he wasn't helping. Whenever either Kermit or I would protest about his giving his portion of food to the canoemen he would say: 'I can't do anything to help and they need the food.' We had to watch him constantly, and reached the point where if he didn't eat all of his share either Kermit or I would take what was left and guard it until a later meal. We had so very little that every mouthful counted at that time.

"Finally, we reached a point in the river where the stream cut its course through a range of hills, rushing down through a very narrow gorge for three hundred yards. The walls of the canyon here were nearly vertical, coming down right to the water's edge. On our arrival at that point we made our camp at the head of the rapids, just before they plunge down through the canyon, while Colonel Rondon and Lieutenant Lyra went ahead to make an examination, to see if it would be possible for us to get our four remaining canoes down. I shall never forget the look on Colonel Rondon's face when he returned and reported: 'We will have to abandon all our canoes, and every man fight for himself!' Had we abandoned the canoes at that point I don't believe that any member of the party would have come out; it would have simply been folly. The Indians were on all sides; although we were never attacked. But the fate of a later expedition that the Brazilian Government sent down through the same stream has proved that the Indians would have been very hostile. They were hostile to the second expedition, in fact annihilating the party completely.

"That night Colonel Roosevelt called Kermit and me to him and said—he was unable to walk—he turned first to me and said: 'Cherrie, I want you and Kermit to go ahead. We have reached a point where some of us must stop. I feel I am only a burden to the party.' He was prepared to make the great sacrifice. . . .

"All credit should be given to Kermit for our finally getting our canoes through the narrow canyon. We worked there nearly a week, and succeeded in getting three canoes down safely. The few supplies still remaining had to be carried over the divide or range of hills. I assisted the Colonel, and we spent the entire day making the trip over the hill and down to the foot of the rapids. We had learned long before that wherever the stream entered among the hills we were in for trouble. From the top of this range we could look down and see the River of Doubt (at that time it was the River Roosevelt; we had long before passed the point where Colonel Rondon had rechristened the stream), like an arrow of light between the walls of green forest, finally disappearing among the hills in the distance. I am sure every member of our party, as he looked from the top of that divide and saw where the river disappeared, felt his heart sink with dread. We were so weak from the lack of food, the lack of proper food. We had been eating a great deal of the tops of the palms at that time and eating it raw. It tastes a little bit like celery when fresh. We had nothing else a good many days. We could not possibly have made another long carry or fight with rapids.

"During the night when we camped at the foot of the canyon, Kermit was on his watch; I could have reached the Colonel from my hammock. I had been dozing off, and was awakened with the murmur of voices, the Colonel and Kermit talking. The first thing I heard was the Colonel saying to Kermit: 'Did Cherrie have a good dinner tonight?' As a matter of fact we hadn't had very much of anything. Kermit said: 'Yes, father, Cherrie had a fine dinner.' 'That is good,' said the Colonel, and there the conversation dropped. . . .''

On April 10, the expedition was still battling rapids, with hours of weary portage for every few minutes of downstream run on the water. Ill-suited for either, the heavy dugouts—of which several had been hollowed out en route, to replace five of the original seven which had been swamped or crushed in the fast water—moved T.R. to a lyric passage in his own subsequent account of the journey: "How I longed for a big Maine birchbark, such as that in which I once went down the Mattawamkeag at high water! It would have slipped down these rapids as a girl trips through a country dance. . . ." Finally, on April 14, they camped for the first time in weeks out of earshot of rapids. The next day, they encountered an initialled post and then a rubber worker's "newlybuilt house in a little planted clearing" that made it clear that they had at last safely reached the fringes of civilization. There followed a few days of relatively easy paddling; and a placid cruise by steamer down the Madeira—for it was into this that the Duvida eventually flowed; and then the broad Amazon to the port of Belem and the voyage home.

When, on his return from this grueling excursion, T.R. reached New York on May 19, there was no harbor full of welcoming boats, no twenty-one gun salute, and no parade up Broadway and Fifth Avenue between sidewalks lined by cheering crowds. Only a handful of old friends were on hand when, fifty-five pounds lighter than when he had left, and so weak he leaned heavily on a cane, he hobbled slowly down the gangplank. T.R. went first to Sagamore Hill and then, less than a week later, to Washington to call on the President, and speak before the National Geographic Society. What the expedition had actually accomplished was the exploration of an unknown river approximately a thousand miles long—the biggest affluent of the biggest affluent of the biggest river in the world—which, theretofore, had been totally unknown to the world's cartographers and which was now rechristened the Rio Roosevelt. In reviewing T.R.'s story, first published in *Scribner's* and later in book form, the *Bulletin* of the American Geographical Society described the voyage as "a first class piece of real exploration." In 1916, T.R. received the David Livingstone Centenary Gold Medal for it. Roosevelt's own best summation of his feat was perhaps that which he later confided to Owen Wister: "I had to go. It was my last chance to be a boy."

In April of 1913, a few months before T.R.'s departure for South America, Ethel Roosevelt had married Dr. Richard Derby, an Oyster Bay surgeon who was also a graduate of Harvard where, like T.R., Kermit, and Archie, he had been a member of the Porcellian Club. The wedding was a quiet affair, the list of guests at which, as T.R. explained to his friend "Winty" Chanler, had been somewhat curtailed by political considerations: "We did not send invitations to Root or Taft or Nicholas Murray Butler. . . . I shall never forgive the men who were the leaders in that swindling." In May of 1914, a few days after his return, he left for Madrid to attend the wedding there of Kermit to Belle Willard, daughter of the proprietor of Washington's Willard Hotel who was then the U.S. Ambassador to Spain. On the way back, he stopped for a few days in London to visit his old friend Arthur Lee, at his house *Checquers*, later presented to the government as the official country residence for Prime Ministers, to talk with an array of other resident notables, including Grey, Selous and James Bryce, and to address the Geographical Club. By June 25, he was back at Sagamore

Hill and ready once more to plunge into the commotions of domestic politics.

As usual, these provided a plenitude of problems of which the most pressing was the future of the Progressive party which had been causing T.R. grave concern ever since the defeat of 1912. The party had attracted strong support from two opposing elements. One of these consisted of reasonably solid citizens like Publisher Frank Munsey and Morgan partner George Wallridge Perkins, whose essential motivation was so far as possible to preserve existing institutions by effecting appropriate reforms. The other consisted of radicals, most notably Gifford Pinchot and his brother Amos, who were emotionally hostile to conservatism generally and to the conservatives within the Progressive party in particular. By the time the 1912 ballots had been counted, the Pinchots and their friends were badgering T.R. to demand the resignation of Perkins as the Party's national chairman. In a letter to Kermit, discussing the possibilities of his trip to Brazil the next year, T.R. had, in December of 1912, described his position in the dispute:

"At the moment my chief task is to prevent the Progressives from fighting one another. The good Pinchots and their kind, the advanced radicals, want to fight Perkins and others, who as a matter of fact have been even more useful than the Pinchots in helping us in this fight. I think I shall be able to keep both sides together. But it is very weary work, and it is irritating now because I ought not to be required to do such work. As I have said so often before, this whole business of leading a new party should be for an ambitious young colonel, and not for a retired major general."

To Amos Pinchot himself, T.R. had gone into the matter with more tact and greater detail:

"Now, my dear Amos, you speak (what I know you feel)

with great sympathy of the task that I am trying to carry through, the task of taking a part in leading a great movement and in keeping its supporters together and planning for the future. Moreover, I absolutely agree with you that this Progressive Party, with its thousands of earnest men and women giving their strength to the cause of humanity, and with the millions of struggling people who see some hope in a cause dedicated to economic justice instead of to politics, offers something very fine and very full of possibilities of real usefulness to our country. I moreover agree absolutely with what you say as to the Progressive Party's claiming to be something different from and better than the old parties, and standing not only for political victory but to establish social and economic justice. As you say, our purpose is to free the industrial slave as Lincoln freed the chattel slave. But I utterly differ with you as to your belief about the source of the dangers with which we are threatened. I believe that our vote would have been cut in half at once if we had not been able to persuade two or three millions of good men and women that we were not engaged in an assault on property, or in wild and foolish radicalism. I believe that the suspicion that we were overradical, were jeopardizing property and business, cost us a million or two of votes. I further believe that if we put out Perkins, and then did the only logical thing by putting out all the men like him, we should gain one or two hundred thousand votes and lose two or three million. I mean in all sincerity that I think that if the policy you advocate had been adopted at the outset of this campaign—for of course Perkins is simply a symbol, and it is idle to put out Perkins if you don't put out all the men of the same stamp—that we would have been a rival to Debs in the running, and would have lost every particle of power to fight for a good cause."

If, as is possible, T.R. had hoped that in his absence on the River of Doubt the squabbling factions in the party would adjust their differences and reach amicable agreement among themselves, his hopes were doomed to disappointment. By June of 1914, on the contrary, Amos Pinchot was circularizing the National Committee to secure the resignation of Perkins whom he described as "monopoly's ardent supporter and one of the most distinguished opponents of social and industrial justice." Meanwhile, quite aside from the personal feuds within the party, there was increasing friction as to what role T.R. should take in the autumn's elections and what policies the Progressives should stand for in the various states. Even such a usually sane and dependable member of the group as William Allen White, for example, was in favor of government ownership of railroads and Prohibition. T.R. lost no time in setting him right on these matters:

"I am very pleased that Mrs. White likes the jaguar skin. But, my dear fellow, I think it would be very unwise for us to go into government ownership of railways, or national prohibition. . . . I have just come from England, where they have government ownership of telephones, and the service is not to be compared with the service in this country. . . . As for prohibition nationally, it would merely mean free rum and utter lawlessness in our big cities. Worthy people sometimes say that liquor is responsible for nine tenths of all crime. As a matter of fact foreigners of the races that furnish most crime in New York at the present time do not drink at all. . . . I do not believe that the American people can be dragooned into being good by any outside influence, whether it is a king or the majority in some other locality. . . ."

But even the schisms and cliques within his own party were not the main problems that confronted T.R., still intermittently wracked by the fever contracted in Brazil, in the late spring of 1914. Now, for the first time since Grover Cleveland, theretofore the only President to represent this party since the Civil War, there was a Democrat in the White House. This meant that the policies and purposes which T.R. had stood for would be not merely misunderstood and mismanaged, as they had been under Taft, but that they would be for the most part disregarded, disdained, or derided.

Roosevelt and Wilson had first met, and liked each other, when, with the former a Police Commissioner of New York and the latter a lecturer at Johns Hopkins, they had shared the platform as speakers at a meeting in Baltimore. In later years they corresponded intermittently. As Governor of New York, T.R. found one of Wilson's early speeches "admirable in every way" and invited him to visit Albany. In 1902, when Wilson became President of Princeton, T.R. was delighted. "Woodrow Wilson is a perfect trump," he said, and sent outspoken congratulations: "As an American interested in that kind of productive scholarship which tends to statesmanship I hail your election as President of Princeton." By 1907, the incipient friendship had begun to cool but upon T.R.'s part, respect at least endured through the campaign of 1912; and even in the winter of 1913 he was able to say: ". . . if he is big enough to master his party he may make a great record and rivet the attention of the country. . . ."

The first indication of what the new administration might presently mean to T.R. in terms of personal frustrations, indignity and injustice was delayed until the spring of 1914. Then, on his emergence from the jungle, he learned that on April 6, at almost exactly the moment of his most painful difficulties on the River of Doubt, Wilson's Secretary of State William Jennings Bryan had signed, and the President had approved, a Treaty with Colombia which, in effect, denounced the means by which Roosevelt had made possible the building of the Panama Canal. The Treaty proffered "sincere regret that anything should have occurred to interrupt or mar the relations of cordial friendship that had so long subsisted between the two governments," promised Colombia an indemnity of $25,000,000, and gave that nation rights equivalent to those of the U.S. in using the Canal.

Roosevelt's reaction was as instantaneous as it was indignant. In an article for *The Outlook,* which appeared only three days after his return to the United States, he expressed incredulity that "Mr. Wilson has so far forgotten the dictates of honor and his duty as a citizen . . . to pay $25,000,000 or any other sum . . . Not one dollar can be paid . . . with propriety, and it would be an act of infamy to pay even a dollar to a nation which, in crooked greed, tried by blackmail to smirch the good name of America."

Early in July, T.R. suggested that he be requested "to appear before the Senate Committee on Foreign Affairs and give them the full history of the dealings of my Administration with Colombia concerning the acquisition of the Panama Canal." The Senate failed to call T.R. but in response to leadership by Cabot Lodge, and in an action which might have served the President as a warning of things to come, it did block passage of the Treaty. Seven years later, after the death of T.R. and under the Presidency of Warren Harding, a somewhat similar treaty was nonetheless passed—this time with Lodge arguing in its favor—primarily as a means of persuading Colombia to extend certain privileges to U.S. oil companies.

What with the uproar over the Colombia Treaty, the schisms in the Progressive party, and the marked lack of excitement created by his return from the River of Doubt, there was little to encourage T.R.'s convalescence from his jungle fever with the possible exception of the progress being made in Washington by the young relative whose wedding he had attended in 1905. T.R. had already congratulated Franklin Delano Roosevelt on his appointment as Assistant Secretary of the Navy, "another place which I myself once held." In a subsequent letter he had warned his young namesake against the danger of dividing the fleet. To this counsel the latter's enthusiastic reaction was to urge his distinguished predecessor to write magazine articles so as to arouse popular support along the same lines. T.R. enthusiastically replied:

"All right! I will do that. I will get at it as soon as possible. . . . Give my dearest love to Eleanor and the blessed children!. . ."

T.R.'s letter to his namesake was dated July 23. By that time, it was almost a month since a fanatic, with better aim than the one who had fired at T.R. two years before, had emptied his revolver into the inoffensive person of the Archduke Ferdinand whose travail in reaching London for King Edward's funeral T.R. had recorded in 1910. By late July, the great powers of Europe were exchanging final notes and ultimata. A few days later the guns would start to speak.

XIV

"THEN there would have been no war?" I asked.

"There would have been no war," he said.

This startling exchange between T.R. and Mary Roberts Rinehart, relating what the former thought would have happened had he been in the White House in 1914, was recalled by the latter as having taken place early in 1917. It parallels T.R.'s conversations with, and letters to, many others to the effect that, had the President of the U.S. acted vigorously at the right moment, the First World War could easily have been avoided. Precisely what T.R. would have done just before the German invasion of neutral Belgium he explained in a letter to Cecil Spring Rice on October 3, 1914:

"If I had been President, I should have acted on the thirtieth or thirty-first of July, as head of a signatory power of the Hague treaties, calling attention to the guaranty of Belgium's neutrality and saying that I accepted the treaties as imposing a serious obligation which I expected not only the United States but all other neutral nations to join in enforcing. Of course, I would not have made such a statement unless I was willing to back it up. I believe that if I had been President the American people would have followed me. But whether I am mistaken or not as regards that, I am certain that the majority are now following Wilson."

T.R.'s reasons for making this distinction were later spelled out, in a conversation with another young writer, Julian Street:

"It is with the people of a country much as with a regiment. There is an old saying that there are few bad regiments but plenty of bad colonels. No matter how good a regiment may be, if, in the stress of a great fight, its colonel advises each man, as a matter of duty to do whatever is best for his own comfort and safety, and if the colonel, still uttering lofty abstract sentiments, then marches to the rear, it may be taken for granted that the regiment will follow."

Roosevelt's accomplishments during the Russo-Japanese War, the Algeciras Conference and the Venezuela crisis, coupled with his lifelong habit of candor in such matters, place his comments on this subject outside the class of ordinary hindsight. To the cynical or the timid historian, thinking of human beings as puny incompetents at the mercy of vast impersonal forces, it may seem outrageous even to suggest that one man, by a few words at the proper moment, could have saved humanity all the immense suffering caused, directly and otherwise, by the First World War. Contrary-to-fact conditions in history can never be completely reliable but nonetheless the weight of evidence clearly suggests that T.R. would have done precisely that.

Though in marked contrast to what T.R. might have done to prevent the First World War, what he actually did in it

was perhaps noteworthy enough. This was eloquently
summed up by Elihu Root in a speech to the Century Association in February, 1919, a month after T.R.'s death: "He
was denied his dearest wish to fight upon the battle front
with the four strong sons whom he had trained in all the
traditions of heroism. He had no source of influence save his
life, his character, his intense convictions; but it was then
that he rose to the greatest height of his wonderful career.
Day by day and month by month he appealed with passion
and power to the people who had loved him; and that clear,
insistent call to courage, and honor, and duty, and the noble
ways of a nation's life, did more, I think, to bring America
in arms to the battlefield before it was too late and to defeat
the autocracy of Germany than any public officer—civil or
military—for whom the flags are dipped as the victorious
regiments pass in review."

Roosevelt's call to courage was deferred until—as suggested
by the analogy of T.R.'s cautious colonel—it became unmistakably obvious that Wilson had no intention whatsoever
of providing one. "For the past sixty days, I . . . supported
Wilson . . . on the assumption that he was . . . correct in
his statement that we had no responsibility for what had been
done in Belgium," T.R. later recalled. Only when he had
examined the Hague conventions himself had he seen that
"they did demand action on our part." In the first weeks
of the war he wrote to Arthur Lee: "I am an ex-President;
and my public attitude must be one of entire impartiality."
To a newspaperman, he said: "What we have to do is not
to put obstacles in the way of the administration."

In the autumn of 1914—writing for the *Metropolitan* which
had by then replaced *The Outlook* as his literary rostrum—
T.R. began with increasing urgency to stress the importance

—now that it was too late to prevent the war—of preparing for possible involvement in it. Lunching with T.R. in New York in 1915, Joseph Medill Patterson, then publisher of the Chicago *Tribune,* asked him a basic question: "You even seem to want to get us into war on the Allied side. Is it just Belgium, or do you feel that America itself is menaced?" T.R. answered that, if Germany won, she would eventually threaten U.S. interests in the Caribbean and added: "In this way, we would be thrown into hostilities with Germany sooner or later and with far less chance of success than if we joined with the powers which are now fighting her."

Meanwhile the President's view of the situation developed in the opposite direction. He urged the nation to remain "impartial in thought as well as in action." In his annual message of December, 1914, careful not to mention T.R. by name, he said: "We shall not alter our attitude . . . because some of us are nervous or excited." He spoke grandly of the way in which the war "affords us opportunities of friendship and disinterested service which should make us ashamed of any thought of hostility or fearful preparation for trouble." A nation, he said, could be "too proud to fight."

On May 1, 1915, the New York *Herald* carried an advertisement for the sailing on that day for Europe via Liverpool of the *"Lusitania*—fastest and largest Steamer now in Atlantic Service." Directly below this was a sinister warning:

NOTICE!

TRAVELERS intending to embark on the Atlantic voyage are reminded that a state of war exists between Germany and her allies and Great Britain and her allies; that the zone of war includes the waters adjacent to the British Isles; that, in accordance with formal notice given by the Imperial German Government, vessels flying the flag of Great Britain, or of any of her allies, are liable to destruction in those waters and that travelers sailing in the war-zone on ships of Great Britain or her allies do so at their own risk.

IMPERIAL GERMAN EMBASSY

Washington, D.C. April 22, 1915

The warning went largely unheeded. On May 7, a German submarine torpedoed the *Lusitania*—which was later found to have been carrying munitions as well as passengers—off Kinsale Head, on the Irish Coast. She sank in 18 minutes with the loss of 1198 lives, among them 114 Americans including such varied notables as Charles Frohman, Alfred Gwynne Vanderbilt, and Elbert Hubbard.

Wilson's just reaction to the sinking of the *Lusitania* was the celebrated speech in Philadelphia which referred to the U.S. as being "too proud to fight." His next was to send a note to the German government through diplomatic channels, protesting the action. In June he sent a second note. In July he dispatched a third one. When the German response to these communications proved "very unsatisfactory," he went one step further by declaring that hereafter the sinking of unarmed merchant ships would be considered "deliberately unfriendly."

When T.R. received word of the sinking of the *Lusitania*, he was engaged in another suit for libel—this time as the defendant. During the campaign of 1914, he had asserted that William Barnes, Jr., successor to Tom Platt as New York's Republican boss, was as crooked as his Democratic opposite number, adding that "the two bosses will always be found on the same side openly or covertly, giving one another such support as can with safety be rendered." Barnes's lawyer had stated that, when the case came to trial, in Syracuse, New York, he would "nail Roosevelt's hide to the fence." Elihu Root had replied with a gentle warning: "I know Roosevelt and you want to be very sure that it is Roosevelt's hide you get on the fence."

On the Barnes case jury were two German-Americans who, like a considerable portion of the rest of the U.S. population, were presumably anti-Ally. Nonetheless, when wakened by a telephone call from a New York editor, requesting a statement on the sinking of the *Lusitania*, T.R. paused only long enough to learn the salient facts of the disaster. "That's murder!" he said, "Will I make a statement? Yes, yes. I'll make it now. Just take this:

"This represents not merely piracy but piracy on a vaster scale than old-time pirates ever practiced. . . . It seems inconceivable that we can refrain from taking action in this matter, for we owe it not only to humanity but to our own national self-respect."

As usual, T.R. was entirely specific as to the action he had in mind. It was immediately to seize all interned German ships in U.S. harbors and to end all commerce with Germany. He added that, had he been in the White House when the German Embassy warned prospective passengers against taking passage on the *Lusitania*, he would have ordered the Ambassador to leave on the same ship. The morning after issuing his statement, Roosevelt told his lawyers that it had probably offended the two German-Americans on the jury but that "There is a principle at stake here which is more vital to the American people than my personal welfare is to me." As things turned out the jury decided that his comments on Barnes had been completely justified—thus nailing the boss's hide to the fence so securely that he presently ceased to be a major factor in New York politics.

The issue of whether or not the U.S. should or should not prepare for war lasted until late in 1915. Then the President cut the ground from under his own feet in a note stating

that Germany would henceforth be held to "strict accountability." This made it obvious that, as T.R. had been saying
and the President had been denying, there was a strong
possibility of U.S. involvement and that accordingly the
nations should get ready to meet it. By the fall of 1915, the
pacifist Bryan—who had resigned as Secretary of State after
the second *Lusitania* note, which he considered too provoca-
tive—complained that even the President was preaching the
Roosevelt gospel. But now the issue between Wilson and
T.R. became that of the way in which Wilson was conduct-
ing the preparation which even he had been forced to acknowledge was essential.

By this time, T.R.'s feelings toward the President had developed from mild disapproval to bitter contempt. In the
summer of 1915, Alice Longworth, visiting at Sagamore Hill,
observed that the President had sent another protest to Ber-
lin. "Did you notice what its serial number was?" asked
T.R. "I fear I have lost track myself; but I am inclined to
think it is No. 11, 785, Series B."

"I do not believe," he said when calling for the seizure
of Germany's interned ships, "that the firm assertion of our
rights means war, but, in any event, it is well to remember
that there are worse things than war." When Wilson finally
adopted the policy of preparedness which T.R. had been
demanding for a year, T.R. distrusted his motives: "Wilson
. . . has come to the conclusion that there is a rising popular
feeling for preparedness, and, seeing votes in it, is prepared
to take it up."

The President inspired T.R. to heights of disdainful eloquence in a letter to Owen Wister: "Nothing is more sicken-
ing than the continual praise of Wilson's English, of Wilson's
style. He is a true logothete, a real sophist; and he firmly
believes, and has had no inconsiderable effect in making our

people believe, that elocution is an admirable substitute for
and improvement on action." Wilson's use of the phrase
"universal voluntary military training" moved T.R. to the
invention of one of his most celebrated epithets:

"When a weasel sucks eggs the meat is sucked out of the
egg. If you use a 'weasel word' after another there is nothing
left of the other. You can have universal training, or you
can have voluntary training, but when you use the word
'voluntary' to qualify the word 'universal' you are making
a 'weasel word'; it has sucked all the meaning out of 'universal.' "

Late in 1916, when Congress belatedly and grudgingly
passed a National Defense Act raising the size of the standing
army from 100,000 to 220,000 and strengthened the National
Guard, T.R., not without considerable justification, called
this "as foolish and unpatriotic a bit of flintlock legislation
as was ever put on the statute books."

The issue between T.R. and the President was partially
tested in the Presidential elections of 1916. Roosevelt's original hope had been to bring back the Progressives into the
Republican party, nominate a strong candidate who would
be acceptable to both wings of the party—if not himself, then
possibly Governor Hiram Johnson of California—and run
him on a platform calling for entry into the war. Though
the scars of 1912 were too recent to make such an outcome at
all probable, T.R. wanted the nomination for himself. At the
same time, he wanted it, as always, on his own terms and
went to considerable lengths to make these clear. ". . . It
would be a mistake to nominate me unless the country has
in its mood something of the heroic—unless it feels not only
devotion to ideals but the purpose measurably to realize
those ideals in action," he insisted in one public statement.
In May, he went on a speaking tour of the Midwest where

he chose St. Louis as the appropriate locale for a denunciation of one of his favorite targets, the so-called "hyphenated"
Americans. "It is our purpose this fall to elect an American
President and not a viceroy of the German Emperor," he
announced a week before the Republican Convention—
where German-Americans were sure to be strongly represented—met in Chicago. The Convention nominated Supreme Court Justice Charles Evans Hughes.

Hughes, though committed to preparedness, based his campaign mainly on the theory that a stronger policy than Wilson's would be an even surer method of staying out of the
war. T.R. declined the Progressive nomination, so as not to
assure the President's re-election by again dividing the Republican vote. He then campaigned without much enthusiasm for a candidate whom he had at various times described
as "not an attractive personality . . ." "a very, very self-
centered man" and "another Wilson with whiskers." While,
true to his cautious legalistic character, Hughes pussyfooted
on the major issue of the day, T.R. made forthright speeches
which alarmed the Republican National Committee. Its decision not to have T.R. speak in California, where his erstwhile Progressive running-mate Hiram Johnson was the
popular governor, perhaps hurt the ticket in that state even
more than Hughes's celebrated failure to call on Johnson
when the two stayed overnight at the same hotel.

On the last night of the campaign, T.R. made his climactic
speech at the Cooper Union. Its most eloquent passage was a
bitter castigation of the President then living at a New Jersey
summer residence called Shadow Lawn:

"There should be shadows now at Shadow Lawn; the
shadows of the men, women and children who have risen
from the ooze of the ocean bottom and from the graves in
foreign lands; the shadows of the helpless whom Mr. Wilson

did not dare protect lest he might have to face danger; the shadows of babies gasping pitifully as they sank under the waves; the shadows of women outraged and slain by bandits. . . . Those are the shadows proper for Shadow Lawn; the shadows of deeds that were never done; the shadows of lofty words that were followed by no action; the shadows of the tortured dead."

Hughes, who went to bed on the evening of Election Day thinking that he had won the election, awoke to learn that the late returns from California had swung the result the other way.

"The President's great message of April 2 was literally unanswerable. Of course, when war is on, all minor considerations, including all partisan considerations, vanish at once. All good Americans will back the President with single-minded loyalty in every movement he makes to uphold American honor, defend American rights, and strike hard and effectively in return for the brutal wrong doing of the German Government."

The sharp contrast between T.R.'s Shadow Lawn speech and his response to the war message to Congress which Wilson delivered on April 2 was due to the rapidity with which events had moved in the interim. In late January, Germany had resumed unlimited submarine warfare and announced that only one clearly marked American ship a week would be allowed to pass through the war zone each way. Early in February diplomatic relations between Germany and the U.S. were broken off. Later that month, British Naval Intelligence revealed the existence of a telegram from Germany's Foreign Minister Waldeman Zimmerman to the German Ambassador to Mexico, proposing a German-Mexican alliance whereby Mexico might recover all the territory lost in the war of 1848. Wilson now used the bold phrase "armed neutrality" but when, in March, more American ships were sunk, it was clear that, proud or otherwise, the U.S. would soon have to fight.

A strong contrast also marked the reactions of the nation's two major leaders to the changed condition. Meeting on March 20 with his cabinet which urged him to declare war, Wilson was reluctant to the last. "Every reform we have won will be lost if we go into this war," he lamented. "War means autocracy. The people we have unhorsed will inevitably come into the control of the country for we shall be dependent upon the steel, oil, and financial magnates. They will run the nation." To Editor Frank Cobb of the New York *World,* he confided further misgivings. "To fight you must be brutal and ruthless, and the spirit of ruthless brutality will enter into the very fibre of our national life, infecting congress, the courts, the policemen on the beat, the man in the street. . . . If there is any alternative, for God's sake, let's take it."

To T.R., on the other hand, the Zimmerman telegram and the new wave of sinkings called for immediate action. "I am as yet holding in," he wrote Lodge, "but if he does not go to war with Germany I shall skin him alive." To the recently hostile Union League Club in New York—a large and far from exclusive organization, not to be confused with the smaller Union Club, whose socially impeccable members had doubtless felt even more outraged by Progressive policies—T.R. put the matter in his usual forceful style on the same day that Wilson met with his cabinet. After pointing out that the U.S. was, in effect, letting England fight its battles, he summed up the situation: "Let us dare to use our own strength in our own defense and strike hard for our national interest and honor. There is no question about 'going to war.' Germany is already at war with us. The only question for us to decide is whether we shall make war nobly or ignobly."

Roosevelt's expression of enthusiasm for Wilson's war message was understandable enough. Not only did this represent complete confirmation of the viewpoint that he had been stating with all the considerable emphasis at his command for the previous two and a half years. In addition it appeared to open up possibility of realizing a project that had been taking shape in his own mind since the autumn of 1914. At that time, in a meeting at the Harvard Club, Roosevelt had first broached the idea, in the event that the U.S. entered the war, of raising a division of mounted infantry. By January, 1915, the idea had assumed more definite form when Theodore, Jr., brought to Sagamore Hill his friend Colonel Gordon Johnston of the regular Army, who later recalled:

"I found Colonel Roosevelt . . . suffering from one of his attacks of fever. . . . He was walking the floor and talking about the war, our failure to come in and his unavailing efforts to influence the Administration. He mentioned how much he would like to have a part in it, and that gave me a clue to make a suggestion, partly to divert his mind." The Johnston suggestion was that Roosevelt start organizing the division at once. T.R., always eager for action, welcomed this plan and began listing names of possible officers. For the next two years, organizing the division had occupied much of his thoughts.

By February 2, 1917, T.R. felt sure enough of eventual U.S. entry into the war to write Wilson's pacifically-minded Secretary of War, Newton D. Baker, to explain what he had in mind and try to enlist Baker's support. What he proposed was a volunteer group more or less along the lines of the Rough Riders only considerably bigger and one in which "the bronco-buster type will be very much lacking." The division was to have "one brigade of cavalry and one or two brigades of mounted infantry." He had, he explained to Baker, already chosen the officers he wanted for major staff and command positions: mostly regular Army men for field grade and business or professional men below. Baker's reply was haughty but not conclusively negative: "No situation has arisen" requiring such a division: T.R.'s letter would be "filed for consideration should the occasion arise."

As the crisis grew more intense, the correspondence continued. On February 7, Roosevelt specifically requested the appointment of Captain Frank McCoy as his chief of staff, with the rank of Colonel. Baker's reply was that action of this sort could not be taken "without the express sanction of Congress . . . under its own conditions." A month later, T.R. explained his program in more detail. He needed one regular officer for each eight hundred or a thousand volunteers: the division could leave for France after six weeks and undergo final training in France. Baker remained coldly noncommittal but now shifted his ground so far as to permit some inference that the occasion *had* arisen, saying that general officers "for all volunteer forces are to be drawn from the regular Army." Roosevelt's reply to this was more spirited:

"I am a retired Commander-in-Chief of the United States Army, and eligible to any position of command over American troops to which I may be appointed. As for my fitness . . . I respectfully refer you to my three immediate superiors in the field, Lieutenant-General S. B. M. Young (retired), Major-General Samuel Sumner (retired), and Major-General Leonard Wood. . . .

"The regiment, First United States Volunteer Cavalry, in which I first served as Lieutenant-Colonel, and which I then commanded as Colonel, was raised, armed, equipped, drilled, mounted, dismounted, kept two weeks on a transport, and then put through two victorious, aggressive fights in which we lost a third of the officers, and a fifth of the enlisted men, all within a little over fifty days."

"The patriotic spirit of your suggestion is cordially appreciated," replied the Secretary, perhaps somewhat taken aback. The sincerity of his appreciation was, however, suggested by a conversation later recorded when Baker showed the President one of T.R.'s letters, perhaps suspecting that this would provide the chief executive with an opportunity to display the kind of academic condescension in which he found special relish: "This is one of the most extraordinary documents I have ever read," said the President, "Thank you for letting me undergo the discipline of temper involved in reading it in silence."

The spinsterish glee with which Baker and Wilson contrived to reject T.R.'s wholehearted offer of service to his country was even better exemplified later on. Roosevelt, never one to stand on seniority, thought he might do better if he talked to Baker directly and requested his young relative, Franklin D. Roosevelt, to arrange an appointment. The Assistant Secretary of the Navy thereupon invited the Secretary of War to pay a call on the former President at the house of Alice Longworth, where he was staying. The Secretary accepted and later gave an account of the visit:

"I found the house filled with visitors on the first floor, most of them Senators and close friends of Colonel Roosevelt. The former President was in the dining room with a crowd, all the rooms being full of people, and seemed to be in high spirits. He came out when I arrived and greeted me cordially, put his hand through my arm and took me upstairs to one of the bedrooms. He then described his hopes for leading a division in France.

" 'I am aware,' he said, 'that I have not had enough experience to lead a division myself. But I have selected the most experienced officers from the regular army for my staff.' "

T.R. also recorded his impressions of the meeting: "I had a good talk with Baker. I could twist him about my finger could I have him about for a while."

Finally, the negotiations led to a memorable meeting with the President on April 9th. "He received me pleasantly," T.R. later told his newspaperman friend, John Leary of the New York *Tribune,* "and we had an hour's talk. I complimented him on his war message and told him it would rank with the world's greatest state papers if it were made good and I told him I wanted a chance to help him make it good. I found that . . . there was a confusion in his mind as to what I wanted to do. I explained everything to him. He seemed to take it well, but—remember—I was talking to Mr. Wilson."

As usual, T.R. knew his man. This time, the President, in discussing the meeting with his secretary, Joseph Tumulty, who was also present, surprisingly and to his credit, refrained from jeering at his predecessor. He seemed genuinely moved, as people usually were by T.R., and echoed the comment which had been made by Cecil Spring Rice so many years before, when T.R. had been in the White House: ". . . He is a great big boy. I was . . . charmed by his personality. There is a sweetness about him that is very compelling. You can't resist the man."

The President was, however, able to go on resisting T.R.'s request, without providing any reason. In May, T.R. was still pleading for a chance to raise or to help raise one division, or even two divisions, in which he would be glad to accept "the junior brigadier-generalship." Wilson's acknowledgment of the offer was a carefully worded sneer: "It would be very agreeable to me to pay Mr. Roosevelt this compliment and the Allies the compliment of sending an ex-President but this is not the time for compliments or for any action not calculated to contribute to the immediate success of the war . . . the business in hand is undramatic, practical, and of scientific definiteness and precision."

The implication that Roosevelt was interested in showing off without regard for the success of the war was soon refuted by personages whose scientific knowledge of the subject far exceeded that of a historian specializing in economic annals. General Joffre, the hero of the first Battle of the Marne, who headed a mission to the U.S. in the spring of 1917, spoke on Roosevelt's behalf at a dinner at which his remarks were later suppressed, presumably by State Department censors. Georges Clemenceau, soon to be France's Premier, precluded the chance that his comments would be thus treated by putting them in the form of an open letter to the President: "At the present moment, there is in France one name which sums up the beauty of American intervention. You are too much of a philosopher to ignore that the influence on the people of great leaders of men often exceeds their personal merits, thanks to the legendary halo surrounding them. The name of Roosevelt has this legendary force in our country . . . you must know, Mr. President, that more than one of our *poilus* has asked his comrade: 'But where is Roosevelt?' Send them Roosevelt. It will gladden their hearts."

T.R.'s enemies, as well as his friends in the Senate and elsewhere, also came to his defense. Henry Watterson of the Louisville *Courier-Journal* wrote that "The appearance of an ex-President of the United States leading American soldiers to the battle front would electrify the world." The Democratic Governor of Louisiana, J. M. Parker, likewise appealed to the President. Such entreaties were of no avail.

"I am not playing politics," the President protested. ". . . Colonel Roosevelt . . . and many of the men with him are too old to render effective service, and in addition to that fact, he as well as others have shown intolerance of discipline."

What game he was playing was perhaps best revealed in his own comradely remark to Tumulty later on, when— without ever showing rancor openly, no doubt because he was too proud to do so—the President had effectively made it clear that Roosevelt's ambition to serve his country in one last great effort was to be thwarted. By this time, Congress had spent two weeks wrangling over a selective service law that would enable T.R. to raise his divisions for which some two hundred thousand volunteers—enough for ten divisions —had already sent in their names. Wilson—the President who three years later was to feel much aggrieved by persecution at the hands of the U.S. Senate—confided coyly to his secretary that ". . . I really think the best way to treat Mr. Roosevelt is to take no notice of him. That breaks his heart and is the best punishment that can be administered."

For his own bitter disappointment at being refused permission to fight for his country, T.R. found one considerable solace. That was the record made by his four sons and his son-in-law, Richard Derby. Theodore, Jr., and Archie had gone to the Officer's Training Camp run by General Leonard Wood at Plattsburg in 1916. Kermit followed them in the spring of 1917 and Quentin was about to join a flying squadron. By summer all four were overseas—Ted, Jr., and Archie commissioned in the A.E.F., Kermit—through T.R.'s connections with Arthur Lee—with the British Army in the Middle East and Quentin with the U.S. Air Force.

In New York one day, T.R. encountered his good friend Finley Peter Dunne, who remarked: ". . . the first thing you know your four sons will put the name of Roosevelt on the map." Quoting the remark in a letter to Ted, T.R. added: "They have done it; and if I had to choose, I would rather have had you four stand at Armageddon even than stand there myself." Archie was the first to be wounded—shrapnel in one leg and a broken arm—and was awarded the Croix de Guerre. "I can't begin to say how proud we are of you," T.R. wrote. "Our pride even outweighs our anxiety. . . . I have received dozens of newspaper clippings and scores of letters about your wounds and the cross. I really think that our people generally felt a genuine pride in your 'proving your truth by your endeavor,' and thoroughly understand my pride in you; and a good many felt that, inasmuch as you were going to recover, they were rather glad that one of *my* sons had the dangerous honor of being among the first to be wounded in battle."

Last of the four boys to reach the front was naturally the youngest, Quentin. On the fourth of July, 1918, he was reported as having taken part in a patrol by an American pursuit squadron that had brought down twenty enemy planes in combat with Baron Ferdinand von Richthofen's famous "Flying Circus." A few days later, the New York *Times* reported that he had brought down his first plane. It was on July 16, only a fortnight after his first fight, that Phil Thompson, the Associated Press reporter assigned to Sagamore Hill, came to the door of the library one afternoon with a copy of a censored cablegram saying merely: "WATCH SAGAMORE HILL FOR—"

"Have you any idea, Colonel, what it means?" he asked.

The Colonel shut the library door before answering. "Something has happened to one of the boys. It can't be Ted or Archie, for both are recovering from wounds. It's not Kermit, since he's not at the moment in the danger zone. So it must be Quentin. His mother must not be told until there is no hope left."

The next afternoon, Thompson brought the verification of T.R.'s deduction. Attacked by two German planes, Quentin had fallen inside the German lines. The papers wanted a statement from his parents. T.R. entered the house and returned a half hour later with a brief message which he handed to Thompson.

"Quentin's mother and I are very glad that he got to the front and had a chance to render some service to his country, and show the stuff that was in him before his fate befell him."

Hermann Hagedorn, Roosevelt's close friend and later his able biographer, found him at his office at the *Metropolitan* magazine the next morning. He wrote that the "old side of him is gone, that old exuberance . . . the boy in him had died." T.R. wrote his son's obituary, without mentioning his name, as an editorial for the Kansas City *Star* called *The Great Adventure:*

> Only those are fit to live who do not fear to die; and none are fit to die who have shrunk from the joy of life. Both life and death are parts of the same Great Adventure. Never yet was worthy adventure worthily carried through by the man who put his personal safety first. . . . In America today all our people are summoned to service and to sacrifice. Pride is the portion only of those who know bitter sorrow or the foreboding of bitter sorrow. But all of us who give service, and stand ready for sacrifice, are the torchbearers. We run with the torches until we fall, content if we can then pass them to the hands of the other runners. . . .

T.R.'s political fortunes had reached their lowest point since his departure from the White House shortly after the start of the European War, some five years after his triumphal return from Africa. As he had perceived, Wilson's eagerness to stay out of the fight was shared by most of his compatriots; and the campaign for preparedness seemed to many merely a backhanded way of trying to persuade the country to go to war. Roosevelt's call to "courage, and honor, and duty" thus fell largely on deaf ears. Meanwhile his position in the Republican party was still the wholly thankless one of the man who had been chiefly responsible for its defeat in 1912.

By 1916, his status within the party had risen considerably, through his efforts to bring his Progressives back to its ranks and his support of Hughes. By now, too, there was a general acknowledgment that he had been right, and the President wrong, about the chances that the U.S. could stay out of the fight. If Wilson's war message of April 2, 1917, was, as T.R. had said, potentially a great state paper, that was precisely because, as he also pointed out, it contradicted everything that the President had been saying for the previous three years. U.S. entry into the war confirmed T.R.'s reading of the situation as a whole; and now the consequences of the Administration's resolute refusal to consider what war might mean in terms of men and weapons also began to be increasingly apparent.

As the months went by after the U.S. declaration of war it became obvious that the Administration's failure to prepare was now being compounded even more inexcusably, by hopeless inefficiency in its efforts to rectify the omission. In November, 1917, Roosevelt was writing to Ted, Jr., in France: "Our national army, the draft army, has only begun to learn the rudiments. The spirit of the men is simply fine; but the shortage in even the most necessary arms and equipment is appalling. . . . The infantry regiments average about one rifle to every four men, taking the camps all the way through; and most of them have had no target practice whatever. When the most elementary training is thus lacking, you may imagine how little had been done in the real war training of the kind that is needed at the present day. . . . The trouble is fundamental and two-fold. The Administration has no conception of war needs or what war means; and the American army has been so handled in peace that the bulk of the men high up were sure to break down in the event of war. If three years ago we had introduced universal military training, if we had then begun to build quantities of cannon, machine guns, rifles and airplanes, and if, two years ago, we had begun an extensive series of large scale army maneuvers, we would have made all our blunders and suffered all our delays at a time when they did not count— and the war would have been over now. Well, I am not merely wise after the event—I advocated all this at the time! Which is a pointless boast."

In a letter to Quentin, he had amplified the same points:

"I am the only man, seemingly, who dares try to wake our officials out of their stupor of fatuous complacency, who dares to point out a few of our more vital shortcomings, and endeavor to get them remedied and to speed up the war. The horrible delays, mismanagement and inefficiency about the army have been matched by what has been done in such matters as shipping, transportation and coal. Nine tenths of wisdom is being wise in time! We ambled deviously into this war without one particle of preparation; and we are paying a bitter price now."

Writing now in a new outlet, the Kansas City *Star*, in which he published over a hundred widely syndicated pieces, T.R. blasted the Administration's conduct of the war from coast to coast. When he found that men in the camps were coming down with pneumonia at six times the normal civilian rate, he admitted that administrative blundering was partly to blame but "the prime cause is the failure to prepare in advance." When the Germans opened a major offensive in January of 1918, the Secretary of War attempted to reassure the nation by stating that "the French and British Armies can be relied upon to withstand the shock." T.R. drew attention to the celebrated willingness expressed by Artemus Ward "to sacrifice all his wife's relations on the altar of his country." He then spoke scathingly of a system which "leaves our small army at the front with no artillery except what we get from the French and an army at home with batteries made out of telegraph poles and logwood."

Criticisms by a former President who had sent the U.S. fleet round the world without a hitch compelled attention. By 1918, even the pro-Administration New York *Times* was confessing that: "All our bustle and stir doesn't hide the fact that, through incompetence and lack of organization and system, we are far behind in our preparations to supply rifles, ammunition, machine guns, airships, uniforms." The climax came when the Chairman of the Senate Military Affairs Committee—Oregon's Democratic Senator George E. Chamberlain—started an investigation of the War Department. "Congress is investigating," T.R. wrote to Ted, Jr., "and, of course, has instantly found that all I said was true." The consequence of the investigation was a New York speech to the National Security League in which Chamberlain said that the military establishment had "fallen down because of the inefficiency in every bureau and department in the government of the United States." The next day, he introduced a Senate bill to create a war cabinet. The President was moved to call Chamberlain's speech a "distortion of the truth."

When Roosevelt arrived in Washington two days later,

in the midst of the uproar created by Chamberlain's proposal, he again stayed with the Longworths. This time the flood of callers included not only reporters—his hostess counted thirty-three of these "fairly stacked" in the small hall—but major politicians representing both parties, and both wings of his own. "No doubt seems to remain," said the New York *Times,* "that Theodore Roosevelt has become the leader of the Republican Party."

T.R.'s sudden re-emergence in this role was more dramatically defined a few months later when a pair of politicians—one a professional from Connecticut, the other a former California Progressive—called together at Sagamore Hill to ask T.R. if he would run for President in 1920. His reply was that he would "if the people want me, but only if they want me. I will not lift a finger for the nomination. I will not make a contest for it. It will have to come to me. It would be worthless on any other basis."

"Colonel," said the professional, "it will be yours, without strings and on your own terms."

To New York's Barnes, who in 1915 had sued T.R. for libel, a Western political leader said:

"I suspect we are going to nominate T.R. in 1920 by acclamation."

"Acclamation, hell!" replied Barnes. "We're going to nominate him by assault."

XV

W HAT might have happened
had T.R.—instead of Warren Gamaliel Harding—been nominated by the Republican party in 1920, by assault or otherwise, is one more of those tantalizing historical conjectures
upon which it may be permissible to speculate. If it is con-
ceivable that Roosevelt could have prevented World War I
had he been in the White House in 1914, it is reasonably
certain that, had he been President in the 1920's, postwar
history would have taken a very different course. That there
would have been no Teapot Dome Scandal goes without saying but T.R.'s influence might also have served to change
many of the more fundamental developments that led so
rapidly and directly to World War II. Hitler, for example,
owed his rise largely to chaotic conditions in Germany
brought about in part by the effects of the Versailles Treaty.
Leadership such as T.R. could have provided, had he survived in good health, might well have been able to amelio-
rate these effects—not to mention those of revolution in Rus-

sia, world-wide Depression and the compound fiasco of the League of Nations—all of which, in hindsight, seem so deceptively inevitable. One thing at least is fairly obvious: T.R. would have been re-elected had he not died, as dramatically as he had always lived, with his foot upon the threshold of a triumphant return to prestige and power.

Actually, though Roosevelt's death was sudden and unexpected, his health had been failing for some time. Delicate in childhood, and subject to the strain of abnormal exertion uninterruptedly thereafter, his constitution appeared to have been permanently damaged by his experiences during the exploration of the River of Doubt. During the summer of 1914, he rapidly—perhaps too rapidly—regained the weight he had lost but never all of his old-time energy and endurance. Recurrences of the fever he had contracted on the Amazon—perhaps deriving from the slighter fevers which he had suffered intermittently ever since the campaign in Cuba —combined with other minor but annoying ailments, such as rheumatism, gout, and erysipelas, to curtail the ceaseless activity which had provided the basis of his physical well-being. T.R. did his best to disregard such afflictions as thoroughly as he had ignored all previous injuries and dangers but their impairment of his resistance nonetheless made itself increasingly apparent.

In the fall of 1917, T.R. made two trips to the Midwest. The following February, a friend called on him at the Langdon Hotel in New York where he was preparing to visit Roosevelt Hospital to undergo operations for an abscess on his thigh—an injury whose origins went back at least to the trolley accident in Pittsfield—and for abscesses in both ears. T.R. was in a somber mood: "I don't mind having to die," he said, "I've had my good time . . . and I don't mind having to pay for it. But to think that those swine will say that I'm out of the game!"

Some indication of the resurgence of T.R.'s influence and popularity was reflected in the newspaper editorials on his illness. Before his doctors released a favorable bulletin, the New York *Tribune* voiced the nation's alarm: "Theodore Roosevelt, listen! You must be up and well again. We cannot have it otherwise. We could not run this world without you." A few days later, when the news from the hospital indicated that he was making a good recovery, the *Times* spoke of "heartfelt rejoicing throughout the country . . ." and of an "inspiring, a compelling force . . ." whose services in arousing the people "to a sense of the national peril and their duty" was "beyond all estimate."

T.R. himself replied to a personal message from King George:

"The chief reason I wished to get well was in order to resume my work of endeavoring to get my country to exert her great, but lazy and unprepared strength as speedily and effectively as possible. For the last three years and a half I have been preaching to my fellow countrymen their duty as I saw it; they finally saw it the same way but always two years behind-time as regards each phase of the duty; and nine-tenths of wisdom is being wise in time. It is maddening to see Russia break and Germany stride nearer triumph because my country failed to prepare."

When T.R. returned to Sagamore Hill in March, hearing in one ear was gone as well as the sight of one eye. When a friend, who had come to tell him of having seen Archie in the hospital in Paris, remarked on how well he himself looked, T.R. replied: "I feel as though I were a hundred years old and had *never* been young!"

That spring, as the last great German offensive neared Paris, T.R. took to the road again. The journey exacted a severe toll; at St. Louis, erysipelas in his left foot was causing him fever and he was in acute pain by the time he reached Chicago. A doctor joined the train and at Omaha, T.R. stayed in his room all day to get ready for the effort of speaking that evening. After his speech he said to Leary, who was also on his train: "I think I'll get over this thing just by fighting it. Anyway, I've got to go on. Such meetings as this tonight are worth some sacrifice." In Des Moines, he pounded against Wilson's apparent readiness to settle for a negotiated peace: "Unless we knock out Germany, we will have to fight again, probably within the lifetime of men now old, certainly within the lifetime of those now young."

Two days after his return to Oyster Bay, T.R. was in Hartford, to receive a degree from Trinity College and to speak, on Sunday, on a text from Kings I, XX, II: "Let not him that girdeth on his harness boast himself as he that taketh it off." His theme again was the Administration's complacent incompetence: "Last fall we were announcing that there would be twenty thousand airplanes with Pershing's army in the spring, and the boast took in our own people. It took in the Germans, too, but, unlike our own people, they built airplanes to meet it."

Writing to Ted Jr., T.R. raged at ". . . my impotence to be of substantial service to all of you at the front. . . . I feel that while you face inconceivably wearing fatigue, hardship, work, responsibility and deadly danger, I sit at home ignobly in comfort and uselessness." In fact, one of these self-accusations was as false as the other. The blow of the news about Quentin that arrived a month later did not serve to lighten the load.

T.R. took the blow, in line with his lifelong principles,

without flinching. A letter to Arthur Lee summed up his feelings: "It is very dreadful that Quentin should have been killed; it would have been worse if he had not gone." He went on with his writing for the Kansas City *Star*—reminding his readers five weeks after his son's death of the debt the nation owed to England and the Allies. "If she had not controlled the seas, not an American battalion could have been sent to the aid of France . . . or any of these Allied nations to whose stern fighting efficiency we owe it that this earth is still a place on which free men can live."

During the late summer and fall of 1918, T.R. spent many hours alone on the porch at Sagamore Hill. Once, as he sat there looking out over the Sound and watching the sun go down, James Amos, his valet, heard him murmuring to himself: "Poor Quenty-quee, poor Quenty-quee." Sorrow for the death of his youngest son was uppermost in his mind but there must have been other memories also crowding his thoughts. The view from the porch, widening in autumn as the leaves fell on the slope below, looked across the water beyond the old house Tranquillity, where he had spent the summers as a boy. In the early evenings he could see the lights along the narrow causeway to Centre Island over which he had portaged his boat on days when a row across the Sound and back was merely a good morning's exercise. After that had come the days of camping in the Maine woods and the time of his courting Alice Lee and later on the winters on the range in the North Dakota Territory of which he had written:

"When the days have dwindled to their shortest, and the nights seem never-ending, then all the great northern plains are changed into an abode of iron desolation. Sometimes furious gales blow out of the north, driving before them the clouds of blinding snow-dust, wrapping the mantle of death round every unsheltered being that faces their unshackled anger. They roar in a thunderous bass as they sweep across the prairie or whirl through naked canyons; they shiver the great brittle cottonwoods, and beneath their rough touch the icy limbs of the pines that cluster in the gorges sing like the chords of an Æolian harp. Again, in the coldest mid-winter weather, not a breath of wind may stir; and then the still merciless, terrible cold that broods over the earth like the shadow of silent death seems even more dreadful in its gloomy rigor than is the lawless madness of the storms. All the land is like granite; the great rivers stand still in their beds, as if turned to frosted steel. In the long nights there is no sound to break the lifeless silence. Under the ceaseless, shifting play of the Northern Lights, or lighted only by the wintry brilliance of the stars, the snow-clad plains stretch out into dead and endless wastes of glimmering white."

Now the ranges were fenced and the frontier gone—and with it much of the old American scheme of things. Its passing and the growth of the great cities had made a new sort of nation, with vast new perils of its own. The questions now were to bring balance and toleration between contending groups, interests, races. The Brownsville riot of 1906—for which he had had to dismiss three companies of colored troops, in one of the hardest decisions that ever faced him, was a straw in the angry wind. Bitterness between colored and white was sure to grow rather than diminish in the coming decades.

"I preach the gospel of hope . . . I ask that we see to it that the line of division in the deeper matters of our citizenship be drawn, never between section and section, never between creed and creed, never, thrice never, between class and class; but that the line be drawn on the line of conduct."

That was what he had been trying to do in those first years at the White House—a residence that was not big enough, really, to hold the whole family when they first moved in. He and Edith had made the plans to do the place over and then got Congress to grant two hundred thousand dollars to put them into effect. It meant pulling down a green house and building executive offices in their place. That left space enough in the upper floors for a man with half a dozen lively growing children. They had done over the interior too— moved the staircase toward the front door, refurnished most of the rooms, enlarged the dining room to hold a hundred people, and given it a new fireplace. The architect had put lions' heads on the pillars under the mantel but there were no lions in America outside the zoos. The pillars had been changed quickly enough; buffalo heads did better.

The second term, too, had been full of challenge and glory. That was when the whole world had really begun to understand what America meant to it.

"Our nation is that one among all the nations of the earth which holds in its hands the fate of the coming years. We enjoy exceptional advantages and are menaced by exceptional dangers; and all signs indicate that we shall either fail greatly or succeed greatly. . . . Here is the task, and I have got to do it."

He had done it, too, and in his own fashion. "My ambition is that, in however small a way, the work I do shall be along the Washington and Lincoln lines." It had been along their lines so far as that went and it was not over yet.

"I have only got one more fight left in me," he had said not long ago, but he still had that, and as things were shaping up, it would come in 1920.

When President Wilson announced the famous "Fourteen Points" on which he proposed to base a just peace, T.R., with his customary contempt for fine phrases that were unapplied or inapplicable, analyzed them in detail. One Point called for removal "of all economic barriers and the establishment of an equality of trade conditions among all the nations." If this meant anything, T.R. remarked, it meant that the U.S. could have "no tariff of its own." Yet Wilson had informed a Democratic senator that the section did not restrict "the free determination by any nation of its own economic policy." If a private citizen had attempted a similar repudiation, T.R. wrote, "there was not a court in Christendom that would not adjudge him guilty of having used language with deliberate attempt to deceive."

In October, T.R. went as far West as Billings, Montana, to speak for the Liberty Loan. He returned in time to celebrate his birthday at Sagamore Hill on the twenty-seventh and then the next night, at Carnegie Hall, to deliver the last important speech of his career, a smashing attack against Wilson's appeal for a Democratic Congress: "He explicitly repudiates loyalty to the war as a test. . . . He asks for the defeat of pro-war Republicans. He does not ask for the defeat of anti-war Democrats. On the contrary, he supports such men if, although anti-war, they are pro-Administration. He asks not for loyalty to the nation. He asks only for support of himself. . . . We Republicans pledge ourselves to stand by the President as long as he stands by the American people, and to part company from him at any point where in our judgment he does not stand by the people. This is the people's government, this is the people's war, and the peace that follows shall be the people's peace."

On Election Day, T.R. was back at Sagamore Hill, suffering now from lumbago which did not, however, prevent him from going to the village to vote. The next day, the papers revealed results of which T.R. wrote to Rudyard Kipling: "We did an unparalleled thing and took away the Congress from him, on the issue that we stood for forcing the Germans to make an unconditional surrender. I took a certain sardonic amusement in the fact that whereas, four years ago, to put it mildly, my attitude was not popular, I was now the one man whom they insisted upon following and whose statements were taken as the platform."

It was on the day the war ended, November 11, that T.R. was taken to Roosevelt Hospital again, this time to undergo a treatment for inflammatory rheumatism that lasted for seven weeks. Warned now that he might have to spend the rest of his life in a wheel chair, he gave a stoic reply: "All right. I can work that way too." In his hospital room he proceeded to do so in the intervals between visits from old friends. Assured by these that he was certain to be the Republican nominee in 1920, T.R. stuck to his previous answer: "Since Quentin's death the world seems to have shut down on me. But if I do consent, it will be because as President I could accomplish some things that I should like to see accomplished before I die."

Still in severe pain, T.R. returned to Sagamore Hill on Christmas Day and there for almost two more weeks went on working at top speed. On January 5, his schedule included dictating a letter to Kermit, correcting proof of an article for the *Metropolitan,* and scribbling a memorandum to himself about the new Chairman of the Republican National Committee: "Hays—see him; he must go to Washington for ten days; see Senate and House; prevent split on domestic policies."

The words of this memorandum—amply indicative of T.R.'s full resumption of power within his party—were the last he ever wrote. Late in the afternoon, Edith Roosevelt who had been sitting beside him in his bedroom rose to leave. T.R. looked up from the book he was reading to say: "I wonder if you will ever know how I love Sagamore

Hill." That evening, he went to bed earlier than usual. A little after eleven he called James Amos, saying: "James, will you please put out the light."

Those were T.R.'s last spoken words. Between four and five o'clock the next morning, Amos, sleeping in the same room, noticed that his respiration was uneven. He called for the nurse but before she could come, the breathing had stopped entirely. T.R. had died in his sleep, of an embolism in the coronary artery.

News of T.R.'s death circled the world rapidly. From Archie, now invalided home, went cables to Theodore, Jr., and Kermit in France saying: "The old lion is dead." Reporters on the train that was carrying Woodrow Wilson to Paris for the Peace Conference got off to stretch their legs at the Alpine town of Modena and glanced through the window of the President's car. He was reading a telegram, and as he did so, his expression seemed to reflect surprise, concern, and then a sort of triumph. Later, they learned what the telegram had contained: word of the death of the man who, at the moment, seemed to be all that stood between Wilson—hailed in Europe as the saviour of the world—and the place in history which he so avidly desired.

T.R.'s funeral followed two days later at the hillside cemetery near the little Cove School where he had sent his children and where he had been the central figure in so many Christmas ceremonies. Distinguished pallbearers—Leonard Wood, Elihu Root, Taft and others—carried the coffin up the steep path. A brief service was read by Mr. Talmadge, the rector of Christ Church in Oyster Bay. Then the coffin was lowered into the snowy grave.

Acknowledgments

This book was undertaken in the effort to provide a reasonably complete short biography of Theodore Roosevelt for the contemporary reader. As such it does not purport to provide new information on the subject but rather to make more accessible that contained in previous books which are longer, more specialized or both. The author wishes accordingly to acknowledge an unusually heavy obligation to such works, among which the major items are listed in the *Selected Bibliography;* and to thank Doubleday & Company, Inc., the Harvard University Press and Charles Scribner's Sons for permission to quote from material contained therein.

The author would like also to express his gratitude to Miss Helen MacLachlan of the Roosevelt Memorial Association; Mr. Robert H. Haynes, Curator of the Theodore Roosevelt Collection in the Harvard College Library; and Dr. Richard H. Meader of the Theodore Roosevelt National Memorial Park at Medora, North Dakota for their kind interest, assistance and advice. Finally and most especially, he would like to thank Mr. Hobart Lewis, Executive Editor of *The Reader's Digest,* for the encouragement and comment which were largely instrumental in bringing the project to completion.

T. R.—A Chronology

October 27, 1858	Born at 28 East 20th Street, New York City.
1880	Graduated from Harvard College. Married Alice Lee of Chestnut Hill, Massachusetts.
1882–1884	Member of New York State Assembly.
1884	Alice Lee Roosevelt died, daughter Alice Roosevelt born.
1884–1886	Ranchman in Dakota Territory.
1886	Republican candidate for Mayor of New York City; married Edith Kermit Carow.
1889–1895	Member of the United States Civil Service Commission.
1895–1897	President of the New York City Police Board.
1897–1898	Assistant Secretary of the Navy.
1898	Lieutenant-Colonel and Colonel, 1st U.S. Volunteer Cavalry (The Rough Riders), on active service in the Spanish War.
1899–1900	Governor of New York.
1901	Vice President of the United States.
1901–1909	President of the United States.

1909–1910   Hunted big game in Africa; toured Europe; represented United States at funeral of Edward VII.

1910–1914   Contributing Editor *The Outlook.*

1912   Formed Progressive Party and became its candidate for President.

1913–1914   Explored and mapped 1000-mile River of Doubt in Brazil.

1914–1917   Led fight in the United States for Preparedness in World War I.

1917   Offered to raise division of troops for service after United States Declaration of War.

1918   Hailed by political leaders, press and public as Republican nominee for the Presidency in 1920.

January 6, 1919   Died at Oyster Bay, L.I.

Selected Bibliography

Abbott, Lawrence F. *Impressions of Theodore Roosevelt*. Doubleday &
    Co., Inc., 1920
Ames, James E. *Theodore Roosevelt: Hero to His Valet*. The John
    Day Co., 1927
Beale, Howard K. *Theodore Roosevelt and the Rise of America to
    World Power*. The Johns Hopkins Press, 1956
Bishop, Joseph Bucklin. *Theodore Roosevelt and His Time*. Charles
    Scribner's Sons, 1923
Bunau-Varilla, Philippe Jean. *The Great Adventure of Panama*. Double-
    day & Co., Inc., 1920
Butt, Archie. *Letters*. Doubleday & Co., Inc., 1924
Dennett, Tyler. *Roosevelt and the Russo-Japanese War*. Doubleday &
    Co., Inc., 1925
Goplen, Arnold O. *The Career of the Marquis de Mores in the Bad-
    lands of North Dakota*. State Historical Society of North Dakota
Hagedorn, Hermann. *The Boy's Life of Theodore Roosevelt*. G. P.
    Putnam's Sons, 1918
———. *Roosevelt in the Badlands*. Houghton Mifflin Co., 1921
———. *The Roosevelt Family at Sagamore Hill*. The Macmillan Co.,
    1954
———. *The Theodore Roosevelt Treasury*. G. P. Putnam's Sons, 1957
Harbaugh, William Henry. *Power and Responsibility*. Farrar, Straus &
    Cudahy, Inc., 1961
Hoover, Irwin Hood ("Ike"). *Forty Two Years in the White House*.
    Houghton Mifflin Co., 1934
Johnston, William Davison. *T. R. Champion of the Strenuous Life*.
    Farrar, Straus & Cudahy, 1958
Lang, Lincoln A. *Ranching with Roosevelt*. J. B. Lippincott Co., 1926
Leary, John J. *Talks with T.R.* Houghton Mifflin Co., 1920

Looker, Earle. *The White House Gang*. Fleming H. Revell Co.. 1929

Lorant, Stefan. *The Life and Times of Theodore Roosevelt*. Doubleday & Co., Inc., 1959

Mattison, Ray H. *Ranching in the Dakota Badlands and Roosevelt's Dakota Ranches*. The State Historical Society of North Dakota

Morison, Elting E. *The Letters of Theodore Roosevelt* (8 vols.) Harvard University Press, 1951–54

Pringle, Henry F. *The Life and Times of William Howard Taft*. Farrar, Straus & Cudahy, Inc., 1939

————. *Theodore Roosevelt, A Biography*. Harcourt, Brace & Co., 1931

Putnam, Carleton. *Theodore Roosevelt: The Formative Years*. Charles Scribner's Sons, 1958

Riis, Jacob A. *Theodore Roosevelt the Citizen*. The Macmillan Co., 1904

Robinson, Corinne Roosevelt. *My Brother Theodore Roosevelt*. Charles Scribner's Sons, 1921

Roosevelt, Kermit. *The Happy Hunting Grounds*. Charles Scribner's Sons, 1920

Roosevelt Memorial Association. *Theodore Roosevelt Cyclopedia*. 1940

Roosevelt, Theodore, Jr. *All in the Family*. G. P. Putnam's Sons, 1929

Roosevelt, Theodore. *Works* (24 vols.) Charles Scribner's Sons, 1923

Sewall, William W. *Bill Sewall's Story of T.R.* Harper & Bros., 1919

Street, Julian. *The Most Interesting American*. The Century Co., 1915

Wagenknecht, Edward. *The Seven Worlds of Theodore Roosevelt*. Longmans, Green Co., 1958

Wister, Owen. *Roosevelt, The Story of a Friendship*. The Macmillan Co., 1930

Wood, Frederick S., ed., *Roosevelt as We Knew Him*. The John C. Winston Co., 1927

Index